Hunting Adventures Worldwide

JACK ATCHESON SR.

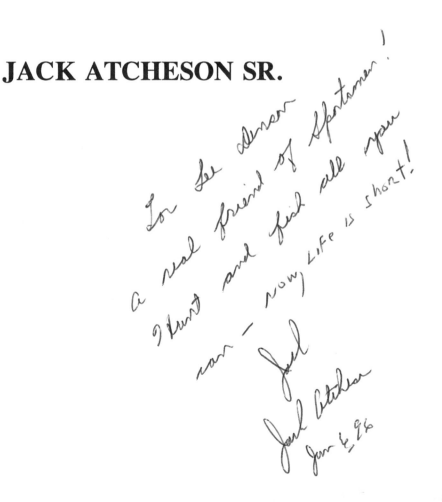

To Lee Anderson

A real friend of Sportsmen!

I hunt and fish all you
can — now, Life is short!

Jack

Jack Atcheson

Jan & 96

Hunting Adventures Worldwide

Jack Atcheson Sr.

ILLUSTRATIONS BY DIANA HAKER

Copyright 1995 by Jack Atcheson Sr.

Published in the United States of America

ISBN 0-912299-60-6

Jack Atcheson & Sons, Inc.
INTERNATIONAL HUNTING CONSULTANTS
3210 Ottawa Street • Butte, Montana 59701
Phone: 406-782-2382 FAX 406-723-3318
In Cooperation With
STONEYDALE PRESS PUBLISHING COMPANY

TO ORDER ADDITIONAL COPIES: A great gift for that special person. For personalized, signed copies sent Priority Mail, same day, contact Jack Atcheson. For Visa or MasterCard orders, include card number and card expiration date. Cost $29.95, plus $4.00 postage.

TABLE OF CONTENTS

My first buck at 12 years old, using a 30/40 Krag.

DEDICATION

This book can be dedicated to only one person, my beautiful wife Mary Claire, who tolerated and actually supported my ambitions and hunting habit. When things went wrong, which was often, she remained always beside me, never seeming to doubt I knew what I was doing. For no other can I ever have such love and devotion.

ACKNOWLEDGEMENTS

I want to thank Jim Zumbo, Dale Burk, Vin Sparano and Craig Boddington for prodding me to pick up my pen, and Lynell Windham and Connie Edelen, who unscrambled my notes and tapes, then Kelly Sullivan who introduced me to commas and periods.

Without the help of Sergeants Vern Hinrichs and Norman Faulk on the Tiger story and Adrian Carr of Zambia on Bongo, I probably never would have completed the texts.

If Jack O'Connor and John Jobson can hear me, "Thanks." It's too bad it took me so many years to grasp all the good advice.

My cheering section, who kept my interest up: my wife, Mary Claire; daughter Kristie; my sisters, Phyllis and Patti; son-in-law, Lee; daughters-in-law, Starla and Cindy; nieces and nephews, Cherie, Patti, Chris and Kerrie; grandchildren, Alissa, Adri, Trevor and Trinda.

A hunting book is meant for hunters and the best I know are my sons, Jack Jr., Keith and Brian, and my oldest grandson, Andrew; along with hunting pals Jim Carmichel, Mike Hanback, Tom Fulgham, Bill McRae, Kerry Constan, Jack Jones, Duncan Gilchrist, Steve Bayless, Henry Budney, Jerry Manley, Tony Schoonen, Bill Holdorf, Vince Fischer and Lee Masters, Bob McDowell, Jim Carkuff, Ron Thompson, Doug Kennemore, Bill Deal, Gene Hughes, Bob Bushmaker, and my Idaho elk hunting partners, Tim, Jim and Chad Magness, as well as Pat Maloney and his two pack horses (especially the horses).

I owe several outfitters a lot — Terry and Deb Overly, Kelly Vrem, Clay Katzmarck, Andy Runyan, Erv Malnarich, Volker and Anka Grellman, Phillip Easi, Max Chase, Ken Robertson, Clark Engle, Bob Curtis, Howard Copenhaver, Jack Wemple, John Cargill, Eugene Yapp, Jim Harrower, Frank Rigler, Gary Duffy, John Coleman, Geoff and Russ Broom, Mike Rowbotham, John Kingsley-Heath, Keith Rowse, Ron Kitson, Jan Oelofse, John Sharp, Rolfe Rohwer, Peter Johnstone, Frank Cook, Bobby Ball and Glen Drinkall — plus a special thanks to Jesus Yuren. When I was not feeling well, Keith and Leah Rush of Lakeview, Montana, found me a room and loaned me a slow and sweet mule named "Sugar" to get me to the top of the mountain.

In 1948 I saw a photo of a sable antelope and determined that, someday, I would hunt them — a wild daydream then, but it happened! When this magnificent sable bull stepped into a clearing years later when I went to Africa to hunt them, I could barely control my rifle.

FOREWORD

It was the kind of hunt you'd like to forget. Jack Atcheson, Vin Sparano, and I were not exactly in the best of spirits. We were wallowing through thigh-deep snow, it was the middle of the night, we weren't sure exactly where we were, and the truck was about 10 miles away. The dark forest we were swallowed up in was foreboding and sinister as we slowly made our way through the timber; the 15 degrees-below-zero temperature didn't do much to improve our attitudes.

It happened that one of the members of our hunting party was supposed to walk our horses down a creek and meet us at dark. A simple plan, but it went awry. The man and the horses weren't there at the designated place and we were afoot. It was not a happy discovery.

"This isn't good," Atcheson said.

"Maybe the guy isn't very far away," Sparano ventured.

"Maybe he's halfway down the mountain," I stated. Murphy's Law is always a fact of life for me.

We were faced with two options: either stay where we were and build a fire, or start walking out to the trailhead. Our outfitter pal, Keith Rush, who had been putting on a drive for us when the horses disappeared, showed up and left the choice to us. He had no clue where the horses were.

"Let's walk," Atcheson said. "We can be down to the road in four or five hours. No problem."

I've always liked Atcheson's positive attitude when things got a little rough in the boonies. The guy was born a couple hundred years too late. He'd have made a great mountain man and Indian fighter.

Hours later we were still walking. I'd like to say we'd made good progress, but we had a bit of a problem. Seemed like we'd gotten a little turned around and were headed for Idaho. Camp was in Montana. A look at the big dipper and a compass confirmed our error, and we made a 180 and headed off in the correct direction. I was especially disappointed because Vin, who is editor of *Outdoor Life*, had been hunting the West with me for years, and hoped he'd score on this hunt. A previous elk hunt in Idaho was a bust.

I marveled at Jack's energy, because he'd been giving it all he had that day and hardly ever seemed to get winded. At one point during the hunt we were faced with a decision. A mountain loomed ahead, and we could either walk around it or hike over the top. (Our horses were tied up, allowing us to slip along quietly.) Atcheson, of course, opted to go over the top. It was another of Jack's ways of meeting a physical challenge. Why go around when you can go over? After all, the mountain was just a minor obstacle. (Vin and I went around!)

Hours later, we caught up to the rest of our party and the horses. They were, of course, most welcome sights.

While trodding along that night in the blackness, water became an important commodity. We perspired heavily from slugging along in the deep snow, despite the bitterly cold temperature.

At one point, instead of eating snow, which isn't a good idea, Jack chipped away at the ice that sealed in a small creek. Retrieving a metal collapsible cup from his backpack, he filled it with water. We drank from it to our heart's content.

The mere act of his having that cup in his pack was a most wonderful treat, and after many other hunts with him I learned that his backpack produces an amazing array of welcome items — things that most other people would never think of. One incident comes to mind, when Jack and Jim Carmichel were hunting in Africa.

Carmichel had shot a huge crocodile, which was lashed securely into a boat. As the hunting party headed back to camp along with the croc, the reptile, which heretofore was believed to be deceased, opened an eye and began thrashing about.

The boat was in the middle of a big lake, and Murphy's Law suddenly struck. The outboard motor died; apparently there was a problem with the electrical system. The croc, still very much alive, caused a great deal of concern among the boat's occupants, including Carmichel and Atcheson. It was impossible to shoot the croc again for fear that the bullet should exit and blow a large hole in the boat. This was not good, because the lake teemed with plenty of other crocs; these also very much alive and willing to dine on human flesh.

Atcheson saved the day when he pulled a tiny set of jumper cables from his pack and started the motor. All present were amazed at this item, but when I heard about it afterward I wasn't surprised. Jack was just being Jack.

A look inside Jack's Suburban vehicle is an eye opener. Jack drives only Suburbans for a good reason — they will hold an incredible assemblage of hunting, camping, and fishing gear that is guaranteed to be of some use somewhere and on some date. Never mind that the date may be five years down the road; the stuff is still handy.

Do you need a sling for your rifle because you forgot yours? Jack will find two or three. Do you need rifle scope caps because it's raining and you don't have any? Jack will have a size that fits your scope. Are you hungry, sick, want to fish, need an extra air mattress? Jack will produce food, medicine, fishing rods, and countless other things...

And just how easy is it for Jack to locate an item? For anyone else it would be an impossibility, because all the stuff is haphazardly arranged in a huge pile, with no semblance of order. Yet Jack goes right to the heart of the disorganized clump of equipment and quickly locates the object of his search.

Jack is always prepared for a hunt anytime and anywhere, and is the most avid, enthusiastic hunter I know. We've trekked many miles for big game together, and I've yet to see him back away from a challenge, even prior to his heart attack.

After Jack recovered from heart surgery, we planned an elk hunt in Montana. I was a bit apprehensive, because I didn't know what to expect. If anything happened on that hunt, I'd be the worst companion to have, knowing next to nothing about first aid and emergency procedures.

Jack scared the hell out of me on that hunt. Declaring himself fit as a fiddle, we climbed a steep mountain in deep snow. Several times I asked if he should be exerting himself that hard.

"Never felt better," Jack said to allay my fears.

Later that day we split up, and he walked at least six miles before returning to our rig. He looked great, said he felt great, and I never remember seeing a bigger smile on his face.

As one of the top booking agents in the world, Jack is the best in the business. He continually strives to work with only the best outfitters, and tries to hunt with each of them to determine their worth. Those hunts have taken Jack around the world many times over.

If you ask him how many times he's been to Africa, he'll shrug his shoulders and tell you he really doesn't know. In reality, he has no less than 30 African trips under his belt, and dozens more in other countries. Listening to Jack's tales about these trips has always been enlightening and interesting. You'll read about plenty of them in this book, along with many amazing stories of clients he's guided over the years.

I don't know exactly when I first heard of Jack Atcheson, but I can tell you it was sometime during my youth when I was a big Jack O'Connor fan. As Shooting Editor of *Outdoor Life*, O'Connor had had many hunts arranged by Jack Atcheson, and the latter accompanied him on several hunting trips.

Little did I know that I'd eventually meet Jack Atcheson and become a close friend. He was, and still is, everything I imagined him to be — a rough, rugged hunter, a superb booking agent, and the kind of person who has a warm smile and is everyone's friend.

But there's another side to Jack that you may not know about. He's also a hunter's champion, defending all the issues of our day that threaten hunters and the sport of hunting.

I can tell you from first hand experience that Jack isn't a fence sitter. He takes one side and defends it fiercely, even though it might be an unpopular view. The management of wolves and grizzlies has become one of Jack's primary subjects of conversation — and action. He minces no words with government agencies, making countless Freedom of Information requests to get the real truth of the issues. Jack's name is a household word among federal and state wildlife officials who don't have the hunter's interest in mind.

Anytime I need information for one of my wolf or grizzly articles I call Jack. Immediately I'm deluged with several pounds of data, all of it literature that he's personally collected from Alaska, Canada, and the continental U.S.

Another major project has been a crusade led by Jack to reform the management of state land in Montana. Prior to Jack's work, millions of acres of public land were posted and off-limits to hunting. Thanks to a major effort by Jack and some of his pals in Butte and elsewhere in Montana, those lands are now open to public hunting — 5.2 million acres of them. It wasn't an easy fight, but then, Jack never backs away from a battle, no matter how big it is.

After a second heart operation, Jack is now semi-retired and has turned most of his business over to his sons, Jack Jr. and Keith. He and his lovely wife, Mary Claire, are spending much of their time traveling and enjoying their family.

You can bet though, that there are many more hunts left in Jack Atcheson. In fact, he and I are currently planning a trip for brown bears and moose in Alaska. I can't wait.

Jim Zumbo, Hunting Editor
OUTDOOR LIFE

HOW I GOT THERE

Deciding which stories I should write for this book from a lifetime of hunting was very difficult. The first hunting I ever did was in Pennsylvania. I was five years old and I shot a cottontail rabbit with dad's old Stevens .32 rimfire rifle. The same year I shot a grey squirrel.

So intent was I, while sitting on a log with my father looking for squirrels, that I apparently fell asleep, but with my eyes open. My father thought I had died. But, I knew I'd done it just because I didn't want to miss anything. My father was primarily a bird hunter, but he also owned a 30/40 Krag, which he had purchased for $2.00. I used this rifle to shoot my first mule deer in Montana. I believe I was 12 years old at the time. I still have both rifles.

When I was eight years old, we still lived in the country. Each day my dog and I would go forth to the forests with my Red Rider BB gun and hunt mice, sparrows, starlings and probably a few species I was not supposed to shoot. There were no kids my age within walking distance, so I spent a lot of time alone hunting, and therefore developed a close and lasting relationship with dogs and wildlife.

In those days kids were supposed to be more responsible — whether true or not, I wandered far afield, usually alone. On more than one occasion I visited the remains of an old house where my great, great grandmother was shot and killed by an Indian's arrow as she was making bread in the kitchen. Some years later, in 1876, Thomas Atcheson would die on the banks of the Little Big Horn River with Gen. George Custer.

I caught my first fish — a carp that was lying between two rocks. I heaved a large boulder between the rocks and stunned the fish, which weighed about five pounds. My mother thought I was a hero. My dog figured we were just wasting time.

My dad encouraged me to keep track of the grouse and pheasant hangouts, forget the "hardrock fishing" and pay more attention to our chickens and ducks, which were plagued by predators. So, I set a steel trap and baited it with bread. I caught dad's valuable white Leghorn rooster. The trap broke his neck; it was to be the only shovel-and-shut-up case of my life.

Those were tough years and my dad had to work from daylight until dark. My mother was ill. One day, just as my father came home in his Model-A Ford, mother fell down the steps. My youngest sister was playing somewhere and we could not find her. We had no telephone and my father

Dad, mother, Phyllis, me and my first dog.

loaded my mother in his Model-A and drove to the hospital. I was left to find and care for my sister. An aunt was supposed to come and stay with us, but didn't arrive until the next day.

After dark I brought my dog into the house and lit the gas lights. We did not have electricity or an inside toilet. I noticed the dog was alert and was looking out the windows and would growl. I knew that particular growl meant there were people outside, but there was no car around and my father's car was also gone. Someone knew we were alone. I watched the house door handle turn and I called out, "Who's there?" There was no answer, but my dog went crazy and roared like a small lion. A few minutes later the back door handle also turned and someone kicked the door.

I had been told to never have a loaded firearm in the house, but I very well recall sitting, with my .32 rimfire rifle in my hands, in a position on a wooden kitchen chair where I could see both doors and the windows that could be forced open. I had a box of shells in my hand with two cartridges ready to load, and the breach was open on the .32 rimfire. Later my father asked, "Were you scared?" I told him, "No. I had my dog and I had a rifle." And, I still do.

In those days doctors would make house calls, even if you lived far out in the country. While visiting my mother during the fall hunting season, the doctor asked me if I knew where there were any pheasants or ruff grouse. Of course I knew. I knew where everything was in the area and had many times crawled through the grass or slipped through the bushes to watch the birds feeding. I also knew where there was a fox who had raised some pups. That mother fox didn't seem to be very afraid of me, but she didn't like my dog. My mother's doctor offered me a quarter to take him to some pheasants. I did, and made my first money for guiding. Later I would be paid for showing the doctor and his friends where to hunt woodchucks and quail, but I kept secret the location of the deer and fox family.

That fall the fox family and weasels killed 35 chickens and 27 tame rabbits in one week. In those days, that was a major hit. My dad taped a five-cell flashlight to his double barrel Montgomery Ward's shotgun and began damage control. About a year later, my mother, using the same big flashlight, hit and knocked out an intruder fighting with my dad. Mother was only five feet tall, but was hell on defense, with strong family ties, as I would have with my wife and four children.

As I reflect back on this, I believe by my tenth year the described events pretty much encompassed the events that would regularly occur for the rest of my life. I would be a wandering hunter.

I have spent an enormous amount of time hunting and fishing for small game and big game in North America, Africa and Asia. I don't know if one should call this hundreds of hunts or thousands of days with many interesting and great people, and some not so great. But, I was there at the right time to see an era end.

After World War II, people had better transportation and more money for hunting. I was only too eager to volunteer to visit world-wide hunting areas and spread the word. The cost, to me, was low, often free tickets and free licenses to better understand the conditions, but those who gave to me expected a lot in return. There were lots of clients, and as many places to go, including Zambia, Botswana, Northwest Territories, British Columbia, Alaska and Tanzania, among others. Argali and bongo were unheard of by most hunters, and the guides, both Indian and especially the Africans, were still part of an age and culture very unlike today. Many of the events that took place during my lifetime of hunting adventures worldwide can never be duplicated; the primitive places aren't primitive any more.

The cost has risen from $45 a day for a British Columbia sheep hunt to $1,500. I paid $600 for a full license in Zambia for 30 species, including cats, sable, kudu, roan, buffalo and elephant. The second elephant was $125. Additional buffalo were $25 each. On my first bighorn sheep hunt, 12 people applied for 10 permits. Last year 2,000 applied. Tough odds.

For various reasons, the tiger story was the hardest to write. Jack O'Connor gave the story its name after our exchange of tiger hunting stories on a deer stand in 1977; in that conversation, Jack told me to write a book, so I did.

Still, it was hard to make a story selection. Sometimes an accumulation of events occurs over a period of years before actually leading up to the final stalk and squeezing of the trigger. Some hunts were incredibly difficult and dangerous. Others have been so easy it's hard to make a story out of them.

Actually, many of the greatest trophies in the world were taken by accident, by people hunting for something else who just blundered onto the world record animal. Luck plays a great part in a hunter's success. Certainly skill and effort is important, but luck or fate, whatever you choose to call it, is the deciding factor — your good luck and the animal's bad luck.

Some of my best trophies, in fact most of them, were taken near the end or actually the last few hours of the last day. Obviously, I had spent considerable time looking over average trophies, looking for a big one or a better one. Sometimes I worked especially hard to see anything at all. For this book, I have selected a cross-section of events that are accurate to the best of my knowledge and fading memory. I spoke with other people on the hunts, and my memory was sharpened by photographs and notes that were taken on the specific hunts.

I did find it interesting that two people who shared the same event saw it so differently, so much so that I wondered if they had been on the same hunt as me. I did not shoot all the big trophies I went out looking for. Sometimes, however, someone else in the party took something spectacular, or we didn't get anything at all and would try again, and again, and again. Some I'm still trying for.

The rules of hunting and the game laws have changed dramatically. Some current laws were always laws, but were ignored by locals in the area, including law enforcement people.

When I was a boy of 15, I left Butte, Montana, and moved to Libby, Montana, in the northwestern part of the state. I lived with an uncle, then alone in a tent and cabin in the woods for a couple of years. I worked for the J. Neils Lumber Company. That may sound rough for a boy that young, but in those days most young men started life early. One day a man I looked up to asked me to help him rob a store. I said no, and forever would suspect that there were two sides to everyone. My idea of a big weekend was to hunt, and on Sunday evening eat a roast chicken and, for dessert, a melted mass of one pound of chocolate, one pound of coconut, about two pounds of walnuts and a quart of butter pecan ice cream.

The Lincoln County deer season customarily opened on the Fourth of July. Deer were incredibly abundant, as were black bears. Elk, moose and bighorn were scarce. Black bears were shot for their fat, which was used for gourmet cooking. Bear meat was eaten if the bear was young. The limit on ducks was 25. I believe it was the same on trout, except brook trout were unlimited. Very little impact, if any, was made on wildlife by people hunting for themselves for meat or sport hunting. Nowadays, laws must be rigidly complied to — many more people hunting in less habitat. But, in most cases, American game animals are now at an all-time high.

I don't think many could repeat my efforts. The opportunity just isn't there, to say nothing of the time and money. I think that not only is that era over, but that times are changing once again.

I hunted with Warren Page when he field-tested Remington's pilot model of the 7mm Remington magnum. I arranged various hunts for Elmer Keith in Alaska and Africa, and traded him a taxidermy job for a rifle and a pistol. I also arranged various hunts with Jack O'Connor in Zambia and Southwest (Namibia) Africa with Volker and Anka Grellman. Namibia was then, and still is, in great demand. These stories are still in my head. There also have been good times with John Jobson, Mike Hanback, Jim Carmichel, Tom Fulgham, Bill McRae, Craig Boddington, and some very special times with Jim Zumbo, the world's best-known elk hunter and a genuinely nice person. Jim and I plan to hunt big mule deer this fall and for cape buffalo next spring.

These stories consist of situations that I thought were unusual or dangerous. Sometimes I took the game, sometimes my friends shot the game, and sometimes the quarry slipped away. And on some occasions, after many years of hunting, when the opportunity did present itself, I declined shooting the animal I had hunted for so long, and shot a younger one right next to him because I prefer to hunt that mountain and see, once again, that familiar track. It is hard to shoot an animal you have "named" or observed on various occasions. But, you also must remove some game to make way for its replacement; that is part of the circle of life.

Jack Atcheson
Butte, Montana
Summer 1995

I GUESS I FORGOT

"Dear Mr. Atcheson: The hunt you arranged for me with Bill Svejkowsky was a magnificent experience for the first seven days. Everything went well. On the eighth day of the hunt, Mr. Svejkowsky suddenly became very aggressive. He cursed me, called me names, jerked me off of my horse and hit me. Then, he jumped up on my horse and rode off and I had to walk five miles back to hunting camp. Needless to say, I am a very disgruntled hunter."

I, of course, approached Bill Svejkowsky and said, "Bill, what happened on the hunt? Mr. Brown says you cursed him, beat him up and then made him walk back to camp because you took his horse. What happened?"

Bill replied, "Yeah, that's right, I was riding up to him and he up and shot my horse. In fact, he shot the heel off my boot and the bullet went into the horse's heart. I guess he forgot to mention that."

I WON'T PAY THE BILL

We had arranged a hunting trip in Zambia for Jack O'Connor, Outdoor Life editor, and several of his hunting buddies. The safari turned out to be very successful and each client had a box of trophies to be processed and shipped to the client who owned them. All of the hunters received their bills, paid them and received their trophies except one individual, who owned a large sporting goods store. We'll call him Paul.

For whatever reason, Paul was being difficult. He would not pay and the safari company would not ship the trophies. The safari company's secretary, Mrs. Baldwin, wrote to O'Connor stating, "Your friend Paul is being very difficult about his trophy shipments and we are wondering if there is any way which you might influence him to clear up this account and resolve this situation so that everyone is satisfied."

Jack took the same letter and wrote across the side, "Dear Mrs. Baldwin — Our friend Paul has been a real pain in the ass on several hunts we have been on, but I will see what I can do to expedite the matter." O'Connor then mailed the same letter back to Mrs. Baldwin. Upon seeing this, Mrs. Baldwin again took the same letter, sent it to Paul, and across the bottom wrote, "See, even your friends don't like you."

Of course, when Paul received it he was furious and mailed the same letter back to O'Connor, and eventually, Jack O'Connor mailed it to me. But, Paul did pay the bill.

JACK O'CONNOR'S LAST HUNT

Published in Outdoor Life, March 1988

When Jack O'Connor asked whether we could hunt whitetails together, I was overwhelmed. Little did I know *this* would be the legend's final outing.

The whitetail buck was enormous, bigger than any I'd ever seen before. Though I'd hunted around the world many times, I'd never been as excited as I was at that moment. The buck's rack was high and heavy, with at least 12 points on each side, and his brow tines were each easily one foot long. As an official Boone and Crockett Club measurer, I knew that the deer was easily a candidate for the record book.

The buck's size wasn't the only reason for my excitement. Jack O'Connor was sitting a few feet away from me, and Jack wanted a big whitetail, bigger than any he'd ever taken.

At the time of our hunt in the fall of 1977, Jack O'Connor was a living legend. Having been *Outdoor Life's* Shooting Editor for 31 years, he was to hunting and shooting what Babe Ruth was to baseball or what Elvis was to rock and roll.

Jack was the king of gun writers. Every shooter had heard of Jack

O'Connor. He was a man so powerful that in a single session at his typewriter, he could sway opinions for or against a particular rifle caliber. Because of Jack's writings, some calibers, such as the .270, prospered over the years, and others died a quick death.

In 31 years, Jack had written almost 400 columns, in addition to 200 feature stories for *Outdoor Life* and more than a dozen hunting and shooting books. I was more than pleased to see that I was one of the people to whom he dedicated a book, "Sheep & Sheep Hunting."

Jack had hunted throughout most of the world and was considered the last word in sheep hunting and rifles. If you had a question about a big-game animal or a gun, you called or wrote to Jack O'Connor. He tried to answer every letter. By his count, he had responded to more than 200,000 pieces of mail.

A few months before the hunt, Jack had called and asked if we could hunt whitetails and pronghorns in Montana. I was overwhelmed at the idea.

I'm a hunter's booking agent. I'd arranged hunts for Jack in Africa, Canada, Alaska and in the continental United States. But this was the first time I'd have him all to myself. I was beside myself with the enormity of it all. I would go with Jack, and my son, Jack, Jr., would go antelope hunting with Jack O'Connor's son, Bradford.

So there we were, sitting on a log in Montana. At least 20 other whitetails were with the big buck, including two other very large bucks that looked like twins but which were easily outclassed by the giant. But Jack was positioned so that he couldn't see the deer.

I knew that the deer wouldn't hang around for very long. In fact, I wondered why they were there at all. Big bucks seldom are so accommodating. The wind was blowing hard, carrying our scent directly to the whitetails. Jack and I were sitting on a log in a fairly open spot, and the deer were milling about in confusion just 50 feet away.

I didn't dare move or talk for fear of spooking the animals. Somehow, I had to call Jack's attention to them. He was sitting on the middle of the log. I was straddling the log so that I could look both ways. Jack was faced one way . . . the wrong way.

My rifle lay on my lap, along with a five-foot walking stick. Carefully picking up the stick, I eased it around and cautiously poked it into Jack's back, hoping he'd realize that I was trying to signal him.

Because the wind was blowing so hard, Jack jabbed back at the stick, thinking that it was the pesky branch of a willow being shaken by the wind.

The herd of deer eyed us suspiciously. I became totally unnerved. I didn't know what to do. Under other circumstances, I would have shot the buck myself, and that made me even more distressed. I wanted Jack to shoot the biggest live whitetail I ever saw.

Our hunt was in eastern Montana, the second part of a double-header. Prior to the whitetail hunt, we'd tried for pronghorn antelope in another area.

As it had turned out, the pronghorn hunt had been frustrating and disappointing, though we'd seen some enormous bucks. The only buck taken had been shot by Jack's pal, Henry Kaufman, who had accompanied us on both hunts. Also along was my friend, Tom Radoumis, who Jack jokingly nicknamed "Zeus" because of Tom's Greek ancestry.

I had done some scouting the day before Jack and Henry had arrived, and I had located a very big pronghorn that I judged to have horns between 17 and 18 inches. Another buck, with 16-inch horns, accompanied the larger antelope. Both were phenomenal animals.

My rancher friend, Albert Newman, had rigged a horse-drawn buckboard from which to hunt for a day. But Jack wasn't feeling well, so we drove the prairie roads in my Suburban.

Both big antelope were where I'd seen them the day before. A third buck, with 15-inch horns, was lying in a draw just below the other two. I had located the trio from a small knoll with my spotting scope, but when I returned to my vehicle with the good news, Jack said that he wasn't up to a long walk.

At that point, I realized that Jack O'Connor was ailing. He was human after all. I was sad, but most determined.

The only chance we had to get close to the antelope was to drive up a creek bottom on an old homestead road, and then try a short stalk from below. A high ridge separated the road from the bucks, and I figured that we could get reasonably close to the animals.

I was in a hurry, probably driving too fast because I was thinking intently about the huge pronghorns. Suddenly, I looked out the window to my left, and there were the three bucks racing along beside the truck. Before I could react, the bucks veered sharply and dashed onto the road in front of us.

It was just a matter of luck that I didn't run them over. What a story; O'Connor's big buck run over by a truck! My quick stop jarred all of us, and that was the end of the pronghorns for the moment.

Later in the day, we saw another good buck, but it was not as big as the large pronghorn we'd seen that morning. The animal was standing close to the road, but was nearly impossible to stalk on the open flat.

"Let's try a trick," Jack said. "Drive past the buck until we're out of sight; then, you and Henry get out. Tom and I will park the vehicle where it's visible. That will hold the antelope's attention. Then, you and

Henry circle around on foot and shoot.

"I've decoyed lots of sheep that way," Jack continued. "A long time ago, I realized that animals can't count people."

Jack's strategy worked, though at one point in the stalk, I was sure we had blown it. We had crawled past a pond full of geese and had alarmed the birds. They had flushed noisily, and I had expected the buck to take off, but his attention had remained riveted on the vehicle. Henry then made a fine shot, and we had our first pronghorn.

For the next two days, we did a lot of driving, and Tom and I did a lot of walking. Jack was feeling progressively worse. He didn't complain, but was obviously in pain. I was worried about what would happen if we found a trophy buck and had to make a long stalk.

Despite our efforts, we hadn't located another worthwhile pronghorn close enough for a shot, and just as we were about to give up, I saw a golden eagle land beside a nest on a little rocky knob. The nest seemed to be unusually large, so I climbed the knob to have a look. I knew that the young eagles were fledged and long gone, but I was curious about the bones and remains of the eagle's prey that would litter the immediate vicinity of the nest.

When I reached the knob, I looked down the other side and was startled to see the monster pronghorn bedded down just 100 yards away. The buck was very distinctive. Not only did he have enormous horns, but he also had very dark cheek patches that almost looked like eyes. I'd never seen an antelope with those markings before. There was no question. It was the same one I'd almost run over with the truck.

I slowly backed away from the knob and ran back to the truck to tell Jack about the antelope. When I reported our great luck, he sat quietly and didn't say anything for a moment. Then, with regret in every word, he spoke.

"I've hunted all my life and never shot a 17-inch antelope," he said. "I'd love to take him, but I don't think I should climb that hill."

I was shocked and disappointed. "My God," I thought to myself, "Jack isn't going to try for the giant pronghorn!"

Until this hunt, I had been sure that Jack O'Connor could climb any hill, make any shot, do the impossible. Now, the realization that the dean of American hunters was old hit me hard. It was a helpless feeling.

"Why don't you go up there and shoot that buck?" Jack said to me. "You've killed two 17-inch antelope. It would be nice to know that a pal of mine is the only man I know of who has taken three." He even gave me some of his .270 cartridges to use for this special event. Today I still have one that I'm saving for a special buck.

Shooting an antelope meant for Jack O'Connor while Jack sat in the truck was not something I could do. So we simply returned to the ranch. A plane would then fly Jack on to the second part of the hunt. Tom and I would drive over the next day.

But now it was a new ball game. Jack was gone and there was still some time left to hunt that evening and the next morning. For the 17-inch buck I dug out my permit and loaded up with the cartridges Jack gave me. It didn't take Tom and I long to head back to the ridge where I had last seen the big buck.

I didn't expect the buck to still be lying there, but I thought he would be somewhere in the vicinity. There was nothing. We decided not to wander around too much, as we might scare him completely out of the area, and it was going to be dark in a few minutes anyway. Reluctantly, we headed back to camp.

The next morning, before daylight, we were back on the same ridge again, as I figured he was not too far from where I had last seen him. We carefully glassed the entire area. We saw a few does, fawns, small bucks, and a couple of coyotes. Tom didn't have a permit, so it was my decision on what to do. I said, "Tom, I believe the antelope may have gone for water last night. I know about a half a mile from here there is a spring that

Henry Kuffman, Jack O'Connor and myself. It was Jack's plan that got Henry his antelope. I sure miss that man.

has quite a bit of green grass growing around it. Let's hike over there and see what we can see."

"Good idea," said Tom. Away we went.

We no sooner looked over the ridge, and there were the three bucks — all within easy shooting distance. But, believe it or not, the big buck had lost a horn. Damn, that was frustrating! I decided we would go back and look around to where he was bedding the previous night and see if we could generally pick up any tracks in the soft soil. Maybe we would see where he had lost the horn. If I could find the horn, I would come back and shoot him. We looked and looked, but no horn. Finally, I decided to go back and look the bucks over again, thinking I might take him anyway and manufacture a horn to match the other one out of fiberglass. "I think you should," Tom said. "Half an antelope is better than none, particularly when you're talking about bucks in the 17-inch category." I was easily convinced.

Again, we returned to the spring. Naturally, the antelope were gone. We eventually located them about a half a mile to the north. The big buck was easily recognizable by the unusually large dark hair on the side of his neck. But, that was all we could recognize, for he had lost the other horn. I then decided to shoot the other buck, which was about 16 inches. He had to be somewhere close by. Sure enough, here came the other two bucks walking up out of the draw. I couldn't believe it! The 16-inch buck had lost both of his horns also.

I decided that I had used up all my antelope luck for the year and would see if we couldn't improve the situation by going to another part of the state and hunting whitetail deer with Jack.

The second ranch, where we hunted whitetails, was in a lovely setting, with old cabins on a bluff above a river bottom surrounded by dense brush, cottonwood trees and lush croplands. Jack was awed at the thought that this area was once home to great herds of bison, elk and large numbers of grizzlies. The ranch belonged to Roy Gentry.

I did some scouting the evening before the hunt and saw at least 200 whitetails feeding in the alfalfa and slipping through the dense underbrush. I had seen some huge whitetails on that ranch on previous hunts, and I fully expected Jack to take the biggest buck of his life in the morning.

Being with America's top gun writer on a giant whitetail hunt would be a highlight in my life. I can remember thinking about where Jack was likely to kill the buck, the kind of shot he would make and how I'd get the buck out. I even envisioned the way the head would be mounted for Jack.

We positioned ourselves in a strategic stand the next morning, waiting for drivers on horseback to push deer around in the brush. It didn't take long for whitetails to show up. Dozens of deer moved by us, including a number of bucks, but none were exceptional.

I'd never seen more whitetails on a drive in my life. They came by constantly, along with foxes, coyotes, raccoons and pheasants. It was a great show. Jack seemed to be enjoying it immensely. We talked of many things.

At one point, he reminisced about driving tigers in India and how often the beaters were mauled by tigers. He noted that if we had been hunting tigers, the situation would have been vastly different for the men on horseback. It was common, Jack said, for tigers to attack elephants and their riders beating the brush. I told Jack of my experience of tiger hunting in Korea. He laughed and said, "That's one hell of a story, 'Hunting Tigers the Hard Way.' You should write a book."

The subject turned to Jack's hunting preferences.

"What do you like to hunt most?" I asked.

"Sometimes, I think I like to hunt tigers, sometimes sheep, and right now, whitetail deer. I guess that I like to hunt everything, as long as the animal has a fair chance."

After several more drives, the day ended without Jack having fired a shot. But he'd had chances at several respectable bucks. Jack had not wanted to shoot an average buck because he'd taken many such bucks. He had wanted something more.

"I'd like to take one really good whitetail buck," Jack said as we walked to the vehicle. "But if a hunter wants to shoot big bucks, he must learn not to shoot the small ones. This may mean you go home empty-handed a few times, but that is the difference between hunting and trophy hunting."

It doesn't hurt to be lucky, too," I remarked.

"And maybe 30 years younger," Jack said, as we headed for my truck.

Before we reached the truck, I pointed to a stand high in a tree and told Jack that a hunter had fallen out of the stand and had been killed the previous year.

"I cannot think of a better way to go," Jack said with a slight smile. "I don't want a long, lingering death; I want to die quickly. I'd like to die while on a hunting trip and have my ashes spread over the sheep country in the Yukon."

Jack's words seemed to reinforce a strange feeling I had that this would be his last hunt. Somehow, I believe that he felt it as well.

The next day, while we were driving to a stand, a very large buck ran across the dirt road in front of us. It stopped and looked back. The deer was so close that I could see his bulging eyes.

Instead of running off immediately, the deer stared at us. Jack had made a hasty effort to get out of the vehicle. But Jack's bulky winter

Jack was best known as a sheep hunter but tigers were high on his list. Jack named my tiger story for me.

clothes hung up on the truck door handle and seat. He cursed his 75 years, the manufacturers of the bulky cloths, Stetson hats and long-barreled rifles.

By the time he finally got out, the buck had seen enough and was running through the brush. Although a shot would have been possible, Jack got back in the car and sat without saying a word.

It was obvious that Jack was terribly frustrated. I felt bad for him. In earlier years, no running buck was a match for Jack O'Connor's incredible shooting.

Finally, Jack started to laugh at the humor of the situation.

"I don't think that deer deserved to be shot," he said, grinning. "Anyone who is so old and decrepit that he can't get out of a vehicle while a deer waits to be killed, shouldn't have shot anyway."

The old hunter had a wry sense of humor, and didn't mind poking fun at himself.

Later that morning, several whitetails appeared before our stand. Some were very fine bucks. Tom and the horseback riders were doing their best to keep deer in front of us. Occasionally, Jack would raise his rifle, look through the scope, and lower it again. When a particularly good buck went by and Jack didn't shoot, I asked him why he was hesitating.

"He wasn't the right one," he said.

Despite bad luck throughout both hunts, Jack kept his good humor and told us more stories of his hunts. I think he perceived my personal frustration that he hadn't scored. He was trying to make *me* feel better. But Tom and I hadn't given up. We were determined to give Jack the best hunt he ever had, with or without luck.

Our next plan was to go to a spot where I'd previously seen a truly big buck. Whitetails normally hang out in the same area, and we hoped to see this particular buck again.

Jack and I walked to the log I'd selected to watch from. I positioned him where he could look down a narrow corridor that had a light background of grass. A heavy frost as bright as snow provided a contrasting backdrop.

Tom and the other drivers were good. Before long, a number of deer ran in front of Jack and me. A dozen does passed through the corridor Jack was watching. Following was a nice buck that bounded through so fast that Jack couldn't react in time. Nor could I.

More deer, including several good bucks, ran through, and Jack looked at me with a pained expression. "I'm rattled," he said. "I must be coming down with buck fever."

I couldn't believe the deer that were running by. I'd never seen more shootable whitetails in my life.

The wind had begun to blow furiously just before the 20-plus deer, including the giant buck and a twin pair of great five-pointers showed up. I firmly believed that the gods were setting the stage for Jack O'Connor's final act.

I'd never been in quite such a predicament before. I was poking Jack in the back. He was grabbing at the stick. And a record-class whitetail was watching our performance.

The first two bucks were alarmed by our movements and ran. They made so much noise that Jack quickly turned and saw them disappear into the brush.

"Damn," he whispered. "How can my luck be so bad?" As soon as he spoke, he spotted the big buck, but it was too late. The animal quickly melted back into the willows.

Suddenly, I saw the twin bucks heading back toward the corridor that Jack had been watching. One of them stopped near a dead snag and stared at us.

"Shoot, shoot," I whispered. But Jack didn't shoot because most of the deer's body was hidden.

"Get ready," I warned. "Here comes the second buck."

I felt foolish telling Jack O'Connor what to do. He was one of the most knowledgeable hunters I'd ever met, and he was indeed ready, but this was not a good day for him. It was like a bad dream. To me, the champion of hunters was now in the ring, under the spotlight, with the crowd cheering.

The bucks suddenly vanished, as happens so often with whitetails. They were gone and no amount of wishing could bring them back.

At that moment, the wind stopped and the woods grew silent. I was never so disappointed in my life. I turned around to pick up my rifle, and was astonished to see the giant buck once again. The great whitetail was in the open, standing broadside, looking directly at me.

Picking up my rifle, I slowly turned my head and saw Jack looking the opposite way. He was still watching for the twin bucks that had made off in another direction.

I whispered loudly to Jack, but my voice spooked the buck. He whirled and crashed into the willows, bounding off in a way I knew was for keeps.

I was heartsick. Why did so many bucks present themselves, and why were we so unlucky?

Then, the impossible happened. The huge buck stopped running and trotted right back to the very place he had just left. It was too much. I raised my rifle, aimed at his heart, but could not pull the trigger. I was staring at what might have been the biggest buck in Montana, but I couldn't shoot. I desperately longed to hear the roar of Jack's .270. There was no reason in the world why that buck should have returned and presented himself for another shot. It was as if the good Lord was giving Jack O'Connor the finest show of his life.

I raised my rifle again, but could not bring myself to fire it. This was Jack's hunt, not mine, even though he had insisted that I shoot it if I had an opportunity.

The enormous buck spun and ran off, this time for good. I turned and was shocked to see Jack standing with his rifle to his shoulder, aiming at the buck. He was grinning from ear to ear, and I realized that he had seen the buck, but for some reason had refused to shoot.

"God, what a buck," he said simply. "What a buck!"

As we left the woods, our hunt over, I couldn't bring myself to ask Jack why he hadn't shot. Perhaps he'd seen me drawing a bead on the buck and wanted me to take it.

Perhaps. Or maybe he hadn't fired because he believed that once you take the biggest buck of your life, there is nothing to look forward to.

Jack O'Connor passed away the next spring, in 1978. I have returned to the whitetail ranch several times since Jack's death. I never saw the giant buck again. Nor have I ever seen the unbelievable number of bucks that we saw on that hunt. Most of the deer there died of Blue

Tongue.

I am convinced that someone up high was pulling for old Jack. Jack was one of the finest hunters and shooting writers that ever lived. It was fitting that he was shown such a superb parade of whitetail bucks the last time he carried a rifle in his beloved American West.

LOCAL HOSPITALITY

I was duck hunting in northern Montana, not far from the Canadian border. The reservoir where we planned to do most of our hunting had pretty well dried out. It was not a good year for geese. Being unfamiliar with the area, we thought we would check around with some of the locals and see if there were some potholes or livestock reservoirs that we could try. What few people lived in the area did not seem to be hunters and weren't exactly helpful. The last assistance we sought brought the message to us very loud and clear.

We stopped to buy gasoline. There were six dilapidated buildings in town, one with an old gas pump in front. The pump was one of those old kind that had the open cylinder glass top. After considerable searching, we found someone with a key. He really looked like someone out of the movie *Deliverance*. A very tall black hat and tattered bib overalls that were cut too short. He was tall and slender with a long black beard. We decided to quiz him about the hunting possibilities. My friend, Jack Jones, of Butte, Montana, talked to him for a few minutes, but the man said nothing. My other buddy, Steve Bayless, of Helena, asked a few questions, too. Then, nothing but silence, although the man would stare intently while the one-sided conversation was being made. I thought at first he might not be able to hear and suggested that they speak louder, which they did.

He then responded in a most menacing way, and at the same time jerking the hose nozzle out of the gas tank and flipping some gasoline in our direction. He said, "I don't hear nothing, I don't see nothing, I know nothing, and you guys want to remember that you are a long way from home."

He snatched my $20, turned and left without another word. We also turned and left without another word, and I have never been back there since. I didn't even ask for my change.

LIGHTS

I have always had a lot of trouble getting children to shut the doors and turn off lights. But one time, it may have prevented a tragedy.

I took mine and a neighbor's children hunting in eastern Montana. We were camping in a tent and hunting out of a vehicle. Three of the boys had their first antelope licenses and the three younger kids hunted rabbits. We were driving on a ridge that had many small finger ridges running down into a big flat basin and where we could see several herds of antelope. One of the boys and myself had not yet shot an antelope. A buck or doe would suffice.

It was the last day and we only had a couple of hours of daylight. It looked like a quick, easy deal. We crawled down a ravine single file, like an Indian raiding party. The antelope moved. We tried to outflank them; the antelope moved again. This process continued until almost dark. Then the wind picked up dramatically and the temperature started to drop. Snowflakes were flying. It was time to leave.

I realized that we had walked several miles and now because of the falling snow, I could not see any landmarks. Everything looked white. There was no depth perception. I knew if we followed the creek bottom long enough we would come to a road, but I feared that we were about to get a severe winter storm. The best idea was to get back to the vehicle. This is the only time in my life that I felt I had put children in a dangerous situation. Many people have frozen to death because of sudden storms in Montana.

We could not wander all night. There was no fuel or shelter and I didn't have my compass or a flashlight. One of the kids was carrying my pack while we were stalking the antelope and had left it laying somewhere.

Without a skyline, the country looked the same in one direction as it did in another. I picked a direction. I was surely betting on my inner instincts like never before, and headed out. But, by then it was so dark we could see nothing. And, it was getting colder by the minute. I had to trust my judgment and wondered how I would ever see the vehicle even if we were just ten feet from it. Then I saw a light a long way off. A house! We had a target.

I said we'd have to move quickly towards the light before the swirling snow blanked it out. As we got closer it looked like a strange looking window. Then I suddenly realized what we were looking at. When we left the vehicle earlier that day, one of the boys left the door ajar and the dome light was on and acted as a beacon. The mistake became our salvation.

THE RULING REPTILE

There was no doubt about it. The boat was sinking. We were about 300 yards from shore, and that is a long way to swim in a crocodile-infested lake. Even if I reached the shore, I was still in big trouble, for a rogue elephant had been following our progress, and for some reason, resented us being there. The old tusk-less cow was making false charges to the lake's shore, her ears standing out and her trunk reaching out as if she were waiting to wrap it around my neck, and then proceed to stomp me between her toenails. My only consolation was that there would be five of us swimming to the shore, which would divide her attention, providing that a croc didn't get us in the water — an incentive to swim fast.

But the crocodile I was really concerned with was in the boat with me at that very moment. The gigantic 1,500 pound crocodile, his tail thrashing like a giant whip and his mouth wide open and lunging with all his strength to reach us. The only reason he didn't have one of us now was because the bulkhead in our 16-foot boat was too narrow for him to get his shoulders through. But, with the boat sinking, he soon would be free to take us all on at his leisure. Damn! I didn't think it was going to end up this way!

No, I certainly cannot imagine how I got into this predicament. It had all started out in a completely different vein. Jim Carmichel, Gun Editor of *Outdoor Life*, and I had been planning to hunt in South Africa with John Coleman and in Zimbabwe with Mike Rowbotham. The objective of the hunt was not crocodiles. In fact, I never even thought of crocodiles, nor did Jim!

Although both of us had hunted in Africa many times, there are certain species we did not have, or wanted to improve on. Jim wanted to hunt some of the more exotic animals in South Africa, like black wildebeest, bontebok, vaal rhebok, mountain reedbuck, bushbuck, nyala and greater kudu. A spiral horned antelope hunt, plus buffalo, of course, were high on our agenda — and, maybe, a big leopard to cover an empty spot on Jim's wall.

My good friend, and great professional hunter, John Coleman, was selected to give us a tour of South Africa, and pick up a few trophies while we were there.

It was an unusual year for that part of the world. The highlands of South Africa were experiencing one of their coldest winters and there was a foot of fresh snow. Although I am noted for having all the necessary equipment, regardless of occasion, I certainly didn't expect snow on that trip! I doubt that many people hunting in Africa have ever spent an afternoon in knee-deep snow drifts, tracking wildebeest. Somehow it just didn't seem right, and the hunt was tougher than expected. Between the snow drifts and mud, some of the areas were just plain inaccessible. Our first attempt failed, and we decided to hunt elsewhere at lower elevations, but we were plagued with wind.

I have noted while hunting around the world that most species are more difficult to hunt in the wind. They are either laid up tight in the thicket, or your scent is picked up and spread into every nook and corner of every valley, and all you see are rear-ends disappearing over the next ridge. We only had so many days to allocate per species, so decided to concentrate on black wildebeest and bontebok and bushbuck. The first two species we collected almost immediately, but the bushbuck were just being plain unreasonable. We could hear them bark, but no way were they sticking their nose out into that kind of wind.

John is an exceptionally good hunter, and knew of a thicket surrounded by a dozen open patches of grass about 10 or 15 feet wide. Ideally, we would have had some sort of tree stand, except all the trees were in the wrong place. So, Jim and John decided they would hike up a small ridge where from the top they could look into the thicket. It was going to be a long shot, if there was any shot at all. While they made their way up the steep slope, I walked down the valley about half a mile where there was a small opening between two brush patches. It wasn't much of a place to sit, but hunting bushbuck is a lot like hunting whitetails, it was as good a place as any.

Any bushbuck that wanted to follow the thicket in either direction would have to go through this opening. I would have to be quick as I only had a three foot space in which to shoot. I would almost have to be aiming at the opening, or I would have no time to shoot. I put my rifle to my shoulder, found a fork in the bushes, and was prepared to do just that. I had been sitting there almost two hours, it was late afternoon, and the sun was setting.

I was thinking about the magnificent game management program that had been accomplished by South African ranchers. Although most areas are completely fenced, many species, such as the bushbuck, come and go as they please — much like a whitetail in farmland country in America. I have seen kudu either jumping over, or sliding between the wire on eight foot fences that prevent species like zebra, white rhino, and wildebeest from leaving a particular area.

Many species in South Africa are on ranches so large that the game is actually free ranging. However, these hunts require more time, for the animals might be there on a given day, or they might not be, but it makes for a better hunt. And, fair chase is paramount to me, or I don't shoot.

I had about given up on bushbuck, and probably wasn't paying attention when a magnificent buck stepped through the clearing, then stopped. I could see his hind quarters plainly and a 250 grain Nosler from my .338 Winchester would have plowed right through his pelvis and put him down for sure. Although an effective shot, even for lions, I personally like to shoot at the shoulders, lung/heart area, regardless of what angle the animal is standing. I hesitated a second too long when I heard the loud crack from Jim's rifle and solid thump of the bullet connecting, and at the same time, my bushbuck disappeared. This was a good example of the adage, "He who hesitates doesn't get a shot!"

It seems that Jim's bushbuck — an exceptional record class bushbuck at that — had been feeding around the edge of a small clearing, but never would quite come out for a good shot. Jim had been holding on him for about 30 minutes and was able to shoot between two trees, about eight inches apart, which is a pretty exceptional shot when you consider that he was over 200 yards away.

By the time we took some pictures, it was dark. We then drove most of the night to another secret area of John's to hunt nyala. Although the nyala is a shaggy looking, spiral horn antelope, it apparently has pretty thin blood and does not move around in cold weather as freely as might other species. The nyala is a very wary mule deer-size antelope if hunted very much, and sticks to thick timber like a wild, wild whitetail buck.

I had hunted Zululand before, and after three days of brush creeping saw a very fine nyala and shot him in his bed. It was my only chance, but now Jim and I both wanted nyala. I wanted one bigger than I had taken before, but I wanted to hunt an area where the nyala naturally lived and where we would have a challenging hunt. We tossed a coin and Jim would get first shot. (He used his two headed coin.) Jim and John Coleman went in one direction, and I and a native tracker in another. The area we were hunting reminded me a great deal of the country around San Francisco — grassy hillsides and ravines full of brush and timber.

We hadn't gone over 500 yards up the hillside when I saw, between two trees, a nyala bull standing and watching us. He had probably the most beautiful long-haired coat I have ever seen. His horns looked especially large, although he was partly obscured in the underbrush. It was too far for a shot, but I could plainly see him through my binoculars. And, it was pretty obvious that he could see us as well and was keeping a close eye on our movements. The only way to reach him was across an open grassy hillside. I did not want to walk directly towards him, as I was sure he would run. Instead, I started angling off to the right, which was also going to bring me within shooting distance. But the nyala evidently was thinking along those same lines; he started to move, walking parallel with my route. So, in fact, I was not getting any closer. One smart animal!

My African friend said he thought the nyala was headed up into a very rocky area where there were a lot of cobras. He quickly added that he had seen a few black mambas there also. These are two snakes I don't like to be around. By now I could see the nyala was extremely large, with horns probably 30 inches long, which is exceptional.

"Damn the cobras," I said. "Full speed ahead!" (But I knew I was lying, and so did the tracker.)

But, sure enough, the nyala knew his business, and when I last saw him, he was following right along the base of the cliff. Either he wasn't afraid of cobras, or he knew I was. The big bull passed out of sight, but my faithful guide felt that he was going to turn downhill, which was the tendency of other nyala in this area. A good guide is what makes the hunt. We decided to head him off at the pass and go directly through several of the wooded ravines where the black man felt we would be able to see him on the opposite ridge. Those are pretty long odds, but this was a pretty big nyala!

It is strange that whenever you have your mind set on one particular animal, you see an abundance of others that are plenty shootable, but you want to hold out for the big one, which is what I did. We saw numerous very good bulls, which ordinarily I would have shot. And, as the evening progressed, I started to kick myself for not shooting one, because we did not see the giant bull again. I might add that we may have done better on the big bull, except that when we got near the ridge we were going to spot from, we ran into a troop of monkeys. There was great squealing and squalling and, in all probability, they were telling the nyala exactly where we were.

Then we heard a shot. Since we were the only hunters in the area, I knew this had to be Jim and decided to head in that direction so we could get some pictures before it was dark, if he had taken his nyala, and I had no reason to believe that he hadn't. Jim is not a guy who shoots unless he feels he is going to hit where he is aiming. We found Jim, John, and their tracker making great circles looking for signs of the wounded nyala. Jim felt it was a good shot, and sure enough it wasn't long before John Coleman spotted the nyala laying at the bottom of the draw. It had been shot through the heart but had run for quite some distance. The bull was considerably better than average. Jim was elated, and so was I!

Now I only had one day left to hunt. We had used up much of our time hunting for other species, when in fact the nyala was one of the main animals I wanted. I had already lost out on the bushbuck, although there was a possibility of seeing others. The next day we started to hunt fairly early in the morning looking for a bushbuck, but didn't see any. After lunch we decided to drive up a side road that was seldom used, where perhaps we would be able to look down into some of the draws when the nyala started to move, but we weren't seeing much.

I thought to myself, "Did I blow my chance by not shooting at one of the other bulls? This trophy hunting for the very biggest animal was not always the best way to hunt. All of a sudden, in front of the truck, standing in the middle of the trail, was a magnificent bushbuck. But he didn't stay there long. In just a second he was out of sight and running up hill. John and I agreed it was a worthwhile project to follow him. We had only followed him a short ways when we could see that he turned abruptly back in the same direction from which he'd come. We turned and followed, down across the road into a brushy creek bottom. We could both see that there was no chance of finding this buck — that's why he was so big and had lived so long. He was damned smart! But we decided to push on for another 100 yards to where John remembered there was a clearing. We were thinking of making a little drive and perhaps running him out where I could get some sort of a shot.

Then, as so often happens when you are hunting one species, you see another! And this was a super sighting! Fifty yards away stood an exceptional bull nyala. Apparently he had been feeding with his head down and had not been visible to us. In an instant he was off and running! I could see he was every bit as good or larger than the bull I had seen the day before. But now he was out of sight.

I noticed he was angling up the mountain towards the same rock cliff the other nyala bull had passed through yesterday. In order to reach that area, he was going to go through a small clearing about 100 feet long and 50 feet wide. It would be about a 200 yard shot. I quickly leaned my rifle up against a tree for support and held on the clearing. Usually when I am really prepared, nothing shows up. But, almost like I'd planned it, he ran right through the telescope and I squeezed the trigger. The 250 Nosler hit him behind the right shoulder and dropped him instantly!

John said, "You made a lucky shot."

"Lucky?" said I. "That was just plain good shooting!"

The bull looked great to me, but as we approached him from the rear, John said, "Jack, that is a big one. One of the best I've seen for a long time."

Although I'm not much on keeping records on inches of horn or antler, John measured the bull and he measured just over 30 inches on each horn. The horns had especially heavy bases. I would estimate that this exceptional animal weighed over 300 pounds and had very long hair and would make a great life-size mount for my museum.

The next morning we flew on to Harare, Zimbabwe, and were met by Mike Rowbotham. Mike is one of the most colorful professional hunters I have ever met, a wonderful storyteller with a wealth of information about the old Mau Mau days in Kenya. From experience, I knew that Mike ran the finest of hunting camps! I was looking forward to a great hunt for buffalo, kudu and leopards. After spending two days at Mike's beautiful farm, we left by charter plane for a long flight to the banks of Lake Kariba, 150 miles long, which was the result of a dam backing water up the mighty Zambezi River, which divided Zambia from Zimbabwe. The area we would hunt was the Chrisa Concession.

As expected, Mike had erected several beautiful permanent huts with thatched roofs, whitewashed walls with beautiful paintings of animals and bushman, on both the inside and outside of each dwelling. We had enough time to go down to the bay just below my hut where I caught a couple of small tiger fish. I hooked a couple of very large ones, but they kept cutting my line in half with their sharp teeth. I was using a No. 5 silver Mepps.

Although we were not hunting elephants, another hunter in the camp, John Walker, was. He had passed up several bulls with tusks over 50 pounds, and that day he had shot a very large buffalo with heavy bases and a spread well over 40 inches. John Sharp was his professional hunter and one of my favorite people in the world. John is my kind of guide. He likes to get out and walk and follow game, and not hunt from vehicles. John explained to me that lions were not particularly abundant for some reason, but there were leopards everywhere.

I can't resist using this photo. I may never again even see a 30-inch nyala.

Jim won the toss for the first leopard, (since then I have my own coin!) so I decided I would put some effort into hunting a big kudu, which also were not particularly abundant in this area, but some very large ones could be found. I believe on our first day of hunting Jim Carmichel shot his finest kudu bull. Jim was batting 1,000 percent.

We decided to take Mike's boat and follow along the shores of Lake Kariba and see if we could spot some game along the shore. We could cover a lot of ground in this way. We were also looking for a big elephant for John Walker, who was hunting a different area that day. We saw a very large herd of buffalo, including one exceptional bull. Mike tied up the boat and proceeded on foot quite some distance — about four or five miles. It was very hot. Occasionally you would see the buffalo, but they seemed to be continually moving. Jim also won the toss for first chance on buffalo.

The tracker and I were quite a ways behind Mike and Jim. We had stopped while I was trying to film a crocodile. While waiting, we saw an elephant that was certainly in the 80-pound ivory class, and so it goes.

Jim Carmichel, myself and one of the world's greatest professionals, Mike Rowbotham, admire Jim's great buffalo.

While the elephant hunter was on one side of the valley, the elephant was on another. It would have been an easy stalk. Unfortunately nobody ever saw him again.

The next day we returned to the same area, but followed up another drainage. We had just started walking when I saw a couple of kudu cows and one small bull. Then we saw a large bull — a very large bull! But, he had also seen us and started to run and was immediately out of sight. Jim started digging for his special coin, but I reminded him he already had a kudu. He said, with a wide grin, "I guess I forgot."

I suggested to Mike that I would go after the kudu and they continue looking for buffalo, which was agreeable to him. A tracker and I had only gone a short distance when I could see the bull walking between the trees. He wasn't going to stop and I wasn't going to have much time to shoot, but it would be a good broadside shot. When the bull broke between the trees, he abruptly turned to the right and was approximately 200 yards away. The 250 grain Nosler struck in between the ribs on his left side, and emerged through the middle of the right shoulder. The bull was the largest-bodied kudu I had ever seen. I am sure he would have weighed over 700 pounds — as large as a bull elk. The horns were enormous — my best kudu ever.

I am thoroughly convinced that if I were using a lighter caliber rifle I would not have shot, which all the more reinforced my theory that you should shoot the most powerful rifle that you can shoot accurately and use a heavy bullet.

Almost instantly Jim and Mike showed up behind us. The buffalo had winded them and they decided to come along with me. We were all pleasantly pleased with my good fortune that night at dinner. Mike broke out a couple bottles of South Africa's finest wine. We swapped hunting tales and ate a reedbuck roast, and the cook baked me a cake with white gooey icing with shredded coconut and little chocolate bits sprinkled over it.

The next morning, like every morning, we would descend upon one of the leopard baits. Then, in the evening, from about 4:00 until dark, we would watch again. We were seeing a lot of leopard sign, tracks everywhere. Apparently they were feeding extensively on duikers, which were very abundant. One morning we arrived at one bait just in time to see a very large male and a female leopard walking away.

Leopard baits are usually placed on a limb of the tree high enough so that other predators or lions can't reach the bait. The bait tree should be anywhere from 20 to 50 yards away from the blind, depending on the circumstance, and placed in such a direction that in the evening, the leopard, which would crawl out on the limb, is silhouetted against the sky. Hopefully, the leopard is shot and instantly drops dead. Tracking wounded leopards through thick brush is extremely dangerous. My concern with this was that I am not puncture proof and have an aversion to deep scratches in my skin. Not only that, there is also the possibility of a wounded leopard jumping in the wrong direction, and your partner shooting you. Great gaping wounds made from double 00 buckshot do not appeal to me either!

One evening I saw an exceptional leopard walk up to the tree and then disappear before I could point it out to anyone. Mike felt the leopard was in the tree before we had reached the blind. I am pretty lucky at seeing leopards and believe I have seen something like 14 just walking around through the forest. That was of course, over a period of years. But my luck was still holding. While I was telling John Sharp about my leopard sightings, I pointed ahead at the brush and said, "As a matter of fact, there's another one right there, a small female."

John was astounded.

Later that evening while we were hunting reedbuck, unsuccessfully I might add, I saw another small leopard lying on a log. We had been following along a river bed that had pretty well dried up. Both hippo and elephants had been digging holes, apparently looking for water. Some of the holes were six feet deep and looked like they had been dug out with a bulldozer. Mike advised that we must be careful, the elephants here were not friendly. Numerous times we made wide detours to avoid conflict.

We came across some very fresh buffalo sign and had not gone far before we saw a huge bull standing broadside looking at us. Buffalo always look at you, it seems to me, as if you owed them money. The bull broke and ran, disappearing down over a steep hillside. Contrary to what people believe, most buffalo are very wary of people. I've hunted buffalo that sounded and acted like a herd of cattle. On other occasions, I have seen a herd of approximately 400 buffalo that knew we were tracking them go into a thick clump of brush and stand there without making a single sound. It is remarkable how the cow buffalo can relay a danger signal to the calves that stops them completely in their tracks. It was almost eerie.

However, if you run across an injured buffalo or shoot one and he gets away, and gets to thinking about it, now you have a whole new ball game to play with. An angry cape buffalo is without a doubt one of the most dangerous animals in the world. And also one of the most difficult to kill once they have been injured. But this buffalo we were following was not so tough. One shot by Jim's rifle right behind the shoulders and the buffalo did not go over 100 yards out in an open field where we could easily recover the meat and take great pictures. I decided that unless I saw a phenomenal buffalo, I was not going to shoot one.

The leopard hunting was not going very well. We had as many as three leopards on baits at the same time, but obviously they were feeding during the middle of the night. Sometimes they would only feed one time and not return. There was too much small game to hold their attention to a bait. The next day we decided that we were going to try a different area and took some of the buffalo meat for leopard bait into the Senkwi River basin. This was indeed the beginning of a very interesting adventure.

I suppose at some time one could call the Senkwi, which flowed into the Zambezi River, a scenic river. But the river was dammed, creating an awesome lake called Lake Kariba. The water level in the lake fluctuates considerably, virtually drowning many trees and bushes which, along with the movement of water and erosion, sculpts a sinister looking environment. All of the trees are dead but still standing. And because of mineral in the water, some trees looked bleach white, while others are black or green, their limbs extended towards the heavens like fingers of demons associated with this particular valley.

As we took our 16-foot boat up the river, I immediately did not like the place. It even smelled bad from the rotting vegetation. With all the soil washed away, there appeared to be strange rock formation and cliffs so unlike the rest of the valley. There were a great number of heron nests, vultures and other fish-eating birds looming down at us as we proceeded up the river.

Jim said, "I don't like this place."

Mike said, "Nor do I. But, there are various tributaries at the headwaters where we have seen some exceptional buffalo, elephants and reedbuck. Worth a look, don't you think?"

We all agreed.

Aside from two klipspringers, there seemed to be little sign of life. I immediately noticed that I didn't hear any birds. You almost always hear birds in Africa. I commented that I wouldn't like to spend a night up here. Ahead I could see an area that had some grass growing, with many logs criss-crossed on the banks. Then there was a loud splash like a heavy body sliding off a bank and dropping into the water.

"A big croc." said Mike. "They like to sun themselves on nice days. There are a lot of crocs on this river, but they are very hard to approach. They are a good trophy." This caught Jim's ear.

"You say they are hard to hunt?" he asked.

Mike answered, "The old ones are."

We stopped and went ashore and waited a couple of hours. Eventually a couple of small crocs rose to the surface. You could only see their eyes and the tips of their noses, but even if you shot one there it would immediately sink. I could not envision any of our trackers, or Mike, diving to the bottom to retrieve one. And as good a friend as Jim is, I told him it was out of the question — I was not even going to go near the water!

I have shot a couple of crocs. The largest, taken in Zaire and which we ate, was about 10 feet long. I was amazed at how fast these reptiles could swim or run across hard ground. I once saw a reedbuck drinking out of a water hole and was astounded to see a great splash and a giant reptile running up the bank and grabbing the reedbuck, and then, in one quick flip, seeing both disappear into the water. It happened so fast it is hard to describe. Crocodiles are responsible for killing thousands of people in Africa every year, mostly native women and children hauling water. You don't see many kids in Africa splashing around in the ole' swimming hole.

The previous year I had hunted in Tanzania with a professional hunter who had a hearty dislike for crocs, and told me that when he was a boy of six he and his partner were fishing in a river in South Africa and a big croc came out of the water and grabbed his friend. They never saw his friend or the croc again.

I think everyone has watched television and seen the crocs in the rivers catching wildebeest migrating across the Serengetti. The crocodile is a member of the family *Archosauria*, or the "Ruling Reptile." The crocodile was first recognizable during the Triassic period, 175,000,000 years ago. Most of the dinosaurs of the same family died out 65,000,000 years ago. The giant river crocodile survived!

Perhaps the crocodile is the Ruling Reptile. The crocodile has a heavy cylindrical body covered with armor, and a massive, wide, flattened tail. With its legs close to its body, it propels itself at tremendous speed, after first quietly slipping through the water without a sound until it is within a few feet of the prey. Many times they will approach with vegetation covering their head to act as camouflage.

Crocodiles cannot chew, and probably the greatest part of their diet is fish. But, big crocodiles feed heavily on cattle and wildlife. They kill by grasping the unsuspecting animal with their teeth and pulling them into deep water where they drown, and sometimes the prey is held in a secure place until it rots and becomes edible. The croc grasps a leg or body and twists around and around until great chunks of meat are torn, which they then swallow. Once the meat is in the stomach, the powerful stomach muscles move the meat, and stomach stones that the croc has picked up for the purpose of grinding up the food, combined with powerful stomach acids, digest the food.

Crocodiles are closely related to the American alligator and can be identified in various ways, including teeth arrangements. Crocodiles have been known to live 50 years.

My best kudu ever. Persistence, a long walk and a heavy bullet brought it all together.

As we watched, to complete the mood, a mist seemed to be rising up and soon we could see nothing. Mike said, "Now it's time to go. We'll be back on a sunny afternoon."

This brought us back to the Senkwi on another day. But this time the fog covered all of the river and hung just below the tops of the trees, which resembled crooked fingers reaching for the sky and gave a very strange appearance to the already sinister Senkwi. We drove slowly up the river.

We would first hunt for buffalo far up the headwaters, and then in the afternoon come back down to look for the Ruling Reptile. Since they are so wary, we left the boat and took a long hike across the peninsula to where we had previously seen a large croc. With me taking pictures, I followed immediately behind Jim as he crawled on his stomach across the sunbaked mud up to the side of a dead tree where we looked over approximately 15 crocs lying on the bank.

At first they are hard to see, as they are very dull colored, and covered with mud and rotting vegetation, they blend in well with their natural environment. Mike had previously pointed out to Jim that you must shoot the crocodile in the brain or break its neck, for they move quickly into the water.

"Shoot him right behind his smile," indicating the shape of the crocodile's mouth, which is somewhat of a straight line, then raises up near the back of the jaw into a sinister smile. "You must hit him in the brain," Mike reiterated.

I could see Jim sliding into the sitting position, leaning up against the tree. He was shooting a 250 grain Nosler bullet in his .338 Winchester. I have seen him shoot clear through a cape buffalo broadside behind the shoulders, and was certain this was all we needed for the croc. At the crack of his rifle, all crocodiles instantly were in the water — just one giant **SPLASH**, then complete silence.

Jim's croc never moved. Mike walked up and said, "Well done. Jolly good!" He then sent Oomo for the boat.

After we crossed the river we had a close up look at the trophy. I had no idea they looked so big. I had been told that an old crocodile of this size weighs about 100 pounds per foot! This crocodile, in a straight line, measured 16 feet over the curves. His body was tremendous!

"Now what should we do with him?" asked Mike. "There is enough crocodile skin here to make you a complete set of suitcases."

"No," said Jim, "I think this is one of the most awesome trophies I've ever taken. I want to do something with the complete animal. I'm going to have the head and body mounted and keep it in the house or on my front lawn to scare dogs and peddlers away." There is no doubt in my mind this crocodile would indeed have a profound effect on social visits to one's home.

I'm sure the crocodile was dead, but its eyes were wide open. They were yellowish with a narrow vertical slit. We did not approach it for some time just to be sure. A swish of its powerful tail could break your legs or fling you right into its mouth. Jim moved ahead and pulled the croc's mouth open to examine its teeth, which were as big as Jim's thumb. I took pictures.

Mike said, "I don't think we have enough time to skin him here. I want to get back to the camp before dark." Lake Kariba is a big lake, and with a little wind, we could run into some giant waves — a bad place to be in a storm.

Mike planned to tow the croc, but Jim said there was too much chance of losing his most awesome trophy. Mike said, "Well, we'll load him in the boat." We tried to put a rope around his head to slide him up on the boat. We couldn't budge him. I had plenty of experience at home loading elk and moose by using a couple of poles, placed under the animal with a man on each side; that way, four to six men could move a lot of weight by working together. But, I guess I was younger and tougher in those days, because it wasn't that easy.

We did manage to get the croc's head and front legs up onto the bow of the boat. Mike had rigged a loop around the crocodile's mouth so that he could grasp the head and pull it as we were lifting. The rope around his nose later turned out to be a real blessing.

When the croc was about half way into the boat we backed off for a few minutes to take a breather. I was absolutely astounded when both the front and hind legs of the crocodile started to move. The giant croc reached up with his hind legs and grasped with his front feet and pulled himself completely into the boat, sliding forward and wedging his head between the bulkheads where the steering wheel was located.

Now this brought a sharp response from all the participants. Simultaneously we all leaped up and back. At the same time, the great croc's tail switched a few times and then went limp. Mike related most calmly, "Reptiles do that often. The nervous system doesn't get the message, which is why a frog's legs kick when it is in the skillet and even when, we know, the croc is obviously dead."

We all agreed, but I noticed nobody wanted to get too close to the croc's jaws which, fortunately, were tied shut. The tail was hanging into the water, and Mike slipped a loop around the croc's tail and pulled it up over the bow of the boat and tied it to the croc's nose. The giant crocodile completely filled the bow section of the 16-foot boat.

We could not move the croc forward or backward, and the boat was front heavy. If we hit any rough water at all, we were going to sink. With some caution we all got into the boat and moved to the extreme rear, which seemed to compensate to a degree. If I had this to do over again, I would have suggested we pull the croc out and come back the next day, although there was a possibility that the other crocs would consume Jim's trophy. Against my better judgment — and, I think, everyone else's — away we went into the setting sun.

Mike spoke to Jason, the boatman, about pulling out the life preservers. Jason responded that they had already pulled them out about a week ago and they were still back at camp. Mike tipped his head up to the skies and closed his eyes.

Jim said, "This is going to make a hell of a story!"

I agreed, but neither of us really knew how much more of the story was yet to unfold.

We seemed to be going along fairly well when Jim commented that there seemed to be an increasing trickle of water flowing out of the crocodile. Mike moved forward, crawling over the crocodile and made us aware that it was not the crocodile but Kariba river water washing in under the gunwale cowling. Jason, who was the boat captain, reacted to this immediately and stopped the engine. We had been moving along at a reasonable speed and the planing lift was lost and the bow of the boat immediately went beneath the waves. Jim made his way quickly back over the crocodile, leaped forward and pulled back on the throttle just in the nick of time.

The bow of the boat raised somewhat and I was bailing water like I thought we were going to sink, which is exactly what we were about to do. We were a long way from shore and I think everyone was thinking about our next move. There was no possible way that we could pull the crocodile out of the boat and dump him into the lake. The three-quarters-of-a-ton monster was wedged in and was going to stay there. There was no doubt in my mind that the Africans could not swim at all, and I'm not a great swimmer. I immediately thought how I would ride on Jim's back and he would take me to shore and save me. But worse thoughts prevailed. Not only were we going to lose the boat, thousands of dollars worth of rifles and video equipment, but we could lose our lives. And, there were crocs in the water and a couple of nasty elephants closely monitoring our progress and keeping parallel to us on the shore. They would undoubtedly be a greeting party to anyone who swam ashore.

In the middle of this, Jim said, "I'd hate to lose this crocodile!" I could see then that Jim wasn't going to save me — he was going to save that damned crocodile!

With Mike now at the throttle, he turned the bow of the boat toward the shore and the waiting elephants, who I suspect thought the churning engine was some sort of a water animal shouting out a challenge — and they were there to meet it. I don't think any of us thought we would make it, but every foot closer we got to shore was one less we would have to swim. Oomo said the Senkwe is an evil river and we would surely die.

Mike knew where he was headed. On the shore I could see a ridge running into the water — a long sloping ridge. Mike was thinking and hoping that this ridge running into the water could be our salvation. The water might be shallow. Squeezing the last bit of energy out of the engine, we suddenly struck a rock. The boat swung around and the engine was cut off. We had made it!

We all jumped over the side of the boat and after doing a lot of baling, we were ready to try again. And, just in the nick of time, because up the shoreline came the old cow elephant and her elephant patrol, hellbent to kick someone's rear end. Fortunately, we got out into the water far enough so that no shooting was necessary.

I thought to myself, "This could have been a bad deal. We were very lucky." Everything looked like a go and we all started to laugh about the situation. Soon we were over deep water. Oomo repeated that the Senkwe river god was not through with us.

It wasn't quite dark yet and I shined my flashlight at the crocodile's head. Jim said, "He just opened one of his eyes." No doubt, it was just another nerve reaction. However, the croc's nose was only about a foot from Jason's legs and Jim brought this to Jason's attention. Jason spoke perfect English and was indeed looking at the crocodile's toothy gumline.

When the croc's other eye opened, Jason and Oomo, with all of the grace of a couple of ballet dancers, leaped onto the gunwale and tiptoed quickly to the rear end of the boat, where Jim, Mike and I were sitting. The throttle was wide open. Jim, who was closest, lunged out toward the wheel; now his legs were next to the croc.

There was another nerve reaction, but this time the nerves seemed to have some direction. The croc's head turned toward Jim and, with a massive lunge, shook the entire boat. Had it not been for the rope around the croc's snout, I am sure it would have taken Jim's leg. Boy, what a story that would make with a great picture of Jim on his one leg, using his .338 Winchester as a crutch!

The rope had worked forward and was slack, and the croc's mouth was open approximately six inches. And there wasn't much doubt he had his eye on Jim. All four of the croc's feet were going and you could hear the claws scratching on the fiberglass surface. The crocodile was twisting and turning, desperately trying to come through the narrow bulkhead, but was wedged in at its shoulders. Then the rope around his snout came loose and I could see the great tail was free and the crocodile let out an awesome roar, which I shall never be able to forget or describe. The Ruling Reptile had spoken! Be it the Senkwe god or bad luck, all hell broke loose!

The giant tail started to swish to the right and left and rotate. My God, the power! The tail was as deadly as the teeth! The boat began to rock violently from one side to the other. The crocodile now discovered his mouth was free and opened wide to impress us with all those sharp teeth and, with another final roar, lunged again. I was sure he was going to bust through the bulkhead and grab someone. Shooting was not an option, despite Oomo's pleas, but I was ready to shove my rifle butt into the cavernous throat.

It would have made a great video. We knew the dance steps, but with little grace we nimbly avoided the clashing jaws. We were all standing on the gunwales, which was really quite an act when you consider that the boat was going full speed, ramming into small waves while the crocodile was rolling and twisting, his great tail rotating around like a giant whip.

With one final roar, the great croc's head dropped down onto the deck, its tail stopped moving and it was dead — again! I suggested to Jim that it was his crocodile and he must control it. Jim said he gifted it to me!

Mike immediately took the initiative and again was in control of the

The Ruling Reptile was 16 feet over curves. Little did we realize this prehistoric monster was not dead at all. Jim Carmichel checked his teeth and commented on bad breath.

boat. We could not shoot the crocodile again, because the bullet would go through the croc and make a hole in the bottom of the boat.

Mike said casually, "This is a most unusual circumstance."

I was quick to agree. Mike then retied the rope on the croc's nose and tail.

Just as we had settled down and begun to relax, the engine sputtered and quit. We were out of gas. Now we were far out in the lake and water began trickling in fast. Fortunately, I had two flashlights. And we did have a spare can of gas, which Jason poured into the main tank, accidently dumping some on the engine, which brought a great gasp from Mike. I expected a giant explosion any minute and we would be blown, burning and disintegrated, into the lake and the croc would indeed be the winner. But that didn't happen.

Jason couldn't turn the engine over. We sat in the middle of the lake with the water lapping occasionally over the side into the bottom of the boat. No one said anything for a few minutes. Then Jim said, "Call 911."

Mike got out his flashlight and helped Oomo look for a paddle and tried to head us toward the shore. I could see it was going to take a couple of hours to get to the shore, if we got there at all. I suggested several of us get out of the boat and, while hanging onto the side, kick and paddle to help propel the boat toward shore. But Mike said we might also attract some crocs and, glancing back again at the giant reptile in front of me, I gave up that idea in a hurry. Besides, even if we got to shore we would have many hours of walking through some pretty hazardous country. I was especially concerned about the cow elephants and snakes. There were no roads and no other boats in the area. Maybe the Senkwi really was a river cursed by the crocodile god!

Things suddenly looked even more grim. Now we discovered that the battery was dead. Jason was fumbling through the compartments, looking for something. I shined my light on him. "Look here," he said. "A new battery, sir."

But there was a small complication. The battery was bolted into the boat compartment and we could not get it loose. Then Mike said, "We've got to have a jumper cable." I replied, "I have one here," and astounded Jim and Mike when I pulled one out of my packsack.

Jim sat back and said, "I will never cease to be amazed at what you keep in that little bag! I am most thankful, but I'm wondering, why do you have it?"

"Actually, I made this up myself to operate my video camera, if necessary, directly off of a 12-volt battery," I replied.

Jim's response was, "Jack, now I know why I really like you!"

Then Jim added, after looking up at the stars, "My God, it looks like we're having some sort of a strange meteor shower or the stars are spinning around us." In the jet black darkness it was obvious that something strange was happening, when Jim started to laugh and shine his flashlight on Oomo, who was working frantically at the rear of the boat with one paddle and was causing us to spin in a circle. Even under the circumstances, this brought quite a laugh from everyone!

Still, we couldn't get the engine started. We were going to have to pour fuel directly into the carburetor. The engine had cooled some, but I didn't like the idea at all, nor did the others. But compared to all of the things that had already happened, this idea wasn't all that disturbing. We all backed off as far as we could while the gasoline was being poured in. Jim was crouched down right next to the dead crocodile. Jim laughed and said, "Surely nothing else can go wrong" and then added, "A good stiff drink would go good right now." I wholeheartedly agreed

"Shine your light on the croc, Jack," Jim said. "Let's see how he's doing."

The instant my flashlight hit the monster croc, we could see both of its eyes were wide open again, and the rope around its snout was gone. The light possibly had startled the croc and with an awesome roar, its mouth snapped wide open. His bloody, giant teeth gleamed like so many knives.

We could not shoot it again, because as I explained earlier, the bullet would go through the bottom of the boat. Jim shouted out, "Is this damn thing killable? Look out for his tail!"

The croc's tail was again free and in the beam thrown by my flashlight we could see the tail swishing to the left and right. We also could hear the croc's awesome toenails grinding into the bottom of the boat.

I thought to myself, "Oh, not again!"

Again, the great tail started to rotate, first to one side and then the other. The croc was trying to propel itself forward through the bulkhead. I thought surely this time the boat was going to turn over. Both Oomo and Jason were standing on the gunwales holding onto the steering wheel to keep from falling over the side, and were screaming for us to shoot. It kind of reminded me of one of those Japanese terror movies with Godzilla going wild. I think if the crocodile had turned more on its side, it would have come right through and had all of us! Then, as if he knew what I was thinking, that's exactly what be began to do!

Jim put a shell in his rifle and, holding the muzzle almost up to the croc's head, said, "If he comes any closer, I'm going to shoot, no matter what." Then the crocodile's mouth snapped shut and it relaxed slightly. Jim obviously had scared him.

Jim took the muzzle of his rifle and picked up the loop in the rope and slowly worked it around the croc's mouth. In the meantime, Mike had worked around the back of the croc and Jim flipped him the rope. Mike was now standing on the crocodile's back with the rope around his nose, which kept its mouth closed and pulled its head up, sort of like a three ring circus master.

The crocodile seemed to be calm now, and it's a good thing, because I think we had all the excitement we needed. Then the humor of the whole situation struck us all and we all started to laugh, except for Jason and Oomo, who obviously felt that white men have a strange sense of humor. And, maybe they thought we would have thrown them to the croc to save ourselves. Finally, our luck changed and the motor started to purr.

Fortunately I took a few pictures with my flash camera just before we arrived at camp — about midnight. Although shaped differently, one must remember that a saddlehorse only weighs about 1,000 pounds and this primitive monster weighed approximately 50 percent more. It took about a dozen Africans to roll him out of the boat at the dock. We placed a heavy chain around its neck and chained it to a tree, just in case it happened to come back to life again.

The next day the monster was dead. When we winched it up onto the bank, there must have been a hundred Africans who had heard about the giant Senkwi monster through the jungle telegraph and had come to see it. Jason and Oomo had told them that the great monster could not be killed with a bullet and had walked into the boat by himself where they and the white men had wrestled the great monster into submission and Jim and Mike had rode on his back. The crowd cheered and Jim raised his hat. The monster crocodile did not die from the bullet, but died from shame, said Oomo.

HUNTING TIGERS THE HARD WAY

When I was in the second grade, which was a long time ago, the teacher sent me home with a note in a sealed envelope. I was to give this note to my mother. I was suspicious, for I figured the contents of this note were not good for me. I was not supposed to open it, but I would anyway, after I was in a safe and secret place and could think up some good answers. I knew just the place. In the woods not far from my home, we boys had dug a cave beneath the roots of a giant pine tree. I kept watching my back trail to be sure the teacher wasn't following me and, once in the dugout, I lit a candle and sat on one of the shovels that had disappeared from my father's garage.

Other loot found in the cave included garbage can lids we used as shields, wooden swords, elaborate guns made out of wood and strips of innertube, which incidentally, would fire a carefully knotted piece of innertube for a surprising distance, and leave quite a welt on the opponents ribs. Other weapons included slingshots, a broken BB gun that one of my friends had pilfered from his older brother and a most prized World War I Army helmet with a bullet hole in it.

Leaning close to the flickering candle, I used my Barlow pocket knife to carefully open the envelope. There were too many big words for me to completely understand, but I got the drift of it. Fortunately, my dad was an avid hunter and I was first born and my mother's favorite son — and the only son. What more need I say. The teacher obviously was wrong, mama said.

Many years later my wonderful mother was to show me the same note (knife slit and all) along with other notes or notations on other report cards that all indicated much the same. It read: "Your son, Mrs. Atcheson, is a dreamer. He could be a good student if he would apply himself. Jack is always looking outside and cannot seem to carry on a conversation without talking about bears, tigers, or other animals that even I have never heard of." And, I suppose, the teacher was right. Then, and even now, I couldn't understand anything being much more important than family, wildlife and adventure. And, yes, I did go on to do a lot of hunting for bears, kudu, elk, etc.

Hunting tigers, however, was one specie that always seemed to evade me. As a booking agent I used to book hunts for tiger, boars and bears in India with famous guides like Allwyn Cooper and Percy Dimshaw. If you did not shoot a tiger, as I recall, they would return 10 percent of your money. These boys would make a tiger out of dirt and straw rather than give back any money. Although I could have hunted tiger with a considerable agent discount, starting a business and raising a family, plus existing opportunities to hunt more species in Africa prevented me from going. For many years, if anyone would ask me had I hunted tigers, I would say "No," but that is not quite true. I have hunted tigers, but under circumstances far different than any hunt over a live buffalo or from the back of an elephant. Now that I think back on it, I risked my life to hunt a tiger. On occasion, I would peek out of a hole dug in the ground to protect me from enemies. But this time, the armament was different. No rubber band pistols. I had hand grenades, binoculars, and an M-1 rifle, and one special clip of 30.06 ammunition that was against the rules of war. I had used a pair of the radio man's side cutters and a file to cut off the points of the ball ammunition to create a soft-nose hollow point that would expand if I had an opportunity to shoot a deer or a tiger. And this time I had my own steel helmet, with no bullet holes in it. I did indeed hunt tigers!

In December of 1951, I was an infantryman in the 25th Division of the U.S. Army in South Korea. And, since I had enlisted of my own freewill, and had completed an infantry leadership course, it was a virtual guarantee I was going to North Korea. One of the sergeants who trained me had been a sniper during the Second World War, and also had been in Korea. He confirmed what the recruiter said — Yes, there was considerable wildlife in North Korea, including bears, deer, pheasants, and tigers. Yes, by God,

Tigers (*Panthera Tigris Altaica*)!

I was to find, however, that recreational hunting in a war zone is nothing like I expected. In fact, war was not what I expected. The spare time hunting opportunities did not exist, nor did the good times and campfire camaraderie as described by the officer who had recruited me to save the world from the cousins of Genghis Khan, whom he predicted were again out to sweep across Asia and the Pacific Ocean, and eventually take over even Butte, Montana. I had to save my mother. I was 18, gullible, and a hunting fool. Fox Company of the 35th Infantry Regimental Combat Team would be my family. I was a greenhorn with a tough bunch of hardened veterans. It was January and bitter cold both outside and inside of my subterranean home. It was situated on a 4,000-foot knife-like ridge called "No Name Ridge," close to Heartbreak Ridge.

The recruiter was right about one thing, there was plenty of shooting, but mostly at 4:00 a.m. I was impressed with eastern North Korea. Much of it reminded me of some of the high mountainous areas of Montana. There were open hillsides, rivers, valleys, and various types of bushes and grasses that I recognized as similar to what I had seen at home. There were pine and other softwood trees of several types, including larch, spruce, fir and juniper. I saw crows, pheasants and magpies, but no sign of all the deer or bears — at least not at first. I was amazed that there was little interest in wildlife by my fellow soldiers. Girls, booze, sex, and getting out of Korea were all they wanted, but I was there to hunt tigers and deer!

Let me share the situation with you. There were no civilians living in the current war zone — therefore, there were absolutely no women in the area. Any buildings that had existed there before were now level with the ground. And the objective of the infantry was to take and hold ground after you blew it up and burned it. You particularly wanted to hold any high ground, which is usually along the face of ridges where you can position the infantry to where they can see down into every clearing or creek bottom. "Just like hunting big game from a stand," said the recruiter.

Before the military takes any ground, there is usually a bombardment of the area by the Air Force and artillery. In our case, at one time we were close enough to the ocean that even the Navy was lobbing gigantic 1,000 pound shells that rumbled over our heads. Some of the higher ridges were actually a couple of feet lower than they were before the bombardment. The Navy supposedly fired more shells into North Korea than they had in all of World War II against Japan. Anything that wasn't turned to rubble was soon incinerated with napalm. Occasionally, a mistake was made and we would catch hell from what is known as "friendly fire." To me, the shrapnel made in America did not seem to be friendly at all. We were shelled several times by mistake in the year I spent there.

Note the huge, snowy mountains. This area had the most deer. The bunker in the left center is where we tied together with the 1st Marine Division.

The first F-51 Mustang airplane that I ever saw was shooting at me with rockets. Thank God for big granite boulders to hide behind. Our positions bristled with barbed wire, land mines of all descriptions, booby traps concocted with five-pound blocks of TNT set in a five gallon mortar shell container full of rocks, shell casings and napalm. Anytime snow would melt, chunks of white phosphorous would be exposed to the air and put out great plumes of white smoke. Forest fires were not uncommon and, on certain days, seeing was difficult because of smoke. I hasten to add, the opposition (Chinese) was prone to dumping great barrages of 82 and 122 millimeter mortar shells on top of us, as well as direct fire weapons that I was told were 76 millimeter and World War II German 88 millimeter cannons. At first it was all very exciting!

Our position was on the main line of resistance (MLR) north of the 38th Parallel near the Punch Bowl, an old volcano basin in the Taeback Mountains. The weather had turned very cold. We were still wearing rubber shoe packs — rubber on the bottom and leather on the top — and they were not insulated. Our gloves were very inadequate and many of the soldiers had frostbitten hands and feet. At that time, when you were on the main line you did not leave. There was virtually no hot food or showers, and the only thing for heat (if you were lucky) was a can of charcoal to burn in the bunkers dug out of the side of the hill. Some people died of carbon monoxide poisoning, or when the rain weakened the ground and the heavy stone roof fell in.

We couldn't do much digging; we just tried to enlarge the bunkers (hunting lodges) that had been built by the Chinese. My hole was not high enough to sit up in. It was five feet wide and about the same length — and this was home for three people. It was like living in a tomb; definitely not for someone with claustrophobia or a fear of rats.

For the most part, we had one sleeping bag for every two men because one guy was on guard all the time. Every two hours we would change, day-in and day-out. Every day. The only way you kept your canteen from freezing was by keeping it inside your coat, which is also where we dried our socks. The C-rations were leftovers from World War II — mostly ham and lima beans, sausage patties and corned beef hash. I never saw fresh fruit. There were lots of lice and rats. But, no deer — yet. I hated that recruiter!

The Chinese* had our area pretty well zeroed in with their live artillery and shells that blew up in the air, dropping leaflets suggesting we surrender or die. And I found out they were serious! Sometimes hundreds of deadly mortar shells would fall on us in just a few minutes. Walking around was very dangerous. One end of the battalion line seldom met with the other end. We were forbidden from leaving our posts, but rumors could pass down the line in minutes.

In front of the line, enemy troops probing for weak spots became a nightly adventure. The Chinese were very tough and determined fighting men, and there were lots of them!

I was in the 60mm mortar section (the infantry's artillery). We also fired thousands of mortar shells at the Chinese. Sometimes the barrels of our mortars became so white hot that the rounds sliding down the tube ignited the propelling charge before it even hit the firing pin, making a very dangerous situation if one was fast loading. The 60mm mortar is a light artillery weapon that shoots a four pound fragmentation shell into the air. They are meant to land near people that are hiding behind rocks where a bullet can't reach them. Upon impact they explode into thousands of pieces that are called shrapnel. These 60mm mortars can fire as close as 25 yards or out to 1,978 yards. A fast loader can have 27 rounds in the air before the first one hits the ground, multiplied by three, since you have three mortars firing at the same target. The shells don't land together, but disperse and saturate as large an area as you wish. Our platoon also had three 57mm recoil-less rifles and two machine guns, a water-cooled .30-caliber and a big .50-caliber with a telescope on it.

---

* Footnote: *The enemy was North Korean in many cases, sometimes with Chinese officers. North Koreans were more brutal towards Americans.*

The main ridge runs west and east of this position. The finger ridges run north into enemy territory. Just over the top of the hand grenades is a timbered knob, which was our outpost where we buried the Chinese soldiers, and where I saw the tiger track. Between the knob and our tank position, to the left, lies the meadow where we made the bullet-stimulated run and my last real effort for the tiger.

We called ourselves Fox Company's Bad-Ass 60's and had our own sign with a skull tied to it. A three-star general stopped one day and had his picture taken by it. I was assistant platoon sergeant and he told me what a great job we were doing. Actually, I don't think he'd ever heard of us before, but he liked the sign.

During attacks, any spare people in our platoon would go on the line as guards and, along with the other infantrymen, shoot endless numbers of bullets. I have seen rifles so hot the wood was smoking. I burned up many clips through my M-1 rifle between calls for mortar fire. Since most shooting was in the dark at enemy gun muzzle flashing, results were vague. It is said it took 50,000 bullets to kill or wound five enemy soldiers. But, like elk hunters, some riflemen were a lot better shots than others...

As the description indicates, the tiger or deer hunting under those front line conditions might be classified as hazardous. And I felt that no wildlife could exist. But, just like the deer population that survive after the initial opening day in Pennsylvania, it could happen in Korea too, and it did. This story evolves around incidents that involved wildlife.

First, you must have all the pieces to understand. I was the assistant

This is a view through a lookout where I spent so much time. The smoke in the background is from the daily air strikes, mostly by F-80 jets and F51 Mustangs.

platoon sergeant. My job as section leader was mostly directing the mortar fire from various lookouts. The company commander, Captain Lawrence E. Spellman, felt that if a little shelling of the enemy was good, then firing hundreds of shells was better. And we did. It was during the daylight spotting adventures that I noticed the tops of all the higher hills were pretty devoid of trees, but down lower, between their line and ours, there were thousands of acres of forests that had no military value and were good-looking wildlife habitat. I decided to watch these areas at dawn and dusk. As section leader I had to be everywhere, and I learned the value of binoculars, as well as how to use them.

I was having about all the fun I could handle, when something happened to raise my spirits! One day I talked to another mortar crew from up the line that had come over to take some spare ammunition and parachute illumination flares that we had. One of the guys was a hunter and told me that he had seen quite a few deer in front of their position — and they had seen a tiger! He was sure it was a tiger — very large and very close to the barbed wire entanglements in front of the line.

He felt that the tiger may have been feeding off dead Chinese, of which there were probably a considerable number in the frozen snow. I went back with him to their position and he showed me the ridge where he believed the tiger to be hanging out in a thick forest about a thousand yards

We called ourselves Fox Company's Bad-Ass 60mm Mortar Section. This photo was taken while we were on Heartbreak Ridge.

down in the valley. And I saw a red deer (*c.e. xanthopygus*), I think. Wow!

But there were so many Chinese on the ridge opposite us that it would be foolhardy to even consider walking out there. Besides that, God knows how many land mines there were hidden in the snow. But, it gave me something to look for. I knew my chance would come. I had hope again! It was just like the opening day of big game season to me.

Since my job was looking for unfriendly people and tigers, I spent considerable time on top of a high, rocky point in an O.P. (Observation Post) — not to be confused with an O.P. (Outpost) or L.P. (Listening Post) or P.O. (Pissed Off) — which we were most of the time. I will describe this O.P. for you. Usually the highest point in the area is where you can best observe the terrain. An observation post is built there. The O.P. is an unheated hole in the ground big enough for two or three people. You enter from the rear. The sides and front are dug into deep ground or fortified with sand bags. The roof and inside of the outpost, if available, are laced with larch or fir logs. A layer of logs, a layer of rocks, another of logs, another layer of rocks, and sandbags, until you have a roof, hopefully four or five feet thick, so that even big shells are more likely to explode before they penetrate.

However, at about chin height, there is an aperture — a rectangular opening about eight inches high and three feet wide. It is from this position that you do what observers do — observe. The same observation point was used by our 60mm mortars, as well as artillery observers for the 105mm and 155mm howitzers behind us. This opening was also a target for Chinese snipers; aside from that, I never had it so good!

On one particular day, the reaction of a couple of deer play a very memorable place in my life. I was in the O.P. The officer with me, Lt. Pierce, had been reactivated and had seen considerable action in World War

II. He had a wife and family and was an old man — about 35, as I recall. I was 19. Lt. Pierce was from Bowling Green, Kentucky. This is how that incident happened.

Using binoculars for observation is a science. Should you be looking for tigers, elk or gun emplacements, you look continually and you look thoroughly. Lt. Pierce was looking for a particular direct fire artillery piece that we believed to be buried in the hillside, and each time the Chinese would fire, they apparently would lift a curtain, shoot a few direct fire rounds at our positions, and then drop the flap again. And, unless you were looking directly into the barrel, you would probably never be able to tell where the shell came from. This particular gun was very accurate, and was raising hell inflicting casualties on our units with alarming regularity.

Lt. Pierce's goal was to wipe it out. I had an idea where the big gun might be — possibly near a wooded area where I daily watched deer feeding. I noticed that twice the deer had run when the hidden gun fired. Twice seemed more than circumstantial. These deer should be used to loud noises and it was strange that they'd spooked to gun firing. I surmised that the muzzle blast was close to them! I reported this, which is why we were there looking at this particular area.

On that day, the area and surrounding mountains were completely covered with fresh snow, and being in this O.P. was like sitting in a refrigerator. I picked up some human tracks in the snow with my glasses, and was following them up a draw where I usually saw the deer. Suddenly the man tracks disappeared, but there sat a stack of cut firewood! Somebody made a mistake! The woodcutter had led me to the door of the secret cave!

While the lieutenant and I were staring at this spot, between two very prominent rock formations, we could see a green-yellow flash and could hear an incoming round screaming off to our right. It hit the ground with a sharp gigantic crack. I was told that if you hear the scream, the shell missed you — maybe!

Although you couldn't see the cannon dug into the hill, we both saw the muzzle blast and had the location pinpointed between the two rocks! Lt. Pierce immediately called the 155s and started bracketing the area with white phosphorous smoke shells. The Chinese figured out what was happening and knew they had been discovered. They also had it figured out where the observers were and that's where they concentrated their shooting — at our O.P.! There were apparently two or three artillery pieces shooting at us. The lieutenant was determined to get our 155mm shells on top of the target, and the Chinese were determined to see that we didn't.

Fortunately, quite a number of the 76mm shells that hit our observation point were duds. But most of them did explode. I could feel each blast right to my bones. All made a horrible screaming sound as they came in, one exploding on top of the other. Some of the shells were hitting three or four feet from our heads. They were virtually shooting the top off the outpost, a rock and a log at a time. There was so much dust that both of us were choking and coughing, and while we were watching, at least one 12-pound shell came right through the aperture, just inches from our heads, and struck the sandbagged wall behind us. It didn't explode, but was interesting to look at if you like that type of exploding decor.

If I hadn't been so young and stupid, I would have been scared. Aside from dirty eyeglasses and a few wood slivers stuck in my neck, I was okay. But they continued firing at us, and I figured the Chinese were going to win this one. Pierce and I were about to be vaporized.

For the life of me, I do not know why it took our 155mm howitzers so long to fire for effect on the target. But, when they did, a multitude of deep penetrating shells came thundering over our heads. I saw two or three hit right on target. The earth heaved and debris flew, and then a flurry of snow crossed the valley and blanked out everything. A few minutes later everything was quiet. The snow flurry drifted past and we could see gigantic black craters all over the Chinese gun emplacement. Obviously some of our shells had penetrated deep into the ground and had wiped out at least one or two of the cannons.

The telltale stack of firewood was still there, but I'll bet their stove was all bent to hell! I could barely hear and my ears have never stopped ringing from that date 43 years ago until today. I have no idea how many shells hit around us, but they had actually shot away part of the roof (remember this part). You could look up and see the sky through a roof that had been several feet thick. If all the shells exploded that hit around us, I am sure the whole observation point would have disintegrated — and us with it. But, we survived, and all because of the deers' reaction and the woodchopper's error. The enemy gun crew took a pounding!

Shortly after that day, my fellow hunter told me he had seen the tiger in front of the same O.P. we just discussed, but in the creek bottom far below me. I would be watching at daylight! Yes, I was to have one final fling at spotting for that particular tiger. And, without a doubt enjoy the most terrifying moment of my life — and a near disaster. *Now*, years later, it seems funny!

About three days after the explosive incident in the O.P. the temperature fell to 20 degrees below zero. The U.S. Army finally got some warm parkas and the new insulated Mickey Mouse boots up on the line. The Korean laborers carried them twenty miles. In that area everything came up on a man's back. There were no trucks, and helicopters were in an experimental stage yet, and then they were only used to move the dead or wounded. We were positioned along a knife-edge ridge with an elevation of about 4,000 feet, or so I'm told. Anyway, we had one parka (extra large) for three small men in our bunker. At 4:00 a.m. I was to relieve the guard in the blown-up O.P. and would begin looking for tiger or deer at dawn, which is also when most serious Chinese attacks began.

The guard saw me coming up the hill and met me halfway, and we traded coats. I slugged my way up through the deep snow drifts, disturbed because you are not supposed to leave your post until the replacement guard has arrived. I gave the guy hell! Especially since there were real and imagined enemy infiltrators passing themselves off as South Korean soldiers who were sticking a bayonet into the guard's eye. I was nearing the O.P. and I vividly remember wishing I had warm mittens.

The moon was full and it was quite light. Now, as you recall, the Chinese had shot the hell out of the O.P. while I was in it and the roof was partly blown off. Anyway, I was carrying an automatic .30 caliber carbine with two 30-round magazines taped together. The sling was on my shoulder and I was cold — cold — cold! As I entered the O.P. entrance, about two feet from me I could plainly see the hat and face of a Chinese soldier. I could see the red star on his hat and the barrel of his burp gun. I tried to pull off the carbine, but I just knocked off my helmet. I grasped at his throat with both hands and threw my body hard onto him with a force only a frightened man could muster. I didn't move him, but I fell down. Now I could see it was not a man — just the moonlight and shadows on the rock!

I got up off the bunker floor absolutely rattled! Then I glanced out through the 8-inch by 36-inch viewing aperture and received another shock! I could see movement and hear the crusted snow breaking. I saw 13 armed men coming in single file and headed right for me. The point man was about thirty feet away. My first thought was that they were an enemy probe since their position was not a normal route our side would use. We didn't have any patrols out and all knew the ridge was laced with land mines and flares which I expected to go off at any time. But, barbed wire in front of the O.P. was pretty well blown up and the route wide open. I also expected our machine gun emplacement to my left to open up. I was just supposed to be there to direct mortar fire (and, of course, look for wild game).

The field phone didn't work and now the first man in the column stopped ten feet away in the tree shadows. Contrary to what you might see on television, or when you reflect back on things, when you're nineteen and expect all hell to break loose in the form of hot lead, your blood pressure goes up and your mind wanders. I figured they had killed our machine gun crew. Why else hadn't they started shooting?

But, that's what war is like. Utter misery and boredom with moments of terror and confusion which some general later calls a planned strategy with acceptable losses. I had to act quickly or become part of the losses! If you're not sure who is approaching, the stateside procedure is call out "Halt!" If they are Americans, they usually respond, "Get screwed, asshole!" Then you relax. But, in Korea, if you suspect it's the enemy, you shout "Chungee!" — Chinese for "Stop." They either stop, or shoot in your direction, and you're sorry you said anything!

The point man was now only six feet away. I was pointing the 30 round automatic carbine intending to shoot at the first three men, then drop down and start tossing out hand grenades like a gone-wild practice tennis ball machine. There were over 100 pineapple hand grenades on the floor at my feet. I admit I was scared, but strangely calm.

At four feet, I started to shout — "Chungee!" But, at the same time the point man said "Goddamn this _____ snow!" I screamed, "Halt, you dumb son-of-a-bitch!" It was a last second miracle! The guy on our machine gun was also ready to give them a 1,000 round burst. They thought they heard someone in the lost squad say something in Chinese and were convinced they were enemy soldiers. The lost squad leader told me that they thought they were still one ridge away from safety and if I had said "Chungee" they would have thought I was a Chinese guard and opened up on me, which would mean every position on our side would have cut loose on them. But, I may also have been dead — all victims of friendly fire!

Shortly after this event a major war erupted. There was considerable activity in our area, but obviously the main body of the enemy attack was towards the company that had borrowed the mortar ammunition and saw the tiger. The next day I was talking to my fellow hunter. The way the story had been reported to me was that after the main attack a disturbance was noted. Something was obviously caught in the barbed wire. The metal C-ration cans they had wired together were rattling and one of the flares we had loaned the mortar section was fired into the air, exposing a tiger standing in the snow. A machine gun opened up and the tiger fell down.

The Chinese patrols normally came back to pick up wounded soldiers or recover some of the bodies of the dead. Perhaps the tiger was wounded, and left on his own (I hope he got away unscathed). Maybe the Chinese took him. A tiger has great spiritual and medicinal values to people living in China — so maybe they just took him and ate him. I think he just moved to safer ground, and I would cross his path again, although much closer the next time.

One day I was looking through my binoculars into a deep valley between our line and the Chinese. Except for an occasional woodcutter, this was a no man's land, which was the big reason wildlife survived. I was watching a thicket near the creek. Magpies were circling, but not landing. Maybe the tiger had killed a deer or a Chinese woodcutter. Anyway, I heard a very loud roar from the Chinese side. I instantly saw two bright

"Long Tom" Thompson drops a round into a 60mm mortar. Vern Hinrichs is the gunner.

lights that looked like eyes attached to a burning monster. It was a B-29, and it appeared they were just clearing the Chinese held mountaintops, but surely would hit the 4,000 foot ridge, close to me. Six or eight parachutes opened. One man jumped late and, before his parachute opened, his body hit the ridge just below me. The plane roared just above us. It seemed so huge and unreal. All engines were on fire, but the pilot did barely clear the ridge into a huge valley behind us. Two more people jumped to safety but the B-29 veered off to the left and near the valley floor hit the headquarters of the R.O.K. (South Korea) Army. There was an awesome ball of fire and explosions.

Later we were told the plane was still loaded with 20 tons of 500 pound bombs and the two pilots who jumped last were okay, but hid out for three days thinking they were still behind Chinese lines. Many South Koreans were killed at the crash site by friendly aircraft and friendly bombs.

After the plane crashed there was considerable rifle fire in the valley between our lines where the first B-29 jumpers floated down into enemy territory. I assume they were killed or captured except for one. His luck was good, then bad.

The next morning at daylight I was looking for survivors and was startled to see a man still in his harness, above the ground and his parachute hooked up in a pine tree, almost exactly where I had seen the magpies the night before. There was some fog around him and I suppose the Chinese had not seen him. At once I started firing 60mm smoke shells around him (white phosphorous) to keep him hidden so we could send out a patrol to get him. We fired all that we and the adjoining company had, but the wind kept blowing the smoke uphill. Eventually the 81mm, the 4.2 mortar and the 105 Howitzers in the rear were lobbing in smoke. The hot white phosphorous started a few trees on fire, but without smoke it was sure death to move outside our line in daylight. Smarter people than I estimated $1,000,000 worth of smoke shells were fired to save one man.

In the meanwhile I had collected additional 60mm smoke shells to give close support to the rescue squad. This was a highly dangerous situation because there is so much room for error due to wind, steep slopes, trees and poor visibility, that we might hit our own rescue squad. I could not see the flyer but on the radio they said they had reached him. I thought to myself, "I'll ask him what he saw in the thicket where the birds were," but that was not to be.

Fate is so cruel! For a man on a machine gun, far up the ridge, did not get the word of what was going on. The smoke lifted so the flyer and the rescue squad were visible to him. The flyer said, "Boy, am I glad to see you guys!" And then he was killed by friendly machine gun bullets. The rescuers brought the body back. I remember he was a very large man. It was a shaking event, especially for the man who accidentally killed him. Some months later the same fellow was shot in the head by a Chinese sharpshooter, but I was told that he was still alive in a V.A. hospital.

We changed areas in a truck driven by a driver who had never been on snow-covered roads. The convoy had no tire chains and it was awesome! There were about 25 men plus gear packed in each truck for most of two days. There were few P-calls — he who had to pee first removed his steel helmet and passed it around. The guy on the endgate would dump it. There was no modesty in the infantry.

A randomly fired Chinese mortar shell landed in one of the other company's trucks and killed everybody in it. We spent some time at Heartbreak Ridge, and at another area close enough to see the ocean — the Sea of Japan, where we hooked up with the 1st Marine Division. The terrain was very mountainous; good-looking hunting country. I saw boar and rabbit tracks in the snow and kept my clip of special 30.06 cartridges ready.

As before, there were no civilians of any kind, except 10 Chinese nurses captured by the Turks while out on a probe. I heard they brought back the heads of men they killed. The dead men were the lucky ones. The Turks were attached to our company and were tough fighters. They always had some trinkets to sell, and drugs, but I never saw anyone use drugs. In fact, I thought drugs were aspirin and iodine, and that's the truth! And a funny story of its own; I must have been dumber than a post!

We did have some Korean laborers who told me they previously lived in the new area and said there were lots of deer, bears and tigers! Another chance for my tiger rug! Even in the higher mountains I saw grouse, and pheasants similar to those in Montana. Once I saw some white-fronted geese flying over our head and wished I could fly with them out of this hell-hole country! The Land of The Morning Calm was not so calm for us. When peace talks faltered, each side would intensify its effort — more probes and more mortar barrages. One crafty enemy patrol got behind our mortar pits and tried to come up a shale slide, but we rolled and pitched hand grenades at them. They were too close for us to use our mortars to fire upon them! Only a fool would try to run up a shale slide, but the Chinese did and kept sliding backwards; any elk hunter would know better!

One day we were firing mortar shells at random to harass the Chinese, as they did us. If you are standing close to the mortar barrel you can see the black form of the mortar shell going into the air. Without warning, a small helicopter that came to pick up two wounded men flew right over our position. We could see the shell just miss the bubble and somehow pass through the propeller blade. We were all lucky. The air burst 20 yards over our heads would have killed us and dropped the helicopter.

But the pilot's luck ran out the next day. He somehow crashed on take-off on the steep mountainside, and in a great ball of fire, he and the wounded rolled down the mountain. There are many accidents in war.

I found a better pair of binoculars in an officer's parked jeep — a pair of 8 power that were made by the Kelvinator company, and located a bolt action 30.06 Springfield with a J 2.5 Weaver scope that I could borrow from another old World War II sergeant in another company. They used it as a sniper's rifle. The Chinese also had snipers. I fired a lot of bullets into caves, apertures and likely places. This must have annoyed them, for my shooting would always draw fire back from the Chinese. One Chinese bullet ricocheted off a machine gun next to Vern Hinrichs' head. Matt Guzik of Pittsburgh had his canteen shot out of his hand. (It was funny then!)

I discovered that their sniper was a damn good shot, so we both called it a draw, I guess. The sniping exchanges ended for a while; I'm sure I gave the Chinese a few thrills too! We also had a J 2.5 Weaver mounted on a 50 caliber machine and would fire it single shot like a rifle. But, a piece of shrapnel knocked off the scope and three fingers of the gunner — a black man who was a basketball player.

As before, I spent a great deal of time observing enemy positions, or looking for wildlife, and since I had been promoted to Sergeant First Class, I could move around freely. Plus, the platoon leader, Master Sergeant Norman Faulk of Rayne, Louisiana, felt my wandering ways were much to the advantage of the mortar section. I knew every ridge and ravine if there

These are the binoculars I found in a Jeep. The word was they belonged to General Matthew Ridgeway. A few years ago I met General Ridgeway here in Montana, fishing. I wanted to ask him if he ever lost his binoculars in Korea, but at the last moment chickened out.

was a call for mortar support, which was all the time. I didn't have to guess, even in the dark. Incidentally, at about dark some of us occasionally saw packstrings of horses or mules being used by the Chinese in the Idaho-type mountain terrain; one day, a white horse wandered into our reserve camp.

I wasn't the only one doing a lot of looking. I recall two men who were more adventurous than others, and obviously, given an okay by the battalion commander. These guys would go out looking for enemy officers. If they brought one back, they got five days on R&R in Japan. And, as I recall, they did capture one but accidently shot him when they reached our main line; they didn't get the five days R&R in Japan. But they didn't give up.

One of these bounty hunters was one of the blackest men I have ever seen. The other was ghostly white. I always thought these two fellows, whom I referred to as being "Mr. White and Mr. Black," reminded me of the old Indian scouts. They had guts and were a little odd. They seemed to have no fear, and obviously were very cautious. I did find out from them that there were indeed quite a number of deer in the valleys below, and I can recall the adrenaline stirring my hunter instincts when they said there was a large lion near where I had seen a small herd of deer. They didn't know much about animals, but I was sure it was a tiger. I never talked much about it to other people. I didn't want someone else to shoot my tiger!

I do recall my good friend, Sgt. Vern Hinrichs, from Sleepy Eye, Minnesota, at one time hearing a squalling roar. But, he didn't see anything except for a few deer, and couldn't get a shot at them. Both Faulk and Hinrichs received Bronze Stars for action months after I rotated out of Korea. They were good men. Vern took my place as mortar section leader after I left Korea. For some reason, Fox Company took a lot of enemy attacks but the men, mostly 17 to 22 years old, were tough and well trained and old for their age — and there was no way out of the damned country, anyway.

I recall one morning, while looking down a finger ridge that led to a river in the valley below, seeing tracks in the snow of what appeared to be a large animal with large feet like a tiger or a bear. There were no tracks coming out of the thicket. I couldn't resist; I put in my clip of hollow point 30-06 shells and advised the machine gun crew on top of the ridge that I was going out front. All I had on my mind was the tiger. My school teacher was right — I was a dreamer — and it almost cost me my life.

To be a good hunter, you cannot stare at your feet. You must look into the distance in front of you, which is what I was doing. But to be a surviving infantryman, you also must spend as much time looking at the ground immediately at your feet for unusual metal objects or wires stretched between trees. Luckily, I did glance to the ground and discovered my left foot was under such a trip wire. I was suddenly aware that I was in a very dangerous situation. I glanced further ahead and behind me and saw other wires that I had missed. Fortunately, the snow was not deep. With the greatest of caution, I stepped backwards into each track I had made coming down the ridge. The machine gun crew had been watching me, and one kid said, "You've got a lot of guts to go out there." But, an older guy who had been in World War II said, "No. He's just nuts!"

Neither one of them was right. I was hunting for a tiger — hunters are like that. The quest for this tiger was going to get me in situations which could have had great influence over my longevity. But, what the hell, I was there for a year and getting $50 a month extra combat pay, plus I had a nice cave to live in!

As I reflect back on this, there were a couple of outstanding tiger incidents which immediately come to mind. One incident concerned an outpost in front of the main line. The main ridge ran east and west at an elevation of about 4,000 feet. In the middle of this ridge was a low saddle and a ridge jutting out to the north, thus forming a T. In this saddle was a dug-in tank with only the cannon and turret visible and pointing out the

Vern was just clowning around with all the hand grenades but a few nights later he didn't have enough.

Myself and Norman Faulk discuss the merits of enlisting in the Army. Norman liked working with machine guns.

north ridge. Immediately in front of the tank was a wide, flat ridge or meadow partly covered in grass which was headed toward a scattered timbered ridge covered mostly with fir, but also juniper and some birch or poplar. At the end of this ridge was a small knob covered with rather large fir trees.

The timbered knob was an excellent listening post or observation point, where one could see in many directions; this outpost, as I recall, was about 800 yards in front of the line. Immediately in front of the outpost, the ridge dropped down abruptly to the valley. The tall grass and fir trees reminded me a lot of good elk country in Montana, but I was not in Montana. I was trying to outfox the Chinese army.

I had previously visited this position, I suppose to check for accuracy where our 60mm mortar shell should land in the event the outpost was attacked. I knew there were no land mines on the sidehills, so I naturally combined a little business with pleasure. I was hunting for deer or tiger sign. I could not go back until after dark so I had all day. It was late afternoon and I was north of the outpost, but on the same T-shaped ridge. I could see this would be the obvious route the Chinese would take if they planned to attack the outpost, but they didn't always take the obvious route.

The side of the ridge was brushy, and noisy, and covered with a lot of shale rock that was difficult to walk on. The ridge itself was fairly open. The Chinese would come up the ridge or come up the bottom of the drainages on each side of the ridge. People and animals are creatures of habit. I would put a mortar impact area on the ridge and along the bottom of the ravines that I marked on my map. The east ravine approach would be my choice, if I were them. I decided to give it a look-see. A surprisingly large stream, with crystal-clear water and watercress growing around the rocks, flowed along the ravine bottom. Along the stream's banks stood tall larch trees, some chokecherry bushes and, here and there, I came across boggy birch and spruce thickets. While I was filling my canteen, I could hear crows and some kind of jays chattering. It was a beautiful setting and I momentarily forgot why I was there, especially when I came across fresh musk deer tracks (*c. capreolus*).

Plan A was to protect men in the outpost. **Plan B** was to hit the enemy when they retreat the way they came. The ravine to the east where I had filled my canteen would be where I would have Vern aim his mortar, which was the most likely route since the upper side of the stream bank was rather flat, almost like a narrow trail that likely had been used by deer and people for hundreds of years. I reasoned that this is exactly what the Chinese would do, since the other ravine was noisy shale rock and the top of the ridge was too obvious. The other two mortars would fire into the other ravine, and on top of the ridge, and so I marked my map. I believe

James E. Young of Alexander City, Alabama, and Ray Willman of Dayton, Ohio, manned the latter two mortars.

The next plan, **Plan C**, was to fire on the outpost itself if the outpost was overrun, and *only* at the defender's request. As soon as the mortars were in the air, and on their way, all defenders would dive deep into the trench. The overrunning Chinese would be caught out in the open above ground and eliminated from the picture. This was, of course, very dangerous and a last resort, but, close support like this saved many Americans. The risk had better odds than sure death from a Chinese bayonet. At one time or another we fired on most every outpost we had, sometimes twice in the same night.

Plan D: The Chinese might overrun or bypass the outpost. But either way, the main line of resistance (M.L.R.) would be aware of a large force heading that way, but since 10 percent of any army never gets the word or seems not to care, or the fact that the Chinese might not pay heed to our clever plan, anything could happen.

With some of our more elaborate plans, the Chinese never came at all or would surprise us. One time we sat out 15 napalm and TNT booby traps and they stole them from us. Talk about crafty people!

As I headed back up the ridge toward the outpost I saw deer tracks and a couple of beds, but saw no game. Skunked again! Then, there it was!

At first glance I thought it was a bear track in the mud. It looked like a bear's front foot, but a closer look quickly convinced me that this must indeed be a large tiger. To a hunter, this was like finding gold. By God, there was another tiger and he had been there just a few hours ago! And, just a few hundred feet in front of the outpost.

I had buck fever! Maybe the tiger was watching me! I said nothing to anyone else, for I figured I would be back here again as soon as possible for some reason. The reason came sooner than I expected, for that night over their portable loudspeakers the Chinese played, *"When I Grow Too Old to Dream"* and *"My Blue Heaven,"* followed by bugles and chimes. There was a small probing action and firefight at the outpost. I could watch from my observation point at the thousands of tracer bullets going in all directions and the greenish-yellow flashes of our exploding mortar shells very effectively circling the defenders. There was no apparent casualty to either side. That day the Chinese let it be known they would kill any prisoner wearing one of the new flak vests. Jealousy, I guess!

We added two light machines and a couple more B.A.R.'s to the outpost. The next night there was another probe at around 4:00 in the morning — this time it was intense with the Chinese very determined to wipe out the position. I do not recall the casualties, but the next morning the captain sent me and a number of other men out before daylight to help with the demolition of the outpost, and lay land mines, as it was now considered too dangerous for patrols. I was expecting to be ambushed before we got there, but, worst of all, the new plan ruined my chance at getting the tiger! That worried me more than dealing with the Chinese.

Let me say now, I don't think young men worry that much about danger. They don't think they'll get hurt, and certainly not killed! And this is especially true if you are a hunting fool.

We reached the outpost just at daylight. I have continually written that hunters invariably shoot too high, which is why they miss. And, it was obvious that the machine guns set up at this outpost position also were shooting too high. The area which had been heavily wooded now had most of the foliage blown off, and the standing trees showed where most of the machine gun bullets were hitting — about eight feet above the ground — too high to hit the Chinese crawling on the ground.

Some of the trees were shot completely off. The seven to ten foot stumps were bullet riddled or gouged with mortar shrapnel. As I stepped over a log, I glanced down and was initially shocked at seeing a dead Chinese soldier with a wide face and dark eyes staring back at me. He had been hit through the heart. Around his neck was a piece of wire with what probably was a good luck charm. It hadn't worked for him. Beside him lay an empty burp gun (a rapid fire machine gun). Empty shell cases were all around him and one unfired cartridge, which I put in my pocket. I still have it today.

Then, there was another body, and another — many bodies. These Chinese had obviously come up the east ravine and circled the outpost and then came down the ridge, exactly the same way I was entering the area, and expected the ambush. They had slid a long pipe bomb (bangalore torpedo) under the barbed wire, blowing a wide gap. The Chinese evidently planned to storm through the opening and overrun our men. But, their plan didn't work. The unfortunate Chinese were poised right in the middle of our mortar impact site. We had effectively dropped a protective ring of flying steel shrapnel around the outpost and broke up the attack. That was our **Plan A**.

The mortar shells saved our men from being overrun. They were nearly out of ammunition. But, judging from the dead, not all their bullets shot high.

We dragged the bodies into the outpost trenches, and started to bury them. I recall a reaching hand was sticking out, above the ground. A man named "Kelm" put a large rock on the open palm to hold it down. I remember that the dead Chinese soldiers seemed very heavy to drag through the brush in their heavy, padded cotton clothes. Before burying them, Vern Hinrichs and I went through their pockets looking for maps or insignia of their unit. They didn't have much, just some rice and ammunition. Vern found a picture in one man's pocket. I could see from the picture that it was him — the dead man below me. Also in the picture was his wife and two children. Although they were the enemy, I suddenly had the feeling that these people were the same as we were — just a bunch of stupid kids who may or may not have wanted to be there, but we were all very human.

I never felt hate, but not much remorse either. Both the dead man and I were people that met under bad circumstances. Nothing has changed much for the infantry. But the incident did change my thinking. From then on I noticed that all oriental people do not look alike. And, I was relieved to see that this particular man had a bullet hole in his ribs and no shrapnel wounds from the mortar shells. The infantry gets to meet the enemy up close; close enough to touch.

While the burial detail was working, I noticed in the mud that a number of bodies had been dragged away. Some down the ridge, others down the steep side hill toward where I had seen the tiger track.

The Chinese seemed very effective at recovering their dead. It is estimated that for each body found, one dead body was taken away, and for each body, two or three men likely were wounded. In the Korean war, most men killed or wounded were struck by shrapnel.

I decided to follow blood trails down the east ravine where Vern's mortar had been lobbing in shells. I worked around the hill very cautiously as there may have been a wounded enemy behind any tree — willing to surrender. But, deep down inside I thought the tiger might be around searching for a body. I looked for several hours. Now it seems kind of dumb. A wounded man could have shot me. God, what a hunter will do to get his tiger! But I saw no tiger — only more dead men strung out down the bottom of the ravine near the creek. In the spruce thicket, one man lay dead in a patch of wild roses and another was lying close to where I filled my canteen. After the small arms fire stopped around the outpost, we figured the Chinese would leave the same way they had come — along the bottom of the ravines on each side of the ridge. I figured it would take them 10 minutes to get there, then fired 300 mortar shells down the ridge and both ravines, mostly along the trail and the stream. It must have been like a long string of huge exploding fire crackers tied to their coattails. That was **Plan B**, as you may recall. It was no longer a beautiful creek bottom; many tree limbs lay on the ground, cut off by mortar shrapnel. It was quiet and creepy there that day and I didn't stay long, but went looking for the tiger.

I was initially surprised that the cat — tiger — would be in an area where there had been so much shooting. But, as I experienced later in Africa, lions often show up in areas where there is shooting because they have learned that is where there is usually dead or wounded game. And, I suspect that this tiger was also educated and wherever there was shooting, there also were bodies or blood trails to follow. I'm told that tigers fared well in Vietnam, also.

We returned to the line after dark, but the next day a squad was going out to finish up and bring back some picks and shovels, or some dumb thing. I asked to go along, intending to look for the tiger; I felt obsessed. I picked up my M-1 rifle and slipped in my now well-worn clip of eight hollow-point 30.06 cartridges. I would go at once to the ravine where all the bodies lay near the stream. I had all day to hunt. For some reason, running into a Chinese patrol out recovering their dead mens' weapons did not seem to bother me. I would just have to be very careful on this stalk. I did not expect to see any live Chinese so I decided not to wear a flak vest; a big mistake!

There was a heavy fog, so dense we waited until after daylight to move out, still invisible to the enemy anyway. As I described earlier, this ridge passed through the barbed wire and minefield and began with a steep downward slope through an open, grassy meadow. Then it leveled off onto a birch, juniper and low fir tree bench. The forest on both sides of the ridge was fairly dense, especially at the now-abandoned outpost — which was about 850 yards from the tank and our M.L.R. The squad leader took his men and started down the ridge. I followed behind the last man about 10 yards. Little did I realize that in 15 minutes I would rethink the notion of sport hunting in Korea.

I was very eager but had big butterflies in my stomach for the first time, maybe not because of fear but the sensation of wondering what in the hell I was doing there! We would be out there until cover of darkness returned. This was my best, and maybe last, chance for a cat. I had to go; I just had to see the tiger! We had almost reached the end of the meadow and were entering the forested area a couple of hundred yards from the outpost, when suddenly a warm wind swirled around us, and the fog was gone! We were looking at a ridge directly to our left and above us. That ridge was occupied by the Chinese. We recognized immediately we were in a bad place — or cold turkey to the Chinese. At that moment the 400 yards back to safety seemed so far that I really didn't think we would make it. Fate had turned the tables and, on this day, I would have a string of exploding firecrackers tied to my coattail!

I was not expecting the sudden and intense Chinese rifle fire coming from the trees near the abandoned outpost and from the opposite ridge. The Chinese had set up an ambush near the trail and we nearly walked into it, but they should have waited until we were closer before they began shooting at us. I don't think they originally planned to meet us on the ridge; the lifting of the fog surprised them, too! Now, however, they had us caught in a deadly crossfire, for now two Chinese machine guns on the high ridge cut loose at us — and they weren't taking any prisoners. I fired my entire special clip of .30-06 hollow-point tiger ammo into the woods at an unnatural color between two fir trees 150 yards away on the left side of the trail. My companions were also shooting and I saw bark flying off a tree. Then our tank crew opened up, very close and just over our heads, with their 90mm cannon and a .50-caliber machine gun at the Chinese in the trees. There was no place for us to hide; turning back was our only option. Meanwhile, our tank was shooting down the forest tree by tree. I bet the Chinese were in as much trouble as we were!

Everyone was thinking the same thing — can we make it back? To my left, and about 100 feet in front of me stood a large pine tree. I heard a loud scream and a gigantic explosion as a direct fire Chinese 76mm shell struck the tree trunk. The entire tree disintegrated as if it had been struck by lightning. I shall never forget that tree — it was like a signal to run! I was angry at myself; I should have glassed the trail! I was determined, however, that I would not die there. We spread out like a flock of flushed quail and I couldn't help thinking that the massive firepower coming at us was way out of proportion just to nail down nine teenage Americans.

Suddenly, from a slightly different direction, another Chinese machine gun started firing. It is truly amazing — even wearing heavy gear and carrying rifles — how fast a young man can run across an open slope if properly stimulated! I could hear incoming 76mm shells screaming and exploding, and the swishing thum, thum, thum of razor-edged shrapnel flying directly in front of and behind me. Sheared-off tree limbs fell on our backs. I recall wishing at the time that I'd worn my flak vest. One of the tank crew was standing on top of the turret. I'll never forget his shouts of encouragement, or the shouts of those who could see us from the other rifle positions. It was as if we were at a football game and carrying the ball for a touchdown. The ground around us was erupting from the impact of ricocheting enemy machine gun bullets and tracer bullets were flying in all directions. It looked like hundreds of illuminated, bouncing ping-pong balls. (I relive this event every 4th of July.)

Safety was on the other side of the tank! From all around us I could hear, "GO, GO, GO!" And, GO, GO, GO we did! I am not a fast runner and a couple of our riflemen passed me as if I was standing still. The tank commander dived into his tank as soon as Chinese mortar shells started to drop around us. I had the feeling that the Chinese saw this as a great sport, and I am sure they were hollering, "GET'EM, GET'EM, GET'EM" — and our side was still yelling, "GO, GO, GO!" For some reason I wasn't scared until I could see safety was only 50 yards away. I cannot really describe the combined and awesome sounds and sights you experience in a major

March 17, 1952. We change positions. This valley was called the Punch Bowl.

firefight — especially when you are one of the targets!

As I passed the tank, a heavy mortar (122 mm) shell exploded in front of me and blew a giant crater on the south slope of the hill. The blast was like an entire door hitting me from feet to my face, actually throwing me onto my back. I immediately rolled into the hole before the acrid smoke had cleared the crater. I remember thinking that, if I could tear the buttons off my shirt to get lower, I would have done it. I couldn't believe I had made it back! And I'd been hit only by flying dirt and pebbles! Lots of bruises but no gaping holes! The Chinese missed us because they were flock-shooting, not aiming at us one at a time — just like a lot of duck hunters I know!

The tank was still firing with both the 50 caliber machine gun and 90mm cannon at the Chinese ambush squad behind us; the tank probably saved us from the Chinese guns closer to us! We started a major exchange over some extra tools left at the outpost and now thousands of Chinese and U.S. tracer bullets criss-crossed in all directions. Tiger hunting was the pits at times, but this was a hunt I will never forget!

The good thing is nobody really got hurt — a bullet through a canteen, one guy's rifle stock was shot off, and I lost my helmet to a large flying rock or maybe shrapnel (there was a loud "clunk" and the helmet was gone, but I didn't bother to go back to look for it). This war suddenly made no sense to me, anymore. And the amazing thing is, everybody, including me, was laughing like it was a contest and we won! War does strange things to people! How we made it through that net of flying steel was a miracle! ***And since that day I have never felt anything was impossible to do.*** (And I hope the Chinese there that day made it too! I never was really mad at them anyway; I just went there to hunt deer and tigers.) Something like this shoot-out happened almost every day or night to someone in our company, but for some reason it didn't seem like a big deal except to the riflemen directly involved. That's how you were trained and what you expected, and I suppose that every man who's been in combat has witnessed or experienced similar events that literally stir your soul.

That was my last effort at tigers. I had been in Korea one long year, almost every day and night in a combat zone, and was soon to rotate home. I had way more than enough points, and now I too was thinking of women and whiskey. I had a nest egg of $600 worth of combat pay to blow on sin! I was getting a little gun shy and if luck was with me, I could be home by Christmas to get in on a post-season elk hunt. And I'm glad I didn't shoot a tiger anyway — I didn't have a license.

I suspect that my opportunities and methods of hunting tigers will never be very popular. It would be the worst hunt you ever booked — forget Korea!

Incidentally, while I was waiting for my discharge papers, the guy in the bunk next to mine and I hit it off great. Especially while discussing "terrifying, but exciting" events. We discovered he was part of the lost squad and was the point man just four feet from my rifle! What a small world! I think his name was Sergeant Carlson from some place on the East Coast. Carlson, if you read this, call me, as I recall you owe me a case of beer for not shooting holes in your jacket!

1950-1953

The Korean War was a bloody war, an Infantryman's war fought in rugged mountains, as it was in Italy during World War II. During the three-year Korean War, 54,246 Americans died, plus over 8,000 missing and assumed dead and buried where they fell. An additional 62,000 South Koreans and United Nations soldiers were killed and almost 400,000 Allied and American soldiers were wounded. Millions of civilians were killed. It is estimated that over 500,000 Chinese and North Korean soldiers were killed and 1,000,000 wounded. In the nine years in Vietnam about 58,000 Americans, one of them very dear to me, and millions of Vietnamese died.

In any case, we are now global-tourists trading partners with our former enemies. What was the purpose of it all? Maybe none of us should have been there at all, except for the tiger. But had it not been for the war, I would never have been able to hunt a tiger.

In 1986 my son was a guest of the government of China to promote hunting in that country. What a strange world we humans make for ourselves!

DEATH BY REFRIGERATION

I completed a hunt on the island of Hawaii and was successful in taking an exceptionally fine wild turkey with a very long beard. I decided to have it mounted and went to a local grocery store in Kona and obtained a sturdy cardboard box in which I cut airholes. I set the turkey on some crushed paper with his head under his wing, and was on my way to meet my wife in Honolulu.

When I arrived at the hotel, the bell captain offered to take my rifle, duffel bag and turkey for storage in the basement until we left. I reminded him that the turkey had to be frozen immediately. He said "No problem," and gave me a baggage claim ticket.

Several days passed and we were leaving for Montana. I could see all of our baggage, my rifle and duffel bag sitting outside ready to be loaded into a cab — but, no turkey box. I went to another bell man and gave him the ticket and said, "I have one box missing."

We waited and we waited, and eventually I could see the bell man talking to the manager through the glass window in his office. He was holding the turkey box in his hands and pointing in my direction. "What has gone wrong now," I wondered. "Have we violated some sort of a local code?"

Both people looked very serious. The manager picked up the box and came out to see us.

"Mr. Atcheson, I want you to know that we go to great lengths to accommodate our clients, but I am afraid there has been a serious mistake made, and we don't know how to rectify it." I was puzzled. At this the manager held the box out to me and lifted the top off so that I could see the frosted turkey. He said, "Unfortunately, someone put your turkey in the freezer and he froze to death."

My wife and I broke into laughter. The manager said he did not understand, nor did I until I found out that on the previous day they had a pet show at the hotel where many people brought their rabbits, ducks, parakeets, dogs, cats and so forth. Many participants placed their cages in the same storage area, and the manager thought that I was one of the exhibitors and somehow they had killed my pet turkey.

LION CREEK GOATS

All of my relatives were hunters, but my uncle Ken was probably foremost when it came to big game hunting. He was tough and determined, and could survive on less food and equipment than anyone I have run across. He usually carried a .32 Winchester special with which he disposed of a lot of game. He also wounded a lot, especially large bull elk, which troubled him.

Ken decided to invest in a new .300 H&H magnum. I was even more surprised when he had a 4X Weaver telescope mounted on it. I figured his eyes must be getting bad. But he decided it was time to hunt something different, like grizzly.

I was 17 at the time, and the thought of hunting grizzly bears and mountain goats appealed to me very much. Montana grizzlies and goats were available on an unlimited permit basis and, in those days, not very many people were even interested in hunting them, or anything else that they couldn't shoot from out of the truck window.

We decided to penetrate an area of the Bob Marshall Wilderness where we would follow Lion Creek from the old Seeley Lake highway to the top of the pass. Over the phone we had hired a packer out of Swan Lake by the name of Nevada Bacon. He was to meet us on the 13th of September, pack us into the area, and come back and get us in two weeks. He said he would do it for $100 each, and furnish eight horses.

We promised to clear the trail out and would pick out a good camp site at the top of the pass. Some trails weren't too well marked in those days, and we headed off across country carrying an axe and a cross-cut saw, which Ken had liberated from the Butte-Anaconda Mining Company. After three hours of floundering around thick brush in deadfall, we located some old trail markers and went to work.

The trail looked like it hadn't been used much, but was passable, and we headed on to the pass. It was a lot further than expected — 14 miles to be exact. We had to know the conditions there, as the packer had never been in the area. We found a good place with plenty of horse feed to set up camp. And, we could see a herd of mountain goats within 200 yards of the pass, the first I had ever seen up close. They were bigger and whiter than I expected. I was most excited, as I had never shot a goat or grizzly bear. In fact, I couldn't tell a billy goat from a nanny, but I had seen a few grizzlies in closed-season areas.

There were a lot of berries that year, and a lot of bears. We had crossed both grizzly and black bear tracks numerous times on the way in, and I was impressed by some of the huge bear droppings that had to be made by a big bear with a poor digestive system, as it appeared the berries were passing right through the bear as if he had never eaten them at all. We had long since finished off our lunches, a loaf of bread and ring of bologna, and I was feeding pretty heavy on the berries myself when it came time to turn back. It wasn't real dark, but it still took us until around midnight to get back to the truck.

We didn't have a flashlight and had a couple encounters with bears on the trail, snapping of teeth, huffing, and one awesome growl. But, that didn't bother Uncle Ken. As long as he had an axe in his hand I don't think a grizzly would have stood a chance. In fact, Ken seemed to be looking forward to a good fight. He sure fared well with his fists with the Butte miners. Bears or miners were all the same to Uncle Ken, the bears just had more hair, and maybe they bit harder.

I figured we had walked over 35 miles that day, and was kind of sore when Nevada Bacon showed up before daylight, ready to go. He had a string of good horses, powerful and well-fed. After they were all packed up, four of the horses which were standing around untied, walked down to the creek to get water. They crossed and kept going, but the outfitter said, "Don't worry. They'll come back. I know those horses." It just goes to show, you don't know anything about people or horses, because they just kept going back to the town of Bigfork, which was over 20 miles away.

Nevada said if the trail was okay, he would still pack us in with what gear we had, come right out and find the departed horses, and come back the next day. But like I said, Uncle Ken was used to a spartan camp, and said we didn't need much, so in we went without a tent or sleeping bag, and a few canned goods.

Ken was riding on a big red horse with a beautiful long mane and tail. The horse was determined to lead the way. We had only cleaned out the worst of the trail. But horses in those days seemed to be able to think better and didn't mind stepping over a few logs. But, unfortunately, while my uncle was crossing a rather steep timbered side hill, the horse side-stepped to the left to miss a boulder and Ken's stirrup hung up in the root of a huge log that was on the upper side of the trail. How such wild and crazy things can happen in a few seconds is often hard to describe. I can only say that the horse lunged forward and this huge log started to roll. There were broken limbs sticking out in all directions, real deadly, and from where I was sitting, it looked as if both horse and rider were going to be impaled momentarily.

The horse went off the trail and fell down and rolled. I could see hoofs, mane and tail, a lot of dust, but not Uncle Ken. The log, with its dozens of spoke-like spikes, continued to roll down the hill, poking big holes in the ground. It was obviously going to roll over both horse and rider. I quickly dismounted, honestly expecting to find both man and horse dead, with broken snags protruding from their mangled bodies.

If you can call it luck, they were lucky this time, since both horse and rider had fallen into a hole. The log had rolled over them and continued down the mountain, doing little apparent damage to the horse. I grabbed the horse's reins and tied it up as I saw Uncle Ken, dirty with his clothes somewhat disarranged, get up and begin looking for his hat, the same type worn by Indiana Jones in the movies. We found it, ruined and pinned to the ground by a limb that had broken off. Ken's jacket was torn pretty bad; he dropped his pants to look at his leg.

Although there wasn't a great deal of blood, a limb about an inch in diameter had pushed into his thigh and followed along between the muscle and the skin and formed a pocket. Ken pulled the almost seven inches long stick out and we washed out the area with salt water and iodine. You could see an area of muscle about two inches wide, but Ken said it didn't hurt much — at least not as bad as losing his hat.

We planned to stitch the leg up that night, but in the meanwhile we pulled the skin together with tape and continued on up to the top of the ridge where we built a lean-to. The sewing of the torn skin was quite an event, kind of like something you see in the movies. Ken took a couple of swallows of Four Roses, dumped in some salt and sewed it himself. I couldn't do it.

Then it started to rain. It rained all night and the next day was the first day of the hunting season. There was a lot of fog. Ken's leg was pretty sore, but he could hobble along, and we headed out looking for the nearest goat. We had a can of corn and sardines for breakfast. That's all we had. Late that afternoon we came on to two big nanny goats. Ken's leg was getting worse, and we decided to just take what we could get and spend most of the time hunting grizzly bears, as long as he was feeling alright.

Ken downed his goat with the first shot, whereas I was about to discover just how tough a mountain goat can be. I was using a .270 with 130 grain Remington bronze point bullets. I hit the goat five times. Three of the shots were very well placed, and would have killed a black bear or a buck deer instantly. Both were very large bodied goats, about 150 pounds each. We dressed them out and would come back for them with a horse if Nevada showed up the next day. Hopefully a grizzly would be there on the gut piles to claim the kill — just like I'd read about grizzly hunting.

When we got back to camp it was raining hard again, and we were pleased to see that Nevada Bacon was there with the rest of our equipment, which consisted mostly of groceries and equipment that he and his friend were planning to cache for an elk hunt they had planned for themselves after we left.

All had not gone well for Nevada. The horses were harder to catch than expected and he had not slept all night. By my nearest estimate, he had

Uncle Ken's idea of a first class camp was any cover over your head and the larger boulders moved from where you slept. One meal a day was a balanced diet.

been in the saddle for around 80 miles with no rest for him or his saddle horse. He was one tough packer and an old, old man - maybe 55. I could see that his right hand was bleeding badly and he was attempting to stop the flow with a spare pair of underwear. It seemed that just before reaching camp he ran into a bear on the trail, his horse spooked, and Nevada brushed up against a tree and drove a snag deep into his palm. We didn't have much in the way of first aid equipment in those days, or didn't bother to take it, whichever. That evening Ken and Nevada spent most of their time soaking their wounds in salt water. I was sure pleased to have my sleeping bag. The previous night had been a long one.

In front of the lean-to I had built a big white-man's fire. We brought back the ribs from the goats and I placed them up on a stick where they could slowly roast. It was probably 10:00 in the evening, cold and raining and I could hear horses coming up the trail. By the fire light I could see the shapes of two horsemen come into view. We gave them a hail to step down and have some coffee. The spokesman for the pair thanked us for the invite, and said they were lost and had been riding for hours and were headed for a camp near Big Salmon Lake. We advised them that the trail did eventually lead in that direction, but they were welcome to have some late dinner. He said he appreciated that much, and his partner wasn't doing too well.

I could see that this was probably correct, for he was leaning off to one side and fell directly off the horse, his whiskey bottle crashing onto a rock. I helped him to the fire and he said that he was starved and said the bourbon wasn't sitting well on his stomach, which was probably true. I told him to help himself to the ribs. But before I noticed what he was eating, he did comment that they were very good, but a little tough. I glanced over at him, and in the firelight I could see some blood trickling down his chin, and that's when I realized that instead of the cooked ribs, the gent had picked up some raw ones. I decided not to say anything after he commented that besides being a little tough, they were done just the way he liked them.

We invited them to stay, but they were determined to find their partners and about midnight they continued on to wherever they were going — if they ever figured out where that was.

The next day it started to sleet and there was a great deal of fog. Weather not conducive to bear hunting. But we had to pick up the goats. Nevada led the pack horses and Ken and I took the lead on foot. About 150 yards from the goats we tried glassing the area, but the fog was bad.

We had covered the goats with brush, but a bear had moved one goat and covered it up himself. It is amazing how much dirt and brush a grizzly will pile onto meat. In a situation like this it's a good idea to know where the bear is before getting closer. In this case, a sow grizzly showed

Our first mountain goats. Part of which we shared with a grizzly.

up behind us and the horses. The horse reacted instantly when one of the bear's cubs bawled and she roared. It was amazing how fast the horse and Uncle Ken moved. He kind of hopped on one leg, but with real class.

I've heard that horses won't usually step on you, but these 1,600-pound Percherons weren't sidestepping anything to escape the bear. I was bowled over and my rifle knocked from my hand. I couldn't breath for a few minutes and thought I broke some ribs. Afterwards, I thought the whole incident would have made a great Charlie Russell painting. Anyway, that was it and the bears disappeared, and I was most thankful, but Ken was disappointed.

In time we found the horses and loaded up the goats without further incident. In fact, the horses seemed to have forgotten about the grizzly. Both Ken and I were limping and his leg wound was bleeding and looking pretty bad. We decided to bag it for the year. By the time we packed up there was a foot of snow and it was falling fast.

Nevada left the camp set up and was going to pack in hay for his elk hunt. When he returned, the bears had already wiped out his food supply and torn up his tent, but Nevada and his partner did get two elk — two five-point bulls — as I recall. One was pretty well eaten up, I suppose by the same sow and two cubs.

It is hard to believe the roof of a car can only support one elk.

THE 1956 FORD

Money was tight in the early days. We had one vehicle, a new 1956 Ford. My 1944 Jeep was broken down. You would be surprised where you can go in a car if you have plenty of weight in the rear, and a good set of chains. But, a car is still a car.

A friend of mine and I shot two exceptionally large six-point bull elk. We had an outfitter drag them to a high pole he had attached between a tree and his barn. The whole carcass was hung high enough that the dogs could not chew off the nose of the unskinned animals.

The next day, our plan was to lower one of the elk on top of the vehicle and tie the other across the trunk. The plan was to do it slowly and easy to see if everything was holding out well. Unfortunately, the pulley broke, and both elk came crashing down onto the '56 Ford. One bull landed pretty much on the driver's side. I was amazed at how weak the roof was — I didn't even need a rope to tie the elk to the roof.

Fortunately, I am not a tall person. I had to drive slouched down in the seat because the roof of the car was caved in right down to that level. Things like that might not have bothered me personally too much, but the car belonged to my wife. Things like this are often hard to explain — my wife doesn't understand me. But, on the other hand, maybe she does!

Like I said, ours was not the usual safari with a fine camp and vehicle into land that had not been hunted by white people since 1890.

This is the courthouse of the mighty Chief Suffa. On this day a man would lose his hand for stealing — another possibly his eyes. I declined to watch justice being served.

BONGO IN THE CONGO
The Wildest Hunting Adventure of My Life

Formerly known as the Belgian Congo, Zaire is one of the largest of all African countries. It borders Zambia, Angola, Uganda, Burundi, Tanzania, Rwanda, the Sudan, and the Central African Republic. Zaire is approximately one quarter the size of the United States. It is primitive today, and you can only imagine what it was like 25 years ago. In all likelihood, little had changed in some areas for 500 years before I hunted there in 1971. I've written this story much the way my field notes were, as the events occurred.

Although a few people had been sport hunting bongo in Kenya for many years, the difficulty one encountered discouraged most hunters from even trying. Had it not been for the alleged abundance of heavy-tusked elephants in northern Zaire, the CAR, and the Sudan, the very presence of the mystic bongo in adjacent areas may have remained somewhat of a secret for many years to come. To this day, few American hunters have ever shot a bongo or even know what they are. I consider the bongo, hunted fair chase, Africa's greatest challenge.

Bongo and giant eland have always been high on my list, plus, I was eager to do an exploratory trip into any area to promote business. But primarily I went because I wanted a bongo, an animal so elusive that even today it is rare to find a zoo that has one. The Congo okapi, an animal related to the giraffe, but smaller, wasn't even known to exist until 1900! The Congo is a wild place!

The magnificent bongo (Mbangana), weighing approximately 500 pounds (males), have relatively short legs to better maneuver through dense undergrowth. In Zaire, bongo are reddish-orange to reddish-brown with 12 or 15 vertical white stripes. They also have white patches and chevrons between their eyes and white spots on their cheeks below each eye. There is also a white patch behind their knee, similar to what you would see on kudu, bushbuck, or sitatunga. Their feet are small and their ears are very broad and large. Their hearing is incredible.

Both sexes have horns, the males more massive and forming an upward spiral. Bongo found in Kenya are much darker in color, at least in the adult males. Despite their size, bongo are timid and evasive and generally inhabit dark forest and thick undergrowth, but have remarkable agility, running rapidly through the underbrush, their head held high and horns touching their back. Females and young males live in parties of five to ten, and the old bulls, except when breeding, seem to be off by themselves. The bongo uses its horns as a lever to dig roots and twist limbs off trees and vines searching for choice tidbits. But, like all the bushbuck family, they are extremely dangerous at times, especially if cornered or wounded.

The Africans believe (or so they say) that bongo use their horns to climb trees to hide if they are being pursued, then drop down on you. The bongo will stand on its hind legs to reach a favorite morsel and that may suggest climbing. The Azande people say that in no case should bongo be touched or eaten, for they carry leprosy and are an evil animal known to pursue and rape women. I don't know about that part, but there were times when I did think they either disappeared or escaped into lofty trees!

The bongo is primarily a nocturnal animal, and people are not. I was to find a fair chase bongo hunt to be my most difficult. Our only map proved to be most inaccurate, and assistance solicited from the local inhabitants was questionable, at best. Still it was probably the best they could offer when you consider at that time the local tribes or villages were, and still are, often hostile or suspicious of each other. The local people were limited in knowledge to very small areas of a forest. At that time, their only communication was drums and hearsay from merchants who traveled by boat and local black and Greek hunters, who often told the wildest lies and gave the worst directions so as not to aid the competition. What you could call roads were few, but a government effort was underway to push in new roads to provide medical treatment and education, though I suspect oil and mining exploration was the major objective. Distant villagers were encouraged to move to the roads, and all black residents with a Christian name were ordered to change it to an African name, or else. Don't knock America until you see other places. And, don't be surprised when you go to a primitive place and discover what primitive really means!

The landing strip was red dirt. At the end of the runway one hundred children and fifty pigs, all covered with red dust, screamed and oinked, delighted to see a new white face. The adventure began! Just before our plane was ready to touch down in Asiro, Zaire, the old missionary sitting next to me warned that elephant and bongo hunting must be very important to me to go to such an area, adding that he knew that P.H. Arnold Callins, four years previously, was wounded by four arrows and left for dead. And, even after the tribal war was over, certain tribal members with long memories would only be too eager to remove his head and consume his flesh. Without a smile, he added that we would be hunting in the center of some of the most primitive country left in Africa. "You'll find disease, snakes and volatile tribesmen who are still cannibals. You can go no farther to reach the interior of Africa. Any direction you go, you will be on your way out," he told me. So what was I doing here? Going hunting of course! It's my nature!

According to P.H. Arnold Callins, hunting company owner, former Congo resident and battle-scarred mercenary soldier, opportunities for hunting existed, and with government permission he did some exploratory range and population studies on elephant, bongo and giant eland. In exchange, Arnold would be allowed to take along a few paying clients yearly to cover his expenses, or so the story goes. Anyway, it was now legal to hunt. At least we had licenses, but must receive permission on a local level from each tribal chief.

In the first year of hunting, 1970 I think, the location of a few elephant crop raiders was well known and the terrified villagers were only too happy to point the finger. The elephants' viewpoint was likely different. They had been shot with arrows and musket balls, hated villagers, and were quick to attack anything that smelled like man, including our clients, who beamed at the thought of shooting a truly wild elephant with 100-pound tusks. They consistently underestimated the speed and rage of a festering elephant and we very nearly lost several clients, as well as myself.

Arnold describes an incident where he made a lucky shot, with his .458 fired vertical under a charging elephant's chin. The elephant collapsed, pinning Arnold with his massive left ear and jerking a petrified client to the ground with a massive trunk around his neck and shoulders.

Some exceptional elephants were taken and good numbers of bongo were encountered. As the primary booking agent and representative for Zambia Safaris at that time, which Arnold Callins also owned in part, I naturally fell into the same role in Zaire. We decided this was a rare opportunity and immediately started organizing hunts for brave, enthusiastic hunters willing to rough it. The safari costs were high. Gasoline, food and equipment were scarce, as the country was just over an awesome civil war, which had left millions dead and civil unrest quite obvious. One must remember that in 1970, most safaris took place in east Africa, Kenya, Tanzania, and Uganda. Zambia and Botswana were still relatively unknown, and had it not been for their abundance of sable and kudu, I suspect that it would have been a while before even these fabulous areas became all that popular. From 1950 to 1994, Africa has come a long way. But even today, there are plenty of places where little has changed in the last 200 years — and up to 1,000 years in some cases.

Beside the dusty kids and pigs, Larry Hammer, Henry Budney and I were met by Arnold Callins. We were taken to an old coffee plantation, which was now the new safari company headquarters in Asiro. Once there, were were greeted by P.H., Adrian Carr and Dereck McCloud, and three chimpanzees. The largest chimp carried an empty wine bottle in each hand. The smallest chimp was covered with a blanket that he was never without. The other coughed a lot, and smoked cigarettes when available. If nobody had a light for the cigarette, he would eat it.

Apparently the plantation originally belonged to some Belgian coffee farmers and during the earlier revolution the white family was wiped out. The house was full of bullet holes. A mortar shell had apparently come through the roof and exploded, perforating most of the furniture, including a very large Bible; a piece of shrapnel was sticking through it. I walked through the house looking at the pictures of former occupants; men, women and children now dead.

Tribal war isn't anything new for Africa. Look at the Rwanda situation now. And here on the plantation, the jungle outside was rapidly reclaiming the land. Civilization was in retreat.

None of the professional hunters really knew much about the new areas we planned to explore. Because the weather was drier and hotter than expected, the plan was to hunt elephants first, then go elsewhere after the evasive bongo, which are easier to hunt when the ground is moist and tracking is easier.

Actually, we'd had a few adventurous clients hunt there the previous year for elephants and, after getting their reports, it appeared to

To reach the remote area we crossed many rivers. The old dugout log canoes were once the only form of transportation and still are to some degree.

me that these Congo pachyderms had huge tusks, but must be the most dangerous game in the world. We were continually advised by the natives to be extremely careful. Like the story goes, what do you find between an elephant's toes? Slow Africans, of course! But the truth was, although some great elephants had recently been taken by our clients, many of the tusks had actually been purchased from local poachers, and we would have to explore some new ground. The easy local bulls were dead.

We didn't have a plan. First we were to hunt the Alwee and Anvo area, particularly in previously unhunted drainages close to the CAR border. For money, the locals would remember such things, like elephants with big tusks. In fact, it seemed to me they could tell you anything you wanted to hear, be it fact or fiction, and since Africans relate more to meat than ivory, all elephants were reported as big. As I said, there were a few rough roads, more like tracks, headed into part of the area we were to hunt. Very few white men had ever spent much time in this particular district, and it would be the wildest adventure I was ever on. Just seeing such land and primitive people was a thrill.

My first encounter with tamer Africans' hunting methods occurred while driving down the road toward Anvo. A group of savage-looking black men armed with spears and clubs had strung handmade nets around a meadow and a few large trees that resembled enormous elms. The older men, in particular, had elaborate designs, cuts or tatoos on their faces, arms and chests. A grass fire was built to drive small animals (mostly rodents and duikers) in one direction where there were people inside the net with their long clubs and grass woven cone-like baskets. These were strategically placed here and there under the net to trick some unlucky rodent into thinking he was running into a hole, only to find that the tunnel kept getting smaller and ended with someone standing there to whack him with a club. Within the net corral there were numerous small dogs, mostly red, the type you see with primitive people everywhere in the world. Most of these dogs did not bark, and had a bell around their neck. They were well-fed, but were not friendly to white people, or fleeing rodents.

As we drove on, it was obvious that since the war road maintenance had deteriorated markedly. There were detours and great concern over forgotten land mines. Overhead, towering trees formed a dark, tunnel-like canopy. Soon the road narrowed and became two tracks. There were fewer villages and the people wore less clothing. The adult women wore nothing on top, the little boys wore nothing on the bottom, and seemed to spend a lot of time pulling on their peters as if trying to stretch them for a record. The little girls usually wore nothing at all.

All the children stared, as they were excited to see us. The women were shy and watched from behind thatched roof huts. One man produced a giant set of bongo horns and offered them to us for sale for $30, as much as he could make in a year farming. It was obvious that money overcame his fear of leprosy. Arnold, the outfitter, bought the horns and said he might need them some day. The black man said he killed and sold many animals, most of which fell into pits he had dug. I would see many such pits in days to come, as wire for snares was not available.

I noticed all the soil was bright red, hard and dry. The grass was drying up rapidly, which was good, as our plan was still to hunt elephants first, since they would concentrate near waterholes or streams. Then, after slaying a couple monsters with 100-pound tusks we would proceed to the bongo area, which would be located to the east. An elephant may weigh 12,000 pounds, but is rated by the weight of each tusk. Forty-five pounds is good these days.

My normal good sense of direction did not seem to apply in this hemisphere. I had no idea as to where I was, nor did the guides, as the directions given by the Africans varied to make one believe their world ends where their vegetable gardens met with the jungle. But, this is a part of why I went — to see the unknown.

So far I had seen little small game, and no large wildlife. I suspected the people in the area were good hunters. Most of the African men carried nets and spears, and a few bows and arrows primarily used to kill duiker-size animals at very close range after calling them in with a reed.

Occasionally we would see someone with a muzzleloader. On closer examination, we could see that the muzzleloader barrels had been made out of an old bicycle frame and tubing. This was crude, but very effective at close range. When fired, the black powder cloud would completely envelope the triggerman. It would appear that fingers and faces took quite a pounding. I declined offers to test fire these blacksmithed widow-makers, even though my friend Larry was a doctor and assured me of a Christian burial, or a nice stitching if I lived.

Throughout the hunt we saw many nets set to capture monkeys feeding on the ground. A fire was started and the animals driven into a series of nets by dogs where the monkeys were beaten to death or horribly burned before they could get away. A tough deal for the monkeys, but to the Africans that was the only way to do it. Captured birds often had their legs and wings broken to keep them handy and fresh until ready to eat.

The African said the large river running parallel to our road was good fishing for catfish or perch types. Apparently we were going to use a pontoon-type raft made out of old canoes to float each truck to the other side. I joked at the time about how we were going to get back across, especially if we were in a hurry or being chased by cannibals, a joke then, but the time would come when it wasn't quite so funny.

We crossed the Uele River and on March 18, 1971, we arrived at the mission called Anvo, run by Catholic nuns and nurses. The person in charge, a woman, told me that four years earlier there had been 20 sisters and 24 priests in the area and one of the local chieftains ordered them all to be captured and held in the mission. The priests were put in one room and the nuns in another. The women were raped, and then, along with the 24 men, hacked to death, dismembered with machetes. Fortunately for a couple of survivors, white mercenaries and a friendly Christian chieftain arrived and saved them from slaughter.

The nun described the incident as horrifying and said the survivors were standing in blood up to their ankles that flowed under the door. She returned to Belgium, then came back later that year, only to escape death by hiding in the jungle. But all was relatively calm now, she assured me, then pointed to a couple of gentle-looking men cutting wood and explained that they had helped kill the priests because the witch doctor said it was necessary. I asked her how she could trust them now and she said they are all gentle people and only doing what seemed right, and she added that I might not understand. I agreed with her and thought I would watch out for these "gentle people" and memorize their faces in case we would meet on a lonely trail. Throughout the hunt, my loaded rifle was never more than inches away. I also noticed Larry Hammer, a World War II paratrooper who jumped at Normandy and was a lone survivor, also felt a bit concerned throughout the hunt.

Arnold discovered that gasoline was not available at the mission and that there would be a day's delay. We stayed within the mission grounds. There was a beautiful church, several buildings, and small palm-lined streets. There were numerous orange trees bearing large oranges with incredibly tough skins and huge seeds — also a few bananas and papaya. It appeared that this had once been a thriving town. But now, outside of the churchyard, it was primitive indeed; both the people and the land.

The next day we crossed the river again. I recall the pontoon bridge was made out of very large logs that had been hollowed out into canoes. I was told that these canoes were used to transport goods up and down the rivers until a few years ago. The country and villages now took on a less civilized look. I thought about my last words with one of the nuns, who said we were going to see many primitive people, as the government had ordered distant villages, accessible now only on foot or by canoe, to resettle along new roads where health services and schools could be provided. I was later to find that progress was very slow, and even the finished government buildings proved to be only grass huts or small mud buildings. I am told that I would never recognize the place today. I guess progress is good, but I hate to think that there are no untouched people or places left in the world. There was no doubt that soon there would be an endless stream of logging trucks and mineral exploration in the area. But, for the time being, we were entering old Africa.

The following day we were going to visit the local Azande chieftain of the area, and the man who was responsible for saving the nuns. We were going to ask him, Chief Suffa, for permission to hunt in the area. I was to find that a chief in those days was the almighty in command. Minor squabbles were settled by his decision. Thieving or offending hands were chopped off and eyes punched out when deemed necessary. Needless to say, we were impressed with his awesome power.

The nun had previously warned us that pointing fingers and the lens of a camera could be considered "evil eye" and dangerous, especially if there was an offended witch doctor who felt us a threat, or if the natives were drinking home brew, which was often. But, we won over all hearts with our Polaroid camera and by handing out money — the American way.

Our visit to Chief Suffa, the monarch of the area, was interesting. On that day, Chief Suffa was holding court. A lot of nervous people sat under the circular open air thatched roof courtroom. Suffa was showing off his new bride. I believe this was his 15th wife. He had 25 children, but was still a young man. I had a Polaroid camera and took numerous pictures after the chief said it was okay. He seemed quite intelligent and worldly. We were suddenly the life of the party. The chief insisted that I have my picture taken with his newest bride. She was very shy, and I was nervous. We used up a lot of film, but did get permission to hunt. Like they say, a picture is worth a lot — better than money in some cases. But, as I recall, he took our offer of money also.

On that particular day, the chief would determine the penalty to be laid down on various people for crimes ranging from theft to murder. Punishment could be severe — hands chopped off or blinding in one or both eyes. His theory was, if you can't see you can do very little that is wrong. If you have no hands, you cannot steal. Sounds simple enough. A man was to lose a hand that day, but we decided not to hang around. It could be contagious and was more than I could handle anyway — justice or not.

The chief's interpreter advised us to hunt primarily along the thick river bottoms since there had been very little rain for many months. Again, he warned us that the elephants could be very dangerous and that numerous villagers had been killed while walking through wooded areas. Warnings were extended to watch out for crocodiles and hippopotamus near any water we found, for they too had been knocking off some local villagers, especially women and children getting water. I never saw any kids swimming. Chief Suffa joked that white flesh was probably as compatible to crocodiles as it was to some of the primitive tribesmen. We all laughed at his sense of humor. I have very white skin — I buttoned up my shirt.

Finally we were there! The elephant country was relatively flat with some rolling hills and many deep ravines created by erosion or numerous small creeks and waterways, most of which were now dry. If we were lucky, we would see elephants feeding up on the benches, but the black tracker said this was unlikely and we must hunt them in the streamside thickets. For some reason, the elephants here are large-bodied, but have relatively small feet, so you weren't sure what you were following. The bulls covered many miles when they did decide to leave the river thickets. The hunting was extremely vigorous.

The thickets were indeed thick — an awesome jungle, beginning with a canopy of very tall trees, with huge buttresses to support them during the wet season. The underbrush seemed to be all thorns or hooks. Very little sunlight could penetrate to ground level, which was covered with leaves and a vast variety of insects and birds.

The water in the creeks looked clear, but we used purification tablets, double doses, even in water that we boiled. To my dismay, my professional hunter, Dereck McCloud, drank his water unboiled and was soon ill and very weak. As the safari progressed, I found I was doing more and more hunting on my own. When he eventually returned to England he was found to have five types of internal worms. One type was the worm that would go through your system and come out of your eye in the form of a maggot. Dereck was normally immune to water parasites, but not in the Congo.

I was told about, and observed, a vast array of diseases in this country. Some are incurable, others could be solved simply by taking a little iodine. Many of the Africans had such goiter problems. My friend, Dr. Larry Hammer, described this as a paradise for those wishing to study rare diseases. Hunters really are a determined lot. Why would we take such risks just to hunt an animal?

I was astounded at the number of local people who already knew that we were coming — through the amazing system of drums, which would be heard every time you were near any type of native settlement. Messages coming, messages going. I saw no signs of paper, bottles or cans, and believe in most cases the Polaroid pictures we were taking were the first pictures most natives had ever seen. (I refer to the more primitive people then moving to the new road.)

Upon gaining their confidence and assuring them we weren't pointing the "evil eye" in their direction, they would take their pictures, leaping, jumping and screaming with excitement and running through the

Women did most of the work, cooked the food and carried the firewood. I never saw them drop anything regardless of terrain.

village to show their friends. Then everyone wanted a picture. Fortunately, I had brought a great deal of film, but I could see I didn't have enough to take care of the demand. I was very popular, especially with the women, who were always cleaner and neater than the men. They would adjust their hair and change garments, if they had them, and preferred to pose in an action photo, like pouring water or pounding maize.

The hunting campsite was one of the most beautiful I have ever seen. Above us was a canopy of enormous buttressed trees, but very little underbrush around the tents. The area had been completely smoothed out. Every leaf was swept away each day, assuring that insects and snakes did not penetrate the tent of the great white hunters, which suited me just fine, for I had seen numerous columns of army ants crossing the road. Usually the columns were four to six inches wide, but often larger. The returning column all carried dead insects or leaves. One evening our truck crossed a trail of ants at least ten feet wide. I have no idea how long the columns were, but heard tales of them eating livestock and people. I do know they would bite like hell if you blundered onto them.

Across the dusty road you could also see the trails of various snakes of different sizes. Some were the size of a pencil, others were over a foot wide. No doubt a huge python was somewhere near. Later we were to see many python skins in the villages as the python is a major food source to the Azande. We purchased a few skins that had been stretched and rolled up to dry. Most of the longer skins seemed to be from 18 to 24 feet long. We were offered the skin of one snake, and although probably stretched out of proportion, it was over three feet wide and was 28 feet long. All the skins showed signs of many spear wounds.

The people were eager to sell snakeskins or whatever else we might want to buy — like chickens and fruit. We were offered women that we could buy and own for $2. A chicken cost more than you might pay for a laborer for 12 hours of work. Another black hunter offered a leopard skin larger than any I have ever seen before. The head was missing, but the skin appeared to be the size of a lioness. Later on we were to occasionally see tracks of leopards that did indicate they were of great size. Unfortunately, we never saw one. Lion sign was rare.

Mosquitoes were scarce, but other biting insects immediately became a problem, especially when near any moist area. I could see when the rains started and eggs would hatch it would be a major obstacle to deal with. I suppose that the vast variety of bug life supported the immense variety of birds of most every size and color you could imagine. I could sometimes identify over a dozen calling or chirping at the same time. But sometimes there was no sound — absolute silence. It was eerie!

The new trail we were driving on had just been cut into the area and I was told only two other white people had hunted here. They had a 12-hour walk along with 30 porters to carry their equipment, which reminded me that the nun at the Anvo Mission told me that she had lived there most of her adult life, and had never known of any white men to go hunting in the area Dereck had mapped out. At the time, it made me wonder again just what I was doing there.

It was not a good place to be sick or injured. If snake-bit, you would die or rot before you could reach a doctor. There was no plane to call in, and no radio to call on.

At first we saw a great many buffalo tracks. The buffalo are similar to any cape buffalo, but much smaller in horn and stature.

Besides the elephant, we were looking for camp meat as well as trophies. The first day I got a quick shot at a running bushpig, but missed. Aside from the birds, we saw only one other small pig and one Colobus monkey with long, beautiful black and white hair. The local hunters sure pounded the wildlife near any settlement. All small streams had fish traps and nets of all sorts. These people ate everything that moved or grew, including people at times. Some denied it, others were very open. I was of the opinion that only men ate human flesh. But I'm not sure tribesmen were always truthful. We knew nothing of their customs. Similar events seemed to mean very different things.

God it was hot! But, after the sun went down, it cooled off considerably. So far no tsetse flies. The sound of birds was around us constantly, even at night. We had a day shift and a night shift. I was told that some of the sounds were made by bats. From the sound, they must have been very big bats.

Big game was not at all abundant. We decided to go further afield. We went to the village of Chief Stuify, another Azande, to beg his permission to hunt and to hire some local trackers who knew the area. Without our Polaroid camera, I think we would have been unsuccessful. Again, the pictures were better than money. Permission was granted for a picture of the chief and his wife. The royal family members were well dressed and wore many pounds of jewelry.

Chief Stuify said that although there was quite a variety of duiker-sized animals nearby, anything larger was rare. This was again confirmed by the scarcity of tracks. We saw no snares as there was no wire in the area in those days. But we came across many deep pits lined with sharp bamboo spikes.

While looking around the villages, it was apparent that life was tough for these people. Although there seemed to be plenty of food — pigs, chickens, fish and vegetables — mortality was high; in excess of 80 percent among the children. There were lepers and horribly scarred people. Many were blind. There were few old people. Most people in the area did not live to see 50.

One day we walked about five miles and picked up an elephant track, which we followed into a swamp area where the grass varied from 18 inches to 10 feet tall. Scattered about were a great many large rocks that seemed out of place. They appeared to be the remains of some type of lava flow.

We slowly followed the elephant through the thick jungle bottoms. Stalking was not as bad as I expected there, for the elephant and hippos had made runways and tunnel-like roadways which were easy, but incredibly dangerous, to follow. There were tracks everywhere. I was most concerned if we were to meet an on-coming hippo at extremely close range. I kept my rifle ready to fire at an instant. There were so many birds chattering it would be difficult to hear an elephant feeding or its stomach rumbling, even if he were very close to you, and we were to find them prone to attack immediately. Adding to the problem, the monkeys kept calling us names, and I suppose kept the elephants advised of our progress and despair.

This was what might be called combat hunting — very intense. I expected every unusual sound to turn into an elephant ambush and I noticed Dereck was all eyes and white knuckles. I suppose I looked the same.

There seemed to be quite a bit of vegetation that was like some type of cane growing all around us. Beautiful green ferns, and a small red flower about an inch long that looked like it was made out of velvet. I supposed though, like everything else here, it had thorns or would poison you if you touched it.

I followed behind the tracker, called "Savage 1" — not to be confused with "Savage 2." His teeth were filed to points, or strangely broken. His face was all tribally marked with cuts and designs. We got along great. He would occasionally point out interesting things to me. At that time we had an interpreter I could barely understand, so mostly it was all sign language. Savage 1 pointed to some buffalo dung that was still steaming and indicated we must be careful. Dereck said that most of the hippo and buffalo had been wounded by muskets and arrows and had an intense dislike of people. I could feature bumping into a mad hippo with nowhere to turn.

Adrian Carr, one of the Professional Hunters, and an exceptional one at that, appeared with Larry Hammer, my hunting companion. We were hunting the same area. They had seen a waterbuck, a couple of pigs, and duikers. The bull elephant we were following apparently was now with some cows and calves. We were not sure we wanted to run into angry cow elephants in a jungle so thick that we could not see them until they were three or four feet away.

There were many women with strange-shaped heads. This woman said she had no one to feed her. We gave her money and food but two men immediately took it all from her.

Typical tracker from the primitive area with spear and filed teeth. His clothing is tree bark pounded soft and looks like buckskin. He had only seen a white person once before.

Larry suggested we do an elephant drive. I lost the toss, so Dereck and I went into the maze; not a smart move. We moved quietly. Then the tracker froze and pointed. We heard the rumbling of an elephant's stomach. Then the palm leaves I was watching 10 feet away became an elephant's ear and I could see its trunk up as if testing the air. I could see his great ear fan out and forward. All systems pointed in our direction. Damn!

Suddenly there was a great crashing and screaming of elephants, fortunately going in the other direction. The African tracker indicated that the tusks on the bull were not very large. I really don't think he saw the elephant tusk at all. He was afraid of elephants, and so were we. Thus, we decided to divert our attention to a herd of red buffalo that was part of the stampede. Great idea! Probably 30 or 40 animals had gone up the bank onto a small thicket. For some reason, the African suggested that we go in exactly a different direction. He apparently knew where they were going. This type of reverse tracking puzzled me considerably, but it was a method I was to see applied many times in the future when we were hunting bongo.

We did indeed pick up the buffalo tracks, and followed them for about an hour, applying some real walking power. Eventually we caught up with the buffalo in more heavy brush — naturally! I could see various movement within thirty yards, but no identifiable parts. Dereck, who had been sick all day, but apparently was feeling much better, climbed a tree to see if he could locate a bull. The African suddenly became very excited as two very large reedbuck were walking directly toward us and would likely scare the buffalo. Either that, or a shifting wind — anyway, the buffalo bolted. They sounded just like what they were — a thundering herd of buffalo, grunting, bellowing and leaving many piles of dung to follow. We followed.

This time our stalk was successful, and I shot at a good bull, but he thundered off after the rest of the herd. We found blood. The bull was hit hard and the tracks indicated he left the herd and entered a thicket made up of vines and vicious thorn trees. I was using a .458 Winchester with 510 grain soft points. I was later to find that the early Winchester soft-point bullet did not penetrate very deep. I did the rest of my hunting with solid bullets only.

We reluctantly abandoned the blood trail just at dark and headed back for camp. Although I have a relatively good sense of direction, I could see that, in this hemisphere, without an African, I would never find my way out. I suspect that we tend to use the sun and stars to guide us more than we think. But now I was in a different hemisphere. A good sense of direction is not just a lucky guess. I did have a compass and made my own map as we hunted.

The next morning a tracker reported that we had given up the track just a couple of hundred feet too soon, for they had found the buffalo completely devoured by hyenas and vultures. They did not bring back the horns. What good are the horns if you can't eat them! I could see we needed to school these boys a bit more.

But that was not to be, for as the safari progressed we were to have various other trackers replace those from other villages. It seems they are a bit wary of being in someone else's territory. The best trackers seemed to be the older men. That generation wore only a breechcloth that was made out of a pounded tree bark that looked like buckskin. They each had one or two spears, and some interesting designs and tribal marks etched or tattooed onto their face or chest, and some of them had their teeth filed to a point. Talk about a bad day at the dentist! They looked and acted friendly, but so did the ones who had hacked up the nuns — a necessary task I suppose.

The following day we returned to approximately the same area. This time we picked up the tracks of a very large bull elephant and followed him again into the dreaded thick jungle creek bottom. We cautiously walked up the same little stream, occasionally finding the elephant droppings still steaming. Once I saw a strange-looking snake swimming through some brackish water, then it slid under a log inches from my leg. This was interesting when you consider that I don't like snakes, and I really don't like to hunt elephants where a bayonet might be as effective as a rifle. My clothes clung to my body from the intense heat and humidity and I needed lots of water. The water was a rather yellow color and I doubled up on the Halazone pills when I filled my canteen, deciding this was my big chance to see if they really worked.

My guide, Dereck, had a bad fever. He had to rest often and I would take short side trips with a tracker who never seemed to tire, eat or drink. The elephant must have been very close. Occasionally a broken limb would float down the creek.

At all times progress was slow; carefully placing your feet and carefully moving branches around. Many of the trees were over 200 feet high, with long vines wrapping, clinging or hanging from every limb. Almost no sunlight penetrated. There were dark shadows that took on all shapes. The tracker would often stop, squat down, and listen for stomach rumbling or a limb being torn from a tree. It is amazing how well an animal ten feet at the shoulder, weighing 10,000 pounds can be so hard to see in this maze of bark and trees; they can walk without a sound.

We came upon a couple of dams built by some animal, probably similar in habit to our American beaver. As we walked my thoughts strayed. I thought back to the nun at the mission telling us that they did not believe anyone had been hunting in this area since 1890. Certainly there was no sign of any previous safari. It was obvious that some of the Africans may have seen their first white men when we arrived. This gave me a lot of mixed feelings, particularly at night, when I could hear chanting and the continual rumble of drums sending messages.

My daydreaming came to an abrupt halt when we heard the slight sound of moving brush and a tusk striking a tree. The squatting tracker, now poised as if ready to run, gave us the sign of big tusks, and indicated there were many elephants only 25 feet away. I couldn't see an elephant, let alone shoot him in the head or heart, but then elephants have a way of changing the scenario, which they did. They came at us like it was an ambush. All I could see was a wall of small trees whipping and breaking in our direction. At 10 feet the roaring screaming elephant, regardless of its sex, can somehow test the determined elephant hunter, and like I said, I'm more of a horn hunter. It was over in five seconds. Thank God they didn't stop to look for us. Dereck and I crawled back to a standing position. The native tracker was gone. I heard laughter above us — our black man was 30 feet up a tree. I think he said white men can't climb trees!

We decided to try elsewhere. After visiting with the local chief and taking a lot of pictures and giving away gifts, we had influenced him to allow us to go into an area the chief described as one where no white men had ever been. This may or may not be so, but it excited me. We were finding the people in the village very reluctant to venture into this sinister area, which they described as dangerous with many spirits. Perhaps they were referring to an unfriendly tribe, or it was against their religious beliefs. Now that I reflect back on this, I think we were dumb to continue, but my sense of adventure overcame my fear of the perils, and I was eager to go.

We hired approximately 20 porters and planned to go for 30 or 40 miles. We paid them extra, but had it not been for the Polaroid camera and pictures to trade, I don't think we would ever have made it happen. Plus, we promised meat, like elephant steak and intestines (which they eat raw), to the Africans. No, this was not your normal safari.

The temperature had dropped to about 80 degrees, and the walk to where we would camp the first night wasn't that bad. The only water available was a small bog where the water was a deep yellow. I found the water slightly clearer or thinner in some elephant tracks where the water had a chance to settle. I applied an additional Halazone pill and thought that if someone died in this area, their body would be completely decomposed before we could get back to civilization. I asked our tracker how he would handle this. His simple, unsmiling response through the interpreter was, "In several pieces after being smoked." A good solid reply through his file-pointed teeth, and I thought, "I'll bet the porters would occasionally have a sample." I added another Halazone pill and pulled my .458 closer.

That day we saw a very large warthog, some sort of kob, and several Sing-sing waterbuck; one with 27 or 28 inch horns and a very heavy base.

As the day progressed, walking became more difficult. It was much hotter, over 100 degrees, which is tough on a guy from cool Montana. There were a few game trails, some heavily used, primarily by elephants; mostly cows and calves. Overall, big game was scarce. The next day Larry and Adrian went up the left side of the river and Dereck and I were on the right. Our human pack train was to follow along behind us until we found another suitable place to camp near water.

Apparently we were somewhere in one of the drainages of the Gwanie River, but I'm not sure. Although we were primarily looking for elephant tracks, we were going to shoot some game for camp meat, for it seems the porters were going to go back. They wanted lots of meat, and NOW! — as we had promised them. Larry offered me instead — they laughed. I think they were just being funny — maybe.

This meat hunting further complicated the elephant hunting. Shooting probably alarmed the elephants. But we were forced to collect meat; mostly smaller pigs or duiker-sized game. That's all there was; Africans eat huge portions, and continually!

On the lighter side of things, I have always found it interesting to be around Africans at night. They never seem to sleep and never seem to quit talking. On this particular hunt, they were most pleased to have, as promised, large quantities of meat and intestines, which they would devour, raw or mostly placed on coals and burned to the right color, then eaten. This went on all night.

I occasionally asked what they talked about. It seems the conversation revolved around beer and the girls they planned to bed, and who was related to whom, and of sickness, aches and pains. Just like the folks at home!

I was surprised to see no sign of zebra or many other antelope species. But, we began to see more buffalo sign. I noted how active the termites were in the country. Almost every stick lying on the ground was encased in mud and was being devoured from the inside. The termites also built a strange-looking housing development with a roof. Larry shot another buffalo, so all seemed calm. But we had been advised by one of the trackers that some of the porters might slip away during the night to sleep on more familiar ground. I believe they were afraid or wanted to take meat back to their village. Biltong (dried meat) seems to play a powerful social and political role in the life of the black men.

The buffalo meat disappeared that night. But what could anyone do to reprimand the thieves? Also, the tribe had been promised whole elephants. They wanted us to shoot cows. Why did we want tusks anyway? I could see these people were serious and perhaps dangerous!

We had to move camp. We came to what we thought might be a good camp place, with a beautiful pool about 100 feet across. The water actually looked clear. There were about 10 male waterbuck and a few pigs on the other side. They scampered up the bank and disappeared into the brush before I could shoot. Not too far to my right, and closer, was a smaller pool that appeared to be very dirty. A bull hippo was standing on the other side with a white bird sitting on his back. I took out my camera and started to take a picture. As I tripped the shutter, the picture would later reveal, he lunged in our direction. I turned to grab for my rifle, but the African holding it had slung it over his back and was rapidly going up the bank with me behind him. The hippo wasn't far behind me. I grabbed the rifle and pulled so hard that I broke the sling. Fortunately, Dereck got off a couple of shots with his double .470 as the hippo lunged up the bank. I fired once at his head at five feet. The monster collapsed almost at our feet. His head was as big as a 55 gallon barrel with teeth over 12 inches long. I suppose he weighed 5,000 pounds. More meat! But a close call!

Later that evening we met Larry Hammer who was looking for our camp. It seems they had been charged by a cow elephant and had to shoot her. That night we had hippo cutlets roasted over the coals. It wasn't bad at all. Larry had also seen his first bull elephant, with tusks about 50 pounds per side. With a hippo and an elephant, the meat situation was settled for the time being, but created a new problem. Part of the crew wanted to leave with the meat and sell it in the villages. We insisted they stay and dry it.

Some days we saw a great many waterbuck. Many were having calves. There were also some very nice warthogs. Although abundant around the water, overall game could be considered very scarce in general. Waterbuck in the area had a plain white rump, relatively light grey-colored, and have always reminded me of elk. Waterbuck is generally considered poor quality table fare, but I thought it was okay.

We had a little rain and a lot of wind, making it difficult to hunt; however, fresh elephant sign was scarce. We saw a couple small buffalo and just before dark encountered two elephant bulls with about 45 pound tusks per side. The rumor of herds of 80 to 100 pound ivory was a myth. But, as usual, we kept following the myth. Maybe in the next drainage — or the next.

I shot at and missed a very large and unusual colored kob; a red and black marble color. I set up a target and found the rifle was shooting approximately a foot high. For some reason I could not change the adjustment so I removed the telescope and used open sights. I suspect the

This ancient muzzleloader barrel was made of bicycle frame tubing. Most elephant, hippo and buffalo were full of old lead balls or arrows and were quick to attack anything on two legs.

scope had been damaged when I wrestled the rifle off the African when the hippo charged us. As a boy I had no problem shooting deer at 200 yards with a peepsight. Owning a rifle without open sights as well as a telescope is like having a car without a spare tire, particularly in a remote area as primitive as we were in.

That night the moon came out very bright and seemed so close. It made you feel like you were on another planet. It was interesting to note the Africans, 15 or 20 sitting around a fire, cooking meat. Not far away they had smoke racks set up to dry meat of any animals we happened to shoot. Otherwise, meat spoils rapidly. The natives were louder than usual; sometimes angry and looking at us. I wondered what these people were talking about. I suspected our interpreter was not telling all. I also suspect the dried meat was worth a fortune to them, and they wanted to leave. We were a bit nervous, I'll admit!

There did not seem to be as much bird life in this area, but the frogs and crickets certainly made up for any night sounds we might have been lacking. I do not recall hearing any drums in this supposedly taboo area. I was worried about the Africans and did not sleep much. I had my rifle at my side. We did not have a tent; I just leaned up against a big tree to cover my back a couple of nights.

The next day we found five men had left, taking a huge amount of the dried meat. Not much was left for our crew. We had decided to walk about ten miles up the river, where it was rumored there was a large salt lick. The heat was intense; far over 100 degrees. Everything at a distance seemed to be shimmering. Yesterday I had been sunburned, even through my shirt. All agreed not to hunt that day and we would stay by the river. In fact, we eventually spent the entire day sitting in the river back to back with our rifles in hand, watching for crocodiles. We saw some real monsters. But, it was the only place where it was cool.

Larry Hammer crossed the river and on the way back, he accidently stepped into a deep hole and disappeared. For a moment I thought he had been grabbed by crocodile, but he came sputtering to the surface. He too had been thinking of crocodiles and swam rapidly to shallow water. (I had no idea a man could swim so fast.)

Larry's thermometer registered up to 120 degrees, and that is where it stayed until dark. The following day it cooled down to 119 degrees or so. We hiked up several small tributaries and found an abundance of waterbuck sign. We also saw a lot of fresh elephant sign, and a few kob. We came across a number of potholes and quite a large number of Egyptian geese. If I had a shotgun, I would have changed our diet, which consisted mostly of meat and a few canned vegetables that had been carried by our porters.

The salt lick was a spring, but also a high bank that was a maze of hippo-size holes dug out with tusks, horn and hooves to obtain mouth-size chunks. These elephant can sure play hell with the habitat. We came upon 35 torn-apart trees that had been pushed down that morning. From the tracks, it appeared we were onto a single, big elephant which we followed through some very tall grass for several hours. Then, we crawled up onto the side of a termite mound and in the distance saw a large elephant. He was facing in our direction as if he were watching and waiting for us. The tusks were fairly heavy, but we could not see how long they were. I believe the elephant actually was waiting for us. The wind was in his favor. Obviously he was planning some sort of ambush, probably to even up an old score. The tracker did not want to go any farther — there were no trees to climb. There was some merit to his thinking.

We decided we could not get around the bull. The brush was too thick and there were many snakes in that swamp, or so the tracker said. We decided to try and catch the bull in a better situation, maybe tomorrow. We were a long way from camp. On our return we ran into numerous kob. They were reddish colored with black legs and the horns reminded me of a puku. They were on an open plain and over 250 yards away, which is a long shot for a .458. I missed the first shot, but after figuring out where the bullet was hitting, on my second try, I shot a good kob. We were pleased and the Africans were very happy, for they were completely out of meat.

But the kob, being a deer-sized animal, was not going to last long with our full platoon of porters and trackers. Dereck shot another one. It seemed that our porters had picked up some camp followers in the way of women and children. Biltong (dried meat) overcame their fear of the alleged sacred area I guess.

The Africans cut up the kob, taking every parcel of meat, including the intestines and skin. All that was left was a blood spot. It was a long hard four hours back to camp in the dark. I never cease to be amazed at the Africans. Even while carrying heavy loads, they don't seem to want to stop, nor do they drink any water. Their sense of direction is remarkable — most of the time.

Actually, I was very happy to see the meat myself, for the night before, had it not been for an eagle, we would not have had any fresh meat at all. As it happened, we surprised an eagle that had killed a large rodent the Africans called a cimbaleke, about the size of a large jackrabbit. The Africans said it was very good to eat. When the eagle tried to take off, he couldn't carry the cimbaleke and dropped it. That night the cook ground up the meat into what he called cimbaleke balls. It tasted pretty good. Larry got sick and blamed it on the rodent, but I doubt that was the problem. I was concerned, however, as this was a very poor place to be ill.

Every day seemed to get hotter. Larry's thermometer registered 120 degrees again. The heat was killing me! Nevertheless, we were covering over ten miles a day, but seeing very little fresh sign of elephants. We were out of meat almost continually. One day while walking by a pool of stagnant water, a 10-foot crocodile came rushing down the bank toward the water. It is amazing how fast they move. I shot him in the head. That night he became dinner. The Africans sang a song about my good shooting, or maybe they actually said how lucky I was. But that is what I was told.

I was continually mesmerized by the magnificent trees. There were various types, some with a strange buttress root systems that acted as "legs" to keep them standing during the wet season. Others had limbs that dropped to the ground, I suppose to draw water. Occasionally we would see a snake, generally some sort of puffadder — deadly indeed. Our snake bite kit was interesting. First you had to identify the snake, if possible, then administer the right antidote. If there is a reaction, there was an antidote for the antidote, and so on. I suspect though, if you had been snake bitten, you would die. It is always best to keep an African in front of you. They seem to see the snakes well in advance. Fortunately for me, on several occasions, they did point out snakes. Once near a stagnant waterhole we saw an awesome python slide off the bank and disappear into the dark water; I saw myself being pulled down.

On two occasions, we were crawling through some dense brush on our hands and knees, and my tracker pointed just over my head and pushed me back. At first I could see nothing, but then could see a green snake about 20 inches from my face. It looked almost like the limbs of the trees. My tracker indicated to me, through sign language, that the snake was deadly by making a distorted face and holding his heart, then closing his eyes. I got the message. I hate snakes — even pretty colored ones.

We were continually encountering small columns of army ants. Some going, and some bringing things back, which they take underground to store under leaves if the entrance hole has too much traffic. Later, other ants come out and take the grub or worm, or whatever, back down into the hole. If you put your hand near them, or spit, they seem to sense it immediately and run out to attack. At the bongo area, I was awakened during the night with ants crawling on my face. I jumped up and could see hundreds of red ants crawling around on the tent floor. I had an insect spray bomb and sprayed them. It seemed to kill them instantly. They curled up in little balls and looked like piles of sawdust. On another occasion, I went outside the tent in my bare feet to reach my waterbag just outside, and stepped into the middle of a column of red army ants. They bit the hell out of my feet. From that point on, I was very careful to keep the tent zippered up and hopefully snake and ant-proof.

We had decided to abandon the elephant hunt. Although we were seeing tracks, we had seen very few elephants outside of the thick jungle-like creek bottoms, where they are almost impossible to approach. When you did get close to them, sometimes they ran away. More often, they attacked. All you could see was a wall of trees smashing down, coming in your direction with a great deal of squealing and roaring. It was all we could do to get behind trees to keep out of their way. If we approached close enough to see their tusks, they seemed to sense us and attacked immediately; actually hunting for us. I can assure you that these Congo elephants are nothing like those you saw at the game park!

Hunting elephants in this area was foolhardy, and it was bongo that I primarily wanted. But, the professional hunters seemed to be fascinated in searching for big tusks. After a few more elephant encounters, we seemed to have walked in a big circle and we were back to the truck early in the day.

That night it rained hard. There was great concern about getting vehicles out before all of the small tributaries were so full of water that we could not get across. It was very hot and humid, almost unbearable. The leaves were sprouting from the trees, and you could almost see the grass grow. There seemed to be a considerable increase in insect life and snakes. But here it appeared that everything was eating everything. There were a lot of small, red beetles, carrying other beetles away. All the leaves that hit the ground seemed to be eaten up overnight.

We said goodbye to the chief, left him some biltong and money, and we were off to the bongo area. To hell with this combat elephant hunting, but I admit it was a thrilling adventure that cannot be duplicated. It is an era gone forever. Now I am sure there are roads and farms near all the water. And the big trees are now part of someone's home in Europe.

Occasionally we would see an old person sitting along the road. Apparently they had no family and if no one would feed them, they would starve. We gave them all some dried meat; some wept with appreciation. I could see we were doing nothing but prolonging a life for a few more days. I gave one old woman some money. As I looked back, I saw two men take it from her. She was screaming and crying. Dereck said we couldn't help her — we might be killed. Foreigners had to be very careful not to get involved, especially when a local witch doctor might interpret your efforts as a threat to his turf. It was obvious through the entire hunt that the older people were much more friendly than the more civilization-exposed young men.

We occasionally would see an African with a bicycle, but most everyone walked. Women carried incredible loads on their heads. I never saw them drop anything, even with a baby strapped to their back. One woman told us she was headed for Asiro. She and her children were going to walk over a hundred miles. We gave her some meat and some money. She looked very ill. I wondered who would take care of her kids if she died. Oddly enough we later saw her in Asiro with her brother. She had somehow made it. Life is tough and short for these people.

We came to a coffee plantation and stopped. It was good to see white people again. The plantation owners were Belgian and Greek and had several children. In spite of their concern of another civil war, they said it was their home. The Greek storekeeper seemed to have a lot of cold beer around. We were only too happy to drink it and talk. I drank two large bottles, and the next day had a horrendous headache. I decided to stick to plain water. Beware of Greeks bearing gifts!

The next day we left early. After traveling 20 miles, the brakes went out on our truck and there was no way to repair them. We had lunch under a big tree and pondered our next move. I noticed quite a number of men gathering, all carrying nets around their necks, and each with two spears and a machete. They had with them a couple of Basenji dogs and were very eager to start the day's hunt. The interpreter said they were after duiker and monkeys.

The spears were interesting. Most of them had a point from six to 16 inches long and two inches wide at the middle. At the other end of the spear was a metal cap, somewhat of a chisel, which I noticed was used for digging under the trees to root out hapless rodents. I suppose it was just by chance that they chose the tree where we were sitting. I walked over to their village.

Around each hut was a plot of land about 30 feet by 30 feet that was cleared where they grew corn and sweet potatoes. Through an interpreter I was told that one of the men had acquired a new wife. Here, the selling price for wives was equal to $4 to $6. Since money was scarce, they used some form of wampum for trade, as did our Indians in the United States. The bride looked very young, but very happy.

We finished lunch and moved on. We had only gone a short distance when the radiator started to boil. We stopped and found the radiator completely covered with some of the most beautifully colored butterflies and insects I had ever seen. We decided to camp along the road for the night. It was worth the delay to watch the people. There were numerous traders with goods piled high on a bicycle, or carrying merchandise — cloth, pans, knives, even a couple of radios. Some would walk over 100 miles to find buyers in remote villages. I could see things would change fast for the Azande people. We were lucky to be there to witness the end of a primitive society.

We had breakfast, fruit and crackers, and looked over our maps. A fork in the road, our selection, was becoming just a track. There were quite a number of people walking along the roadside. Whenever we would stop, a throng of people would collect, staring and apparently asking questions about why we were there, and aghast when they found out we were after the dreaded bongo. Most of the little kids hid behind their mothers when they heard we also would eat bongo meat. White men were indeed the work of demons. I noticed that the women's clothing was clean, while the men appeared to be dirty.

Although several spoke poor English, our interpreters helped us carry on an interesting conversation. As usual, the kids were real comedians, particularly two boys who happened to have some fish to sell. We traded photos for fish. There were quite a number of old people in this group, some with pointed heads. I assumed they had been bound when they were children. Seeing the old people saddened me greatly for they are in tears and begging and said they had no one to care for them. No doubt some of it was an act, but I think most of them were sincere. Again, we gave them some dried meat, a few coins, which I am sure were again stolen from them as soon as we were out of sight. The best thing that can happen to old people in this area is an early death.

There were many sick people. They begged for something to ease their pain. We gave out hundreds of pills Larry had brought for that purpose. Some claimed we cured them with one aspirin. But one witch doctor said we had caused some of his patients to die and he was going to put a curse on us — and, in Africa, that's serious!

After a very long drive, we arrived that evening at Dungu. The road had improved considerably. Apparently before the last revolution there were numerous Europeans living in the area running plantations.

When we drove over the bridge at the edge of town, about 50 feet below the bridge on the riverbank, I noticed 20 graves. It was explained that this was where 2,000 rebels had captured 20 nurses, and, after gang-raping them, the survivors were carried to the bridge and thrown onto the rocks below. Later they were buried by Christians (African). Actually, some of the same men who had raped them had also helped bury them, or so I was told.

As it was explained by the first nun that we talked to at Anvo, these people were very simple. Although they may say they love you, they could be completely influenced by the local witch doctors, or by the fact that you may have been leaning toward a closer alliance with another tribe. They had been killing each other for so many years, that I don't think they gave it much thought. If necessary, do it. That's all there is to it.

We had practically no supplies. Fortunately there was a store in this town run by the Greeks. Greeks apparently ran most of the stores in this part of the country and supplied the few other white people in the area with their needs. The Greeks suffered no problems with the rebels, but I was told they paid an enormous fee to be left alone and probably treated the blacks better. I suspect the money factor was paramount. The Greeks were eager for conversation. We had a few drinks and later that evening contin-ued up to the little village called Duro, which was about two hours away.

As we had no real map, and rivers and villages also had local names, there may be some confusion. For those of you with a modern map, 25 years ago it was different world!

We got a late start, but did repair the truck brakes. It rained a little and was cooler. Unfortunately, there were a lot of night jars (birds) flying about after insects, and we must have hit 40 or 50 of them with the truck. They would dive at insects in our headlights. The road had become very rough. We crossed the Nyeka River. It was after midnight when we reached the bongo camp.

The camp had been set up the previous year and was in surprisingly good condition. I was continually amazed at the huge trees and vines that surrounded us. I could hear a bat chirping nonstop and very loud. Larry and I were placed in a tent with good mosquito netting and a cot. I thought about using earplugs to close out the bats — bonk.. bonk.. bonk. It was a maddening sound! But, I was very concerned about some of the Africans, as I understood they were hostile toward whites, and I have an allergy to

Our Bongo camp was a beautiful site except the continual rumble of great log drums throughout the night made sleep difficult.

knife wounds. We were continually being warned by the interpreters. I usually slept with my shoes on and my rifle in my cot. On two occasions I slept on the ground in a corner with my rifle and packsack full of escape items at my side. In fact, I never went anywhere without my rifle. Not even to breakfast — just like in Korea. This certainly was not like a deer hunt in Montana. I was surprised one morning to see Larry sleeping in the other corner. He too was wary. Sometimes we would wake up in the middle of the night and see a man just standing outside the tent, or peering from behind a tree. There was no sound sleeping on this hunt.

At long last, though, I would hunt bongo. We started hunting at daylight and drove down the road, such as it was. Periodically, we dropped off Africans to look for tracks of bongo bulls. When they would find one, they were to return to the road. We would wait at the truck two hours, then drive back until we met someone with a track. Often the tracks they found were cow bongo, reedbuck, or no track at all. Africans would say anything for the reward money. I could see that getting a bongo was not going to be easy, especially with so many people walking with us. I suggested I hunt alone with just one tracker. That was fine with Dereck, who was ill and very tired most of the time.

Arnold Callins had advised us prior to the hunt that we should use nothing but a .458 Winchester with 500 grain solid bullets. Because we were hunting in so much brush that you could never really see the whole bongo — perhaps just a stripe. You need a bullet that will plow through brush and bongo from one end to the other, and keep shooting. But, that was slow in happening. We scared away most everything we followed — mostly on our hands and knees. The bongo loved to punish us and would run down scary, brush-covered tunnels or walk in a stream. The bongo must really be able to climb trees!

I offered Polaroid pictures to the successful African trackers and they were pleased. For some strange reason, they were not surprised by anything that white men can do. With a promise of more pictures, I could see where we could get all of the trackers we wanted until I found one who was outstanding.

We drove along a river called the Byeka. We stopped to visit the local chief prior to pursuing any bongo to be sure there were no problems. The chief had 20 wives and 30 children. All of the adult men had tribal markings on their face and body. Some of the old men had their teeth filed to a point. While we waited for the trackers to come back to the road, I walked down to a cluster of huts. They were swept very clean. I saw no paper or glass, and only a couple of metal pans, which were greatly prized. I noticed their chicken coops were built off the ground and looked like the huts the Africans lived in, but chicken size of course, complete with a little ladder leading up to the doorway so the chickens could walk up. A wooden plug about six inches wide was placed in the opening to keep predators out at night.

I noticed that women were doing most of the work, like burning brush, gathering wood or digging in the gardens. The men were mostly drinking beer or hunting. One of the trackers turned out to be exceptional, almost uncanny. I knew I had found my man. His name was Bittee — sharp teeth and all.

I again suggested the tracker and I hunt alone. Dereck was too ill to decline. Bittee was a friendly, powerfully built man. He spoke no English — none whatsoever. But, through sign language and the language of the forest, he and I communicated very well. When he saw that I was not going to stand around and wait for him to make things happen, he seemed to delight in helping me find the tracks. Sometimes he would see a bruised piece of grass, or a branch a bongo had broken or nibbled on. In the days to come, I picked up a few words of Azande, and he a little English. This man could track an ant across a dry rock.

Bittee was a born actor, and would play the part of the bongo to show me exactly what the bongo was doing according to their tracks. In one particular case, he described three cows watching two bulls, one coming from one side of the clearing, and one from the other side. They circled each other as he showed me — walking and playing the part of each bongo.

At one point they touched noses. One ran away for a short distance and eventually left, leaving what seemed to be the larger bull with the cows. Without any help, I noticed that the bongo, especially the bulls, would enter the brush in a particular place, and if undisturbed, when they came out it would very often be in the same place. Perhaps I had found a crack in their armor.

We didn't see any bongo on our first days of hunting, although we tracked various bulls. But, we couldn't get near them. The brush was too thick. At several points we made drives, but the bongo would somehow get out behind us. Incidentally, snakes and animal capture pits weren't the only dangers to face. One has to be careful when following the Africans because they have a habit of putting their spears with points about 16 inches long pointing back over their shoulder. Running into the back of the guy in front of you, in that case, could get your throat cut.

At night I thought back to some of the things we had seen during the day, such as the termite mounds some 15 feet high. The African women had dug a circle of pits about the size of a five gallon bucket and placed a torch in each one. Periodically, at night, the insects would fly out and fly directly toward the fire where their wings would be singed and they would drop down into the hole. The next day they were scooped out to be eaten! Later, by accident, I was to sample them. They weren't to my liking. Also, some sort of oil was squeezed out of the termite for some purpose — it smelled BAD!

There was no wire so there were no snares like you find all over Africa today. We encountered deep pits that had been dug for various size animals. The small pits were wedge-shaped, so any animal falling in would have its legs pushed together so it was difficult to climb out. At the bottom of the pits, numerous bamboo spikes, sharpened at one end, were set so when the animal dropped in it would be impaled, perhaps being killed on the spot if it were lucky. The larger the pit, the greater were the number of spikes. I remember in one instance, one of the African trackers, I believe it was the one we called Savage 2, showed me a pit by taking his spear and picking up the edge of the grass so I could look down inside the large pit, which possibly was for hippo-sized game.

The water from recent rains had filled the pit about half full. The sharp spikes, dozens of them, could be seen above the water line, and swimming around in the water were several venomous snakes that had accidentally dropped in. I couldn't think of a more horrible place to fall, especially if you didn't like snakes. All the more reason to walk carefully behind an African who knew of the existence of the pits. Most of the time though, you could see a pile of dirt along the side of the pit. Be careful!

Each day we hunted bongo in a different direction where a big bull had supposedly been seen. Once we walked through a small village and I could see a tree had been planted on the main pathway by the witch doctor. On it hung various pieces of bone, feather, animal teeth, and brightly colored stones. At this early hour, the Africans were huddled around the fires, as it was cool. Most of the men seemed occupied with various types of fiber which they were fitting together to make rope by continually laying on new strands while rubbing it across their leg. The rope is remarkably uniform, and looked like something you could buy at Wal-Mart. It was very strong. Most of the rope was used for fish line or for making capture nets.

The main interpreter, Mr. Jeeves, was a Sudanese who claimed to speak seven languages. He had been a teacher in the Sudan before being chased out during a revolution. He explained that the unusually small huts we encountered were used to place a body when someone died. The first day was a day of mourning. After that, they would mourn no more. Then, after seven days, the bones and remains were placed in the ground where they would remain forever, and life would go on.

I suspect much of what I saw has changed with various missionaries, more roads, schools and stores, and even satellite television in some public meeting centers. I wish now I had spent more time photographing the people and asking more questions.

In each village there was a giant drum made from a hollowed-out log, larger than a 55 gallon drum. All day long, and at night in particular, messages are sent to various villages. I asked Jeeves, our butler/interpreter, if it was possible to find out how my friend, Henry Budney, was doing in a camp supposedly a hundred miles away. He told me he would have a message for me the following day. The drums can be maddening at times, as sometimes they are beat all night.

The next day I did get my reply. The interpreter told me that my friend, Henry Budney, had shot a reedbuck and an elephant. He described the elephant tusks being as tall as Wenda, one of the camp staff, and as big around at the base as the thigh of Sota, a tracker in our camp, indicating to me that Henry had shot a pretty good elephant.

Sometimes at night the Africans would bring down some musical instruments they had devised with gourds and wooden boxes with small metal strips they would plink with their fingers to make various musical tones. I was told the metal was made from the spokes of bicycles, although I had not yet seen any bikes in the area.

Most of these people had never been in any vehicle. They knew how to walk! (Fortunately I was in good shape.)

I noticed that the fields (actually small plots) that had been cleared contained mostly corn, cotton (which they seemed to be weaving themselves) and manyok, which is very poisonous until cooked. The leaves of the manyok were eaten like spinach, and the roots appeared to be something like sweet potatoes. There were also some small melons about the size of a fist that appeared to grow profusely around the huts.

We had some rain so the bongo tracks seemed to be more abundant. We crossed the tracks of two bulls traveling together and slowly tracked them through the thick brush. Finally, we saw quick glimpses of movement as they crashed through the forest. Even being close to a bongo sent shivers up my back. I had yet to see one.

We made several drives, but it was like driving an old whitetail deer, and the Africans were scared to death of a running bongo. The hunting was ever more difficult because it was so hot and there seemed to be a lot of wind swirling around through the forest. Despite the light rain, all the vegetation on the ground was very dry and noisy to walk on. The bats chirping at night were enough to drive you loony! I was tired, as I hadn't been sleeping well the previous few nights. It had been a tough safari. Perhaps we should have been looking more into the treetops for the elusive bongo. I have never encountered a tougher animal to hunt fair chase. My friend, Larry, never did get one, but he concentrated more on elephant.

I became concerned about the Africans. Jeeves said to "sleep light" — whatever that meant! Some of the camp staff was unfriendly, but I thought more about snakes crawling into the tents or putting my hand on the wrong limb, or being dragged into a stinking sinkhole by a 25-foot snake!

The interpreter told me that most of the people living along this road had only been there a short time, as the government was encouraging people to leave the more primitive areas. There were always Africans standing around at camp looking for medical assistance. Larry had given out a lot of aspirin and antibiotics. I was afraid to give away too much, for if someone were to get sick or die, the witch doctor could blame us, as in the other area.

We may joke about the witch doctors, but the Africans, even today, take them very seriously. You must be careful not to offend, or appear to be belittling, his efforts. Actually, most civilized white people worry about the number 13, black cats, ladders, etc. I might add that I have seen some strange things that you might think of as unexplained phenomena. For example, we were walking toward a small village. On the trail we met two witch doctors who stopped to chat with the trackers. Jeeves, our interpreter, told me what they were saying, more or less, blow by blow. The conversation was as follows:

"Good morning. Why are you in this part of the forest?" The tracker responded that we were hunting bongo and elephant. The witch doctors wanted to know, "Why do you want the bongo? They are poisonous to touch and can be very dangerous if wounded. During the daylight hours they use their horns to crawl up into trees, and might attack you from above." The tracker responded, "Have you seen any elephants?" The witch doctor asked, "Why do you want the elephant?" The tracker responded, "The white men wish to take their tusks, feet, and ears. We can have the meat." The witch doctor said, "Why would the white men take the feet and ears and not take the meat? Do the white men eat the feet?" The tracker said he didn't know. The witch doctor said, "You are not going to see any elephants today anyway." The tracker said, "Why not?" The witch doctor said, "Because today is the day that elephants are invisible. And, even if two of them were standing on the trail, you would walk between them and not see them." The trackers and Jeeves responded then, "What can we do to find an elephant?" The witch doctor said, "You must give me something that is valuable to the white men." Jeeves asked him what he would require. The witch doctor said he would take one of the cartridges, as he did understand very much what rifles were, even though we had not seen even a muzzleloader in this particular area. Then the witch doctor noticed that one of the assistant trackers, who was carrying our waterbag, also had for himself a soft drink bottle that was badly worn, and which was tied by a string around his neck. He carried it under his arm and seemed to consider it very valuable. The witch doctor wanted the bottle. The African tracker was reluctant to give it up, but we offered to pay him considerably more money and take more Polaroid pictures of his family when we returned to our base camp. The witch doctor then said that tomorrow when the sun is what seemed to be 3 o'clock, we should be at a certain river crossing.

The next day Larry Hammer was there and sure enough, here came the elephant. Larry shot and wounded the animal, but lost the track at nightfall. A swarm of Africans appeared out of nowhere to take the meat and promised to remove the tusks and bring them to our camp if they found the dead elephant. As I recall, we never saw them again, although Jeeves told us the drums said the elephant was found dead and to tell the bald white man — Larry. I assume that is as it happened. Whatever.

The previous night must have been a big party night. I supposed they had eaten a missionary or something like that. The drums beat all night from various directions, people coming and going. There was a great deal of singing and yelling. The next day I noticed all of the trackers were still carrying spears, but all looked in bad shape, like they might be suffering from hangovers and overeating.

When searching for fresh sign, periodically the trackers all came together and seemed to be having a conference, pointing in all directions while we stood and watched. I noticed one of the trackers had his son with him, a boy about 12 years old. He seemed to be very keen on tracking.

Through an interpreter I was told the boy liked to hunt very much. I felt a kinship with him, and took his picture. He was delighted. The father was especially delighted to have a father/son picture.

I found out we were paying the African trackers about 30 cents for a fourteen hour day. The cost of a chicken was about 80 cents per chicken, and about 50 cents for a guinea fowl.

Dereck was quite ill by this time and did not want to walk. I was hunting on my own with Bittee being the primary tracker and several others who would pack out meat, assuming we shot something other than bongo. I could see that getting any bongo, male or female, was a major project.

On one occasion we picked up the very fresh track of a bongo herd moving out through some large clearings, which is unusual for bongo. I think the tracker and I had the same idea, follow this bunch and maybe we would finally have a chance at seeing them. Even with a .458 I thought I could hit one at 200 yards. One track was that of a big bull. But, after hours of tracking, the bongo returned to their old habits and entered the brushy creek bottom. We followed ever so slowly, mostly in a crouched position, carefully moving every branch or vine so it would not scrape against my clothing. At one point, Bittee hesitated and pointed to a stick inches in front of me and indicated that I was to move. After closer examination, the stick turned out to be another deadly stick snake. Bittee kept saying, "Pettee, pettee," which I interpreted to mean bongo very close. Never had I been so anxious to just get a glimpse of a white stripe! I normally am quick to see game.

I don't think I have ever hunted harder or under worse conditions. Sometimes I could hear the bongo or see limbs moving, but no bongo. We often lost the bongo tracks as they seemed to have a habit of walking in the small creek beds. Finding where they came out was extremely time-consuming. If we could not find the tracks, some of the Africans would continually point up into the trees. I have often thought the same thing about elk and whitetail deer.

I observed that the Africans did not like to get too close to the bongo in the brush. It seems the bongo are somewhat like the little bushbuck; when wounded or alarmed, they have the habit of lying flat, then leaping up and punching the pursuer in the belly with sharp horns. I suppose that would get your attention. Were they purposely trying to stay away from the bongo? I wondered. But I think Bittee was sincere and he was also a cannibal.

I stopped daydreaming and noticed that not even a bird was chirping and there was no wind. There was absolute silence. I could feel a strange sensation up and down my back and the hair on my arms rose. The Africans were frozen in various positions, all looking straight ahead. I was sure I was finally going to see the mystical Mbangana. I could sense they were watching us. I wanted a bull, but to start with, any bongo would do. I had two licenses. Just to get a bongo would be most satisfying at this point. Never before have I experienced such intense feeling. Through my binoculars, and through the brush, approximately 30 feet away, I could see an eye, and then a bit of an ear and part of a horn. The horn looked heavy at the base and I was sure it was a bull, but I couldn't determine how he was standing and where to shoot through the brush. There were several thick trees that might divert my 500 grain solid bullet.

I decided I must shoot, and fired where I thought his shoulder would be. A small tree fell over, sliced off by my bullet, then creased the bongo's horn base. The bongo disappeared and I could hear running all around me. The bongo I shot at broke between two trees. I fired and knew I hit it somewhere. A bongo bull flashed between trees and I fired. I could see bark fly on the opposite side of a 12-inch tree. But the solid bullet missed its mark.

The wounded bongo appeared again about 15 feet away and was heading fast in our direction. The African went up into a tree like quail from a fox, and I fired. The bullet hit the center of the bongo's chest and exited by the tail, and it fell to the ground. Everyone was elated. It appeared that the bongo I shot was a cow with an exceptionally heavy horn and body, similar to a bull.

Since I had no interpreter at this time, it was difficult to communicate with the Africans. One man indicated he would go for Dereck. They were afraid to touch the bongo. I did convince Bittee to help with skinning by holding the legs, but before touching the bongo, they would wrap palm leaves around the particular area so their hands never touched the bongo skin or meat. I life-sized the skin, removed the horns, and cut the meat into pieces, which the trackers did agree to carry on poles, provided they did not have to touch it. All this was done in sign language — great waving of arms and facial expressions.

While I was skinning the bongo, the ants were terrible; they crawled into my ears and were continually biting me. Each bite was like a hot match. I had to get an African to get a switch and keep switching around my legs and back to keep the ants off of me.

I knew that the fear of leprosy would not last long, as I had been told earlier by the interpreter that there were several priests in a mission who were encouraging the Africans to kill the bongo for food, assuring them that there was no leprosy. I don't think these missionaries realized they had opened the season on the bongo, and they too would soon be as scarce as other wildlife around the villages. This concern was reinforced when we were informed one night by the drums that an African wished to sell an exceptionally large bongo and a skin, which, when time permitted, we investigated. The horns were indeed very large, and we found the skin amazing.

It appeared this particular African was not afraid of bongos, and had removed all of the flesh from the inside of the bongo through its mouth, anus, and a small hole in the stomach. He made a framework of sticks, grass and sand, and had actually created a life-size bongo mount, claiming that he had cured it somehow or other by funneling smoke to the inside of the animal. It did look strange indeed. We decided not to eat the bongo I shot, or it might give the Africans more encouragement to start killing them.

Larry and Adrian hadn't shot a bongo yet, but as you recall, elephant was their game. They were going to try more drives, which so far had been unsuccessful. There was just too much brush. Dereck suggested they try the dogs and see if we could use them to drive the game through the brush to Larry. The Africans did not think that was a good idea, but said they would try.

One dog that they figured would be better than any was a black and white one that lived near Bittee's village. We were unable to get the dog into the truck. The dog kept leaving. But one of the trackers felt that if he put a net over his shoulder and shook the bell which was put around the dog's neck when they were hunting, this might change things. It did. The dog became very excited and came up to the truck, but still would not get in. Then, he ran away. The tracker ran him down, picked him up, and the dog peed all over him, then proceeded to bite him in the face, on the shoulders and hands. It was obvious this dog did not want to go with a white man in a truck.

Most of the Basenji dogs were somewhat aggressive and I think they would bite whether provoked or not. All the dogs were well fed, and seemed to be well treated.

The next morning, the Africans insisted we take two other dogs, and we walked from the village. We walked for many miles, until late afternoon. This time the dogs did run the bongo for a short distance. I could see the ears and tails of a bongo, but could not tell if it was a bull. I did not shoot. And, I didn't want to use a dog anyway. About dark it started to rain. Perhaps the hunting would get easier.

The rain did not help the situation with the noisy bat living near our tent in a high tree. The continual bonging was so bad I took my .458 and fired up into the tree where the sound was coming from, hoping I would shoot him. It was silent for about an hour, but then he returned with a mate. Now there were two. We even offered a reward to any African who could catch and remove the bats from the tree. For $5, the price of a woman, the witch doctor said he would take care of the bats — and he did!

We continued hunting bongo. At one point, Bittee and I had worked ourselves into a herd of bongo. I could see various cows standing under the underbrush. Then, for some crazy reason, Sota, who had accompanied us that day, walked up to Bittee to ask something, in a rather loud voice — a very large bongo bull disappeared into the underbrush. To say I was disappointed was an understatement. Bittee was visibly angry, and Sota most apologetic. He could speak a bit of English. He was not a hunter, but a city African and did not understand the complexity of the problems we were having. Away went the biggest bongo I would see. Sota suggested I buy a big one. He knew of one that died in a pit.

The next day we hunted half the day because of a death in the village. Through sign language Bittee let me know that he had three children, only one had lived, and that his mother had died just two weeks prior.

We had been in Zaire about a month and only had a few days left to hunt. I must admit we were all ready for the trip to be over.

Larry Hammer's guide's name was Drumo. Near his village we encountered some people who were very black and spoke with a female-type lisp. All had a strange chemical odor, which was most unpleasant. I noticed this on a number of people in this particular area. I also noticed that one of these black Africans had some sort of marker in front of his hut with bird wings, teeth, and feathers attached. I suppose it was some sort of omen. Although all the people seemed very friendly, it was easy to see that under the right circumstances, the situation could change dramatically.

Larry Hammer returned from the shower and told me that one of our crew had been strung up in front of a nearby hut and was being beaten with sticks. We investigated the situation and were advised by Jeeves to stay away, even though it was obvious they would probably kill him. I spoke with Dereck and he said it was an internal problem and told me to forget it. The next day I asked Jeeves what had happened to the man. He told me he had died, but later in the day he acted as if he knew nothing about the event at all. I never saw the man after that — maybe they ate him?

Finally Bittee, through the interpreter, acknowledged that he was a cannibal, and on numerous occasions had eaten human flesh. He would not discuss how the person died. When I asked him what part of the person appealed to him, he raised his arm and rubbed his ribs. I asked if he meant he liked the ribs or the lungs. He did not answer, just smiled and said he wanted me to come to lunch! Now, I had to think about this. Was I going to eat or be eaten? What would you do? I told him I was old and tough but he didn't seem to catch my joke.

We went into Bittee's village that afternoon. I welcomed the

Perhaps my greatest trophy ever. My first Bongo and Bittee, who could track an ant across solid rock and admitted he preferred the loin when eating human flesh.

opportunity to sit down and rest. It was hot and I was very tired, but planned to stay alert. The village was very clean. A woman brought a clay bowl of water for me, but I decided not to drink it, even though I was very thirsty. Somehow or another I had lost my canteen. Then the woman brought me a plate of boiled and raw bananas. I ate about a dozen and she brought more. She brought me a bowl of what I assumed was some type of boiled root and another bowl of a thick white smelly batter, like tapioca. I knew it had been boiled so I thought it was okay. I ate some of the tapioca type food and discovered it was bitter, yet sweet. It turned out to be termites. Bittee ate with great enthusiasm, dipping it by the handful into the smelly portion and smacking his lips.

A young girl came out of a hut with a large galvanized safety pin and was digging the thorns out of Bittee's feet. Besides a few pots, the pin was the first commercial metal object I had seen.

I had previously purchased a small radio to give to the trackers when I got a bongo. I gave it to Bittee. He was most appreciative, to say the least. They finally had their first noise box in the village. I didn't know what he was going to use for batteries when those ran out, but I understood a store was being built in the near future at another village. Things would change dramatically in this part of Africa. The modern world was coming fast. Bittee did not show up for a couple of days. He had gotten drunk and had sold his radio and a shirt I gave him. Later, I saw the shirt on a local prostitute.

Larry, and Adrian, his guide, brought back two baby forest hogs that were given to them by an African who had killed the hogs' mother. I understand if you can get them to civilization, they are very valuable. We tried feeding them with a hypodermic needle and powdered milk, which we squirted into their mouths. By the second day, they caught on, and went for it in a big way. I didn't know what we were going to do with them. Later on, on the way home, we dropped them off at one of the Greek stores and they were going to try to raise them.

Our five-week safari was coming to a close and I had one final day to hunt with Drumo. Bittee was going with Larry on a last ditch attempt. Drumo was not near the tracker that Bittee was, but could speak a bit of English and with the little Azande I had picked up, and a whole lot of sign language, we could carry on a reasonable conversation. But it was obvious he was telling me what I wanted to hear, or was just lying outright, which complicated matters considerably. I decided that we would return to one particular area where I felt that two bulls were, as we had often seen their tracks.

Since it had rained the night before, perhaps we would be able to pick up a fresh track. In spite of Drumo's insistence that we do something else, we went to the area and immediately found the tracks, which we followed on our hands and knees for several hours on the narrow trails the bongo liked to follow. I suspected that, because of this habit, many of these animals would die in wire snares when wire became available to the Africans.

To take one of these bulls, we would have to catch him lying down, which is the equivalent of finding an old, wary whitetail buck snoozing in his bed. Tough odds to be sure but I was getting a lot better at spotting tiny pieces of bongo in the jungle.

There was a slight breeze blowing in my face and for a moment, I thought I could smell a bongo, which I believed was very close. I laid down on my stomach where I could look under the brush, and sure enough, just a few yards away I could make out what I believed to be two bongo lying very close together. I had handed my rifle to Drumo when I laid down and could not get his attention to hand the rifle to me. I had to get to my feet, and when I did, one of the bongo stood up also. I could see that he had exceptionally large horns. The other bongo immediately stood up. They were moving slowly, their horns tipped back. I could see slight movement between the trees. They stopped and I could just make out two bongo about three feet apart. Drumo motioned that the one to the left was the largest, and about 25 feet directly in front of me. I slowly raised my rifle and fired.

A 500 grain solid actually made a bullet path that you could follow through shot-off limbs, but did find the target. I hit the bull squarely between the eyes, splitting the skull and a 500 grain solid exiting through his rump. The other bull disappeared, but not before I noticed that his horns were absolutely enormous. I had shot the smaller one.

Drumo continually insisted that my bull was larger in body, which brought up a problem that I had with Africans and Indians in various parts of the world — getting them to understand that body size does not matter. It was usually the horn that was important. I doubt I ever convinced any of them.

The safari was over and we headed back to Asiro. Larry had bad luck, although Adrian did get him onto a couple of fleeting bulls in thick brush. Henry Budney did very well — a big bongo, elephant and various plains game species. But, a series of events was about to plague us.

We nearly had a dangerous incident with some drunken and armed boatmen who were supposed to ferry us across the river on a raft made out of old canoes. When we arrived in Asiro, there were quite a number of soldiers in the town and it seems that our airplane seats had been taken up by the military. Arnold Callins seemed to be in a great rush to get out of town. Their plan was to drive the vehicles back to Kenya. I suspect there was a problem between Arnold and the local military, most of whom were drunk and carried machine guns.

I had no desire to wait another week to get on the plane, if we could get on at all. We already had tickets, but the plane was off limits to us. A Greek merchant put us in touch with a man who had a boat that eventually would end up in Kinshasa, the capital. The boatman, a black man who spoke French, as did Larry Hammer, determined that he would take us for little money, but that it would take approximately 35 days through malaria-infested jungles.

I confronted Arnold about us going with him to Kenya. He said we could try, but might have visa problems. Besides that, he was afraid they might detain him at the border and, if they did, he was going to shoot his way out rather than fall into the hands of some of the hostile factions. That did not appeal to me.

We pooled our money, as I recall $4,000, and offered to bribe the airport manager to get on the plane. For this he could get us to Kisangani, but did not know if we could get on the plane there. But, at least we were out of what appeared to be a hostile environment. We left all of our trophies with one of the Greek merchants and took the flight. We did get the trophies about a year later. Now, I hear there are many easier places to take bongo, and I doubt that there is such danger or primitive conditions.

When arriving at Kisangani, I found there was a representative of the United States living there — some sort of Peace Corps ambassador-type fellow. He said he was coming to the airport and would help us. He was most unfriendly and enraged Larry Hammer when he arrived. He looked like a beatnik and was distributing communistic literature, but if it had not been for him, I don't think we would have gotten on the plane, and certainly would not have been able to bring our firearms any further.

We made it to Kinshasa. Enroute from the airport, not far from the hotel, we noticed a structure being built, which I thought was to be some sort of podium. The driver explained there was going to be a public execution of some rebels and that we should stay in the hotel. Sure enough, there was a hanging.

The next day Larry and I were able to turn our flights around and get on a plane that would fly over North Africa, ending up in Spain, where we could get a connecting flight to meet our wives in Athens. It was a long flight — somewhere in North Africa the plane made an unscheduled landing far out on the runway.

An army bus took most of the male passengers that boarded in Kinshasa. They took our passports, and then lined us up against the wall. I believe there were about twenty of us. They thoroughly searched each person at gunpoint, shaking up a couple of passengers who did not want to lean up against the wall with arms and legs spread. Then, suddenly, the police officer said they were in error and shook our hands goodbye and gave us each a Coke. I was happy to arrive in Madrid.

I've been to Africa many times before and since, but never had so many happenings. We decided not to tell our wives about all these incidents. Larry said to me, and I believe he was serious at the time, "Atcheson, you SOB, I never want to go on any exploratory trips with you again." But, I think he would. Larry did end up shooting what was then the world record Alaskan moose, so his luck wasn't always bad.

As for me, this hunt, I will admit, was wonderful, different and difficult. But, that's why I went. Would I do it again? You bet I would! That was 25 years ago, and now I don't think there are many such places left in this world. I think I saw the end of ancient Africa.

THE ALASKAN BROWN BEAR

The charging bear's eyes had locked onto mine. His were black and shiny, yet with the overall appearance of blood red. Just before he reached me, his mouth opened wide and his ears went back.

The giant bear and I were on a collision course. The very alders that I had struggled to get through parted like blades of grass for this great Alaskan brown bear. He was coming towards me at an unbelievable speed. My .338 Winchester was cradled across my left arm, and although my response was instantaneous, before I had the barrel level with the bear I knew he was going to be upon me. At the same time, I jumped to the right. I can remember thinking, "My God, he is so big, and if he grabs me I must not let go of my rifle."

How had I allowed myself to get into such a predicament? Well, actually, it was pretty easy. I wanted to shoot a bear, and a big one at that. I'm not the first who's wanted a bear rug with lots of teeth and long claws. Cave men had long been hunting and evicting the vicious and enormous cave bear from its living quarters. Bear meat was not really an important food item to the cave dweller, and the skins of caribou or deer were probably a lot warmer to wear and the animal itself was more readily available at a lot less risk. Obviously the cave man was a sport hunter who worshiped the bear and held him in high esteem. They collected claws and teeth and arranged bear skulls and bones in such a manner that one would believe the hunter was honoring the bear.

Even more recently, Indians of the West collected teeth and claws of bears as a symbol of courage. The hunting of bear with a spear no doubt would be a courageous act, especially since there were no riflemen around to back him up.

I've taken my share of black bears, grizzly bears, and one polar bear, and now I wanted to hunt the giant Alaskan brown bear (the Giant Grizzly). Although the cave bear of ancient times was supposedly much larger and more ferocious, I would think that the Alaskan brown bear that can weigh up to 1,500 pounds would be big enough to impress anyone. When you consider that this would be an animal possibly as large as a big saddlehorse, we're talking about a bear skin rug that could be 10 feet across the paws, and just about as long from his nose to his tail — almost too big for a living room floor. I decided I'd worry about where I was going to put it after I got it.

In May of 1964, I arrived at Cold Bay, Alaska, on the Alaskan Peninsula where the bears were big, and hunters few. I also was going to find that there was plenty of country for a few bears to hide in, in a land famous for bad weather, and the bear liked it that way.

My hunting companion was Bob Hanson of Los Angeles, California. Our guides would be Bob Curtis and Clark Engle. We would hunt northeast of Cold Bay and Beaver Bay, where the base camp was located.

First Bob would pick us up and take us to Beaver Bay. He had explained that the weather was terrible and that there were several other hunters at the base camp, as he was unable to move them out to other locations. Previous to hunting this area, I thought I had seen some bad weather, but I do not believe many places in the world have a more adverse climate. The wind never seems to quit blowing. In fact, a 20 miles per hour wind isn't considered worthy of mention, and I would learn a lot more about a windy day.

Our Helio-courier made a controlled crash landing on the beach in front of the cabin. Apparently we did well, for I could see half a dozen people clapping their hands, which I assumed meant we had put on a good show. The 16-foot by 16-foot cabin was quite comfortable and was constructed out of 4 by 8 sheets of plywood, a tarpaper roof and coat of green paint. The oil stove kept the camp warm. We had a propane refrigerator, an oven, and a good-looking cook, and most important, she was a very good cook. I could see that the quarters were going to be cramped with 10 people in one small room. A blanket was put up to give the cook some privacy.

Sharon did the cooking and we did the dishes and kept the floors clean. Since Sharon could not escape the tainted jokes or the manly bodies brushing close to her, she good naturedly participated with many friendly barbs.

We were there several days and the camp was low on heating fuel. Bob suggested he and I fly over to Unga Island where there was a mission and see what was available. I was delighted to be doing something, although the flight over and back was worse than you can imagine. But Alaskan pilots just take that in stride. Except, I was not an Alaskan pilot and left deep fingerprints, even in metal.

But once there, while Bob was filtering water out of the fuel, I walked up to a small store that was used by the natives. The shelves were full of sweet things, soft drinks, all of the good things to rot the teeth of little children. I remembered Sharon saying that today was her birthday. I thought it would be nice if I bought her a box of candy. Then, I bought a couple of gallons of ice cream for the rest of the crew. I was sure Sharon would be pleased with a gift.

I gave Sharon the box of candy and she said nothing for a few minutes. Then she said, "Jack, we've been together with all of these people crammed together in one small room for almost a week now. Everybody in the cabin has pinched my rear end at least once except you. And now you have bought me a box of candy. Now I've figured you out. You're not any different than they are, you're just sneakier!" No good deed goes unpunished!

The wind continued to blow at about a steady 45 mph, with occasional gusts up to about 80 mph. Trying to hunt was a lost cause. My eyes were so full of tears, along with the stinging raindrops, it was just unbearable and Bob felt that the bears probably were staying pretty much in thick cover themselves. But, every time there was a let-up, our party would spread out, either walking up the creek, or along the beach. As long as you are out looking in bear country, you are likely to see a bear. But, they seldom come to the card table.

One by one, Bob was able to get the hunters into the spike camp. Since I had the most time, I would be the last to go. I got to know the area around the cabin pretty well. There were 75 Emperor geese that would fly in every morning about 10:00. Behind the cabin, in the thick alders, every morning I would see half a dozen giant white tundra rabbits, which are about the size of a very large jackrabbit. There were a few parka squirrels, which became very friendly, chickadees, and a bald eagle that hung out around the creek where I would occasionally fish for dolly varden.

Bob decided to take me out to a place called Gosh Darn Weather

Creek. Bob jokingly said, "We call it this because sometimes the weather gets bad up there." I couldn't imagine it being anything worse than what we were experiencing. But, I was all revved up to go and Clark Engle was standing in the doorway of the cabin to see us off. The wind was blowing steady, but not gusting. We boarded the Supercub. I was anxious to go somewhere and set up a camp.

Bob started to take off, when suddenly in front of us I could see what appeared to be a wall of sand. I heard Bob utter an exclamation, and then it hit us. It is obvious the wind was moving us backwards faster than we were going forward. Bob was afraid to cut the engine for fear the wind would blow us away. Bob yelled to me to jump out of the plane and grab the wing struts. The plane was only about five feet off of the ground so I didn't have far to fall. I am probably one of the few people that have ever stepped out of an airborne airplane.

Clark Engle rushed out of the cabin and grabbed a wingtip while I had the strut. The driving sand was almost unbearable and Bob Curtis yelled out that when the wind let up he was going to stop the engine, but in the meanwhile we were slowly moving backwards. Then, as fast as it began, there was virtually no wind at all. The engine stopped and the plane dropped to the ground.

Bob laughed and said, "Wasn't that something!"

I said, "Yeah, it sure was!"

There was virtually no wind so we decided to try it again. This time we got off the ground and were about to make a turn around the corner to Beaver Creek when another gigantic rolling wind struck the plane, turning it completely on its side. Bob Curtis, being the pilot he was, managed to right the plane. We made a quick circle and landed. That was enough flying for that day. My education had begun!

The next day was relatively calm. Bob decided to show me the area before setting up the camp.

The country was much rougher than I expected and the mountains lofty. The higher mountain elevations were completely covered with snow and I was amazed to see the number of bear tracks coming off these high rugged cliffs, obviously hibernation sites. Some tracks were on slopes so steep that the descending bear was sliding or actually rolling off of the mountain.

I noticed most of the bears seemed to hibernate near a large mountain on the north slope. There was not a tree of any kind in the area. We did fly over a few small bears and quite a few caribou. Most of the cows still had their horns. We also saw a few wolverines.

Bob decided that we would first hunt at Pavalof Bay, not far from Pavalof Volcano and another identical peak known as Pavalof's Sister.

Bear hunting is mostly spotting with binoculars. The bear might be at the highest peak or at your feet.

There was a great deal of smoke erupting from Pavalof, which was obviously so warm all of the snow had melted on the surface of the giant mountain.

We landed the plane, and as we were starting to set up a tent there suddenly was a great rumbling and enormous belch of smoke and fire — the whole ground shook. Bob seemed to pay no attention and said, "That happens all the time. It does make sleeping a little difficult sometimes."

Later I would certainly agree with that. I brought along my sleeping bag and enough equipment and food to last me for two or three days, as you are never without your sleeping bag and rifle anytime you are dropped off in a remote area. It is always possible the plane might not be able to come back.

It was several hours until dark and I decided to look over the area before Clark flew in to hunt with me. I set up my spotting scope and almost immediately located a bear. I knew instantly it was a big bear. The only way you can be sure of the size of the bear is to measure his skin or measure his track. But some bears you just know are monsters! This bear appeared to be very dark. His head appeared small and his body large. He walked with a great shuffling gait and appeared to hurt with each step. Bob had advised, "Look for a bear that seems to have a low tail and towers above the vegetation." This bear fit into the category Bob described.

I was not supposed to be hunting without a guide, but at least I could take a look. I thought I would hurry through the alders up onto a little point for a closer look. This was my first experience with peninsula or Sitka alder. Most of it seemed to be about 10 to 14 feet high and growing downhill on the slopes. And, I might add, growing in every direction. It was almost as if hands were grasping me and pulling me back.

By the time I reached the top of the clearing, the bear could not be seen. I was amazed at how fast these animals could walk across the tundra. I returned to the bottom where I came upon a bear trail, it looked more like a dinosaur trail. The series of footprints indicated that bears had been using it for centuries. Each step being about 40 inches apart and about five inches depressed into the ground. It had taken a lot of big feet to do this over many centuries.

From the air, Bob had shown me a bear carcass and I decided to check it out, being careful that there was not another bear eating it. The wind was at my back and a herd of caribou was crossing the creek, and when they picked up my scent every one of them reared immediately up onto their hind legs, quickly turned and headed for parts unknown.

A caribou is curious and perhaps has poor eyesight, but when they pick up your scent, there is no doubt in their mind that danger is present.

I could see a wolverine coming towards me from the direction of Pavalof. The wolverine was very large and probably the most beautiful I had ever seen. He was loping towards the bear carcass and immediately started to chase away the magpies. I had a license and considered shooting him. He was a beautiful brown and had a bright yellow band around his flank.

The wolverine tore a large chunk out of the bear and ran into a clump of diamond leaf willow. I could also see the carcass was partly covered over, probably by a bear. I noticed the magpies returned, but remained in the trees over the bear, and I assume the big bear I had seen previously might be very close to me. I decided I had better back off and wait for Clark.

Clark arrived about dusk and I went to a creek to fish. I caught about a dozen 14-inch dolly varden and threw them up on the bank. I turned around suddenly and noticed the fish were all gone, and in their place were sitting two red fox, almost at my elbow, waiting for the next fish.

That night the wind started to blow again. We were staying in what Bob called a pop tent; a gumdrop-shaped tent with plastic staves to hold it erect. The wind seemed to be coming from two different directions, and actually crushed the tent in until the sides were almost touching, reversing the staves. I was afraid the wind was actually going to pick up the tent and blow us away. But, Clark had already tied the tent with heavy rope to several alders.

Between the wind and the rumbling of the volcano, neither of us slept much. For the next couple of days we sat in grassy depressions on the hillside to keep out of the wind and watched for bears. But bears don't like nasty weather either, and we only saw a couple of small ones far away. One was eating the bear carcass.

Bob came in to see us about the third day and said he'd decided to move us to a different area, to a place called Balboa Bay. From there we would hike across to Canoe Bay where Bob would pick us up, which was about 20 miles on foot, or 11 miles by air, through very rough country. The next morning we were ready to go. We were wearing hip boots that are ankle fitting, raincoats, of course, and enough gear to last overnight if necessary. Immediately we saw a big bear, and changed plans.

The bear was walking along the beach near a kelp bed. We took after him. Both Clark and I were tough in those days, but I'll tell you, out-walking a long-legged brown bear just isn't done. The bear left the beach and on to the tundra through thick arctic birch and dwarf willow, which was continually tripping us. I do not believe I have ever made a more exhausting stalk. We were never less than 500 yards behind the bear, and I don't think he ever knew we were behind him. While we were out hunting, Bob had flown into camp, left us a pie and fresh-baked bread and peanut butter, and suggested we hunt there another day and then head out to Canoe Bay, where he would pick us up the following evening.

(I cannot emphasize enough that the client should have a very warm sleeping bag and a good sleeping pad. Sometimes you can spend days at a time in the tent. Bring along some snacks and be sure you have enough food. Bringing along a good book to read also helps.)

The next morning we were up at daylight and I walked down to the beach and looked out towards the kelp bed. I looked at my feet and saw a gigantic bear track. I pulled out my tape measure and the back foot measured nine inches wide and 14 inches long. Clark and I decided to follow in the same general direction. A light, wet snow was falling and accumulated to about three inches. The bear wasn't moving very fast and appeared to be feeding. I was sure we were going to catch up to him.

In some thick alders, we somehow lost him. I believe the bear switched back on us. Clark was going to look over one ridge and I would look over the other. I walked to the forward slope of the hill and sat down and took out my binoculars. I had only been there a few minutes when I heard the brush rattling behind me and the wind making a funny noise. I had my parka pulled over the back of my head, and my hearing's not very good anyway. I looked left and right, then uphill slightly, and only about 25 feet away I could see the head of a giant bear — obviously standing on

My friend Clark Engle finally outfished me, but I think he snagged them. Amazing what a guy will do to win a $1.00 bet.

his hind legs. He looked at me, made a loud huffing sound, and disappeared. He stopped about 200 yards away behind an alder patch.

There was a small spot I could shoot through. And, if the wind hadn't been blowing the alder limbs around so much, I may have gotten him. Instead, I shot off an alder about three inches in diameter and snipped a little hair off the top of the bear's back — just enough to get him going fast. He headed uphill.

Clark and I decided to follow his track as long as he was going the same direction we were. Tracking a bear of this size in fresh soft snow is indeed like you are tracking some sort of prehistoric monster. Each step he made was almost four feet apart. The bear was moving fast.

We followed for miles and the wind started to blow as we neared the top of the pass. I do not believe I have ever been subjected to more punishment by the forces of nature. The wind virtually tore at our clothes. The bear track was quickly obliterated. For two hours we stumbled through blizzard-like conditions. It was bitter cold. If someone had broken a leg on this journey, I am sure they would have frozen to death.

It was late afternoon by the time we had reached the other bay. We had walked about 15 miles through some very rough country. We lost the bear track. I looked back up towards the awesome mountain.

Clark was weary too, and jokingly asked, "If you saw a bear up there, would you go back."

I said, "Hell no!"

Just then, we both saw a big bear near the top, and of course, we went back. We saw Bob's plane come and go from the area he was to pick us up. It would soon be too dark for him to fly.

Clark and I decided to continue along the beach back to the cabin. It was going to be a long walk. Walking has always been competition between Engle and I. He is much taller than I am, but in the mountains I could walk him into the ground. I told him I enjoyed seeing his pale face and tongue hanging out. But, when we hit the beach, those long legs had me at a disadvantage! It was my turn to pant! Engle was almost tireless. I think it was because he could smell chicken cooking!

It was nearly midnight and we were about 200 yards from the cabin and I could smell chicken myself. Clark tried to run, but I held on to his coat. He was not going to get to that chicken before I did. Our clothes were wet with perspiration and rain water. I don't believe I have ever been more weary in my life. Clark agreed. We had walked approximately 25 miles and we were barely able to finish the cold chicken that Sharon had dished up for us. But, I did last long enough to eat half of the apple pie, as I was afraid Clark would get it the next morning if I didn't take it now. Clark was that kind of guy. And, I would do the same for him!

We decided to hunt out of the cabin for the next couple of days to recuperate and, hopefully, the weather would improve. It had now been almost two weeks of absolutely horrible weather 90 percent of the time. To the west of the cabin a few miles away, along the beach was a rocky point that we would walk up every day and look on to the high ridges above us. I could see that in the summertime the bears had plenty to eat — cranberries, blueberries, bear berries, kelp beds and probably some spawning salmon, and I'm sure they preyed heavily on the caribou.

It was in this same general area that each day we would have an encounter with a female brown bear and two cubs. Several times she made false charges, but did not get very close, as the cubs were always on the other side of her. Twice Clark and I retreated into the ocean far enough that the seawater raised up over our hipboots and I was afraid we were going to have to shoot the bear. She would walk menacingly up and down the beach snapping and popping her teeth occasionally. We kept thinking she was going to go away, but for some reason she and her two cubs called this home.

To complicate matters, there were numerous pieces of driftwood along the beach. If we came back toward dark, it was kind of a white knuckle hike, as you were never sure which piece of driftwood was going to turn out to be the irate female bear waiting to ambush us at close range.

Each day we would see one or two large boars at the far end of the bay, but by the time we got there, they were lost in the thick alder. I could have shot a couple of smaller bears, but decided I wanted a big one or none at all. It was looking like I was going to end up with just that — nothing! I had waited too long, for tomorrow was the last day. But I had been lucky on last days.

Early the next morning we left at daylight for one final fling. It was actually a pretty nice morning; not much wind. The 75 geese were there, and so were the tundra hares, the parka squirrels, the magpies and the chickadees. And, all of the same faces that I would have to bid farewell to the next morning.

Sharon and Bob were starting to pack up the camp. I'd had a great hunt and had my chance and could live without a bear — I've done that before. But this time I really thought I was going to connect with something big. All of the other clients had filled out and left, although most of the bears were not particularly large.

Bob was going to fly to Cold Bay that day. While we headed up the beach he passed over us and wobbled an acknowledgement with his wings, then disappeared over the mountain. I asked Clark if he thought it might not be a good idea to try something different.

"What's that?" he asked.

I suggested that every day we would see bears early in the day, and they would disappear into a valley full of thick alders. Instead of going our usual route, let's go to the thick alders first and sit there and maybe we can ambush a bear.

Engle said, "You realize the wind is not going to be in our favor."

I said, "Yes, I know. But we can sit up on the hillside and see a considerable distance."

"Good idea," he said. So this was the plan. But first Clark said, "I think I'll walk to the top of that ridge to our right, and you keep your eye on the valley and we'll hand signal each other if we spot game."

I said, "Okay."

I noticed almost immediately that from the top of the hill Clark was waving his arm to me indicating I should go up hill to the same level he was. At least that's what I assumed he meant. Again, almost immediately, I saw what he was pointing at — a large dark-colored bear following a small one, which usually means a boar following a sow. They were headed uphill, and if we hurried straight ahead, we might get a shot.

I started through an area about 200 yards square of incredibly thick alder to meet Clark. I had my .338 Winchester cradled across my left arm, so I was ready. In about the middle of the brush patch I suddenly became aware of an animal in front of me, obviously running directly at me. I thought I could hear a huffing noise. At almost the same moment, I realized that a giant bear was coming directly at me no more than 25 yards away. He was coming very fast and the alders didn't seem to be interfering with him at all.

Brush was flying in all directions and I was looking into the red eyes of the bear. There was no doubt in my mind he could see me well, and I was his target!

His ears were laid back and his mouth was open. I shall never forget that eye-to-eye contact! Quicker than I can tell the story, the bear was no more than three feet in front of me. And, the rifle was only at about a "present arms" position and in no way would I have been able to get off a shot. I jumped to the right. But, for whatever reason, the bear must have changed his mind and passed within six inches along my left side.

He was absolutely enormous! Such incredible speed was more than I could imagine. My first thought was, he is going to turn and bite me, as his head and nose were tipped up towards my left shoulder. He smelled like a wet dog. Either he changed his mind, or I spun around quickly enough to avoid the clash of his teeth. But the bear did not stop. He instantly disappeared into the alders.

I must say I was relieved, but did not know whether I should be moving forward or backward, because I knew there was another bear with him if this was the same bear we had seen a few minutes ago.

About this time, high overhead, I could hear Bob Curtis returning from Cold Bay. He circled, wobbled his wings and continued on. The wind was blowing pretty hard through the brush and was quite noisy. As I broke out into a small clearing, I could see Clark about 50 yards to my right at the same time he saw me and acknowledged me with a wave. Almost immediately, between Clark and me, I could see a large brown bear walking up the ridge, while looking back over his shoulder. Obviously he knew we were there. The bear looked like a good one to me, especially for the last day. It was about 100 yards away and quartering away. I put the 4X Leupold crosshair on his ribs on his left side.

I fired one shot and could hear a solid thump. The bear whirled instantly and disappeared with a tremendous roar. In the meanwhile, Clark had moved down to where I was standing at the small clearing.

"Did you hit him good?" asked Clark.

"I think so," I said. "I aimed at his last ribs on the left side, towards his right shoulder."

We quickly decided to move slightly to the left where we could see better in the event the bear charged us. But, we both actually thought the bear was dead, and I sure hoped so, because it was now late evening with fog and darkness was soon to be upon us. Suddenly, I could see the bear walking to where he had been standing when I shot. At this point I could see all the hair on his body was standing straight up, his ears were straight back tight against his head, his mouth open unbelievably wide. He gnashed his teeth a couple of times and let out roar after roar that I'm sure could be heard a mile away, and then started down the hill in great leaps towards where he had last seen me.

The bear was out of sight in seconds, but we could hear him coming though the willows roaring and snapping his teeth. Both Clark and I had our rifles to our shoulders so we'd be able to shoot the instant he broke through on us. Had we not moved, I'm sure one of us would have been hurt, for this is where the bear broke through the brush. He had honed in on us like radar and pounced out of the alders like a cat (a big cat).

All I could see was that he looked like a jet black hulk with fiery red eyes and a mouth open wider than I thought a bear could manage. Both Clark and I fired instantaneously at near point-blank range, and the bear collapsed with his momentum rolling him out of sight. There was total silence.

Almost instantly it was dark. We could not hear the bear. I was hesitant to reach into my pack for my flashlight, for fear that at that second he would break through the brush only a few yards away. Clark and I were standing back to back. In a few minutes we decided that perhaps the bear was dead. I was sure we had hit him hard.

But what a predicament! We did not know which way to go. I dug out my flashlight and discovered it would not work. Clark got out his and it didn't work either. From that day to now, I have never carried less than two flashlights! But, at that moment, we had to do something — either the bear was dead or he wasn't. I did not want to walk through that thick alder thinking that a wounded bear, was going to grab one of us, especially me.

Clark said it was my bear and I should go first. I responded that a good guide would give up his life for a client!

We decided to move ahead to where we had last seen the bear disappear into the alders. We had only taken a few steps, then realized the bear had not disappeared into the alders, but in fact collapsed into a ball and was laying in a deep depression. He was laying on his back. I could see that much.

We both fired a shot into the mass of hair on his chest at a distance of about 10 feet. I decided that we had lots of thread in the taxidermy shop and suggested we fire again, which we did.

I could see the bear was enormous, but it was so dark I really wasn't sure which end of the bear we were looking at. Clark got out his cigarette lighter and said, "Take this down and find his head and see if he looks dead."

I said, "No Clark, it's your lighter, and I wouldn't want to lose it."

So, we both moved slowly ahead step by step, Clark with his lighter held high over my head and me with my rifle ready at his side. Suddenly we both let out a yell!

While looking for my knife sharpener, I found I did have another flashlight which lasted long enough to skin the bear. Clark loaded the huge skin of the bear in his pack and I took the rifles and other equipment.

I like big guides with great carrying capacity. Now we were ready and started down the beach, which was a terrifying event in itself, for a roar ahead of us let us know that the old sow was on the beach and knew where we were. But the wind was blowing towards her and I'm sure she could smell the big boar we had just killed. This smell may have worried her some. Every time we'd see a dark form we prepared for an attack. A sow often attacks male bears to save her cubs.

To make matters worse, it was obvious that she was moving parallel with us trying to figure out what was going on. Clark and I stayed as close to the ocean as we could get and not be washed over by a wave. As soon as we moved inland she would huff and growl and pop her teeth and charge, roaring like a lion.

This had to be one of my more stimulating experiences, perhaps even worse than the wounded bear charge because it just kept going on and

Until you have been charged by a bear, you have not been properly inspired.

on for nearly two miles until we got to the cabin. Later I was to find that when Bob had flown over me he looked down and saw the bear run past me, turn and run right up almost touching his nose against my back. The bear did this twice and I didn't even know he was there!

Bob said he would have dived down to warn me, except that he was having some engine problems and thought his plane was going to stall and needed all of the altitude he could get to make it to an open area of the beach.

All in all it was a great hunt. The bear squared out at an honest nine feet, three inches. I must say it was one of my more adventurous bear hunts.

This had been my second hunt with Clark and there would be many more. He and I became great and lasting friends, always pulling pranks on each other. I usually was the loser, and I'm the loser again, for a few years ago, just two days apart, Clark Engle in Alaska and my buddy, Jim Ford in Montana, were killed in plane crashes. I sure miss those guys.

AFRICAN QUEEN

Another letter I received came from a young woman from California. The letter went this way:

"Dear Mr. Atcheson: All my life I've wanted to visit Africa, but now I finally realize that financially, I will never be able to handle this on my own and since you deal with so many people going to Africa I thought perhaps you might know some gentleman who would like to have a lady companion with him on his next safari. I'm sure we could be very compatible. I am enclosing my photograph. I recognize that should some gentleman accept my offer that there are certain commitments I may have to fulfill and as long as it is a reasonable number of times at a reasonable hour, I am quite eager to go."

MONGOLIA

For whatever reason, mountain sheep have always attracted hunters. In prehistoric times, pictures of sheep were drawn or cut into rock by early man, usually with bigger-than-life headgear. The ram had its place within the religious belief of many peoples, possibly because of its large horns or huge testicles — which are proportionately larger than any other animal I have seen in the world. Volumes have been written about the sex life of sheep, which is indeed an awesome performance. Many wild sheep rams die every year, because of their lust for the ladies, by wandering far away from the cliffs and ridges where there is safety, down into the river bottoms where they are eaten by bears and wolves. Hunting sheep during the rut also gives the sport hunter an opportunity at seeing or taking larger-horned rams. Nevertheless, the wild mountain sheep of the world have survived and proliferated because the sport hunters of the world have financed enforcement and habitat improvements.

Hunting and taking a great ram is indeed a stimulating experience. For the most part, sheep hunting is not easy. A considerable amount of walking is often required, more or less depending on the area. The more complicated the situation, the more money involved. In some circles, how many sheep, or what variety of sheep that you have taken more or less positions you among your peers. There are many species of sheep and equally as many subspecies, or hybrids, where ranges overlap — providing a pleasant, but unending task for hunters who must have one of each.

For the most part, sheep country looks pretty much the same

throughout the world — similar grass, forbs, birds and mammals. Though sheep generally don't live in as rough a country as do mountain goats, sheep can develop the knack of hanging out in deserts or thick timber specifically to annoy hunters and, probably for other scientific explanations as well, depending on what you want to hear. Wild sheep, for the most part, can be readily tamed and will hang out around people. Desert sheep near Las Vegas are fond of the green grass in the yards of the country folk — which pleases some and disturbs others, depending on how you feel about your flowers and shrubs being devoured, or your front yard being cluttered with sheep dung and urine.

A real hunter considers this a form of perfume, and I believe I have heard of people who have rubbed sheep urine on their body trying to fool the sheep. Hunted sheep are smarter than that and, regardless of the odor, sheep consider anybody walking on two legs, be it a hunter or a gardener swinging her rake, a possible danger. One big ram I know of used to sun himself on the office porch at a sawmill near Thompson Falls, Montana, until the foreman fell over him, and both the ram and the rider went through the porch railings and roof support.

I have seen sheep in Canada and various places in Montana wandering throughout the city trying to chew tires and licking the salt off of vehicles. Tame mountain sheep don't do much for me. I like to see wild sheep in wild places.

For various reasons wild sheep hunting can be costly. But, usually, if you are willing to spend the money, you can get a sheep. Or, if you keep applying for permits, and you're lucky, you will eventually draw. Then, you can do it on your own, if you wish.

However, some sheep are not available to everyone. There are expensive airplane tickets involved, costly licenses, unbelievable red tape and complications, huge guiding fees and disappointments. Who you know is sometimes important, and a fistful of extra dollars can help out a lot.

There has always been a nucleus of people hunting North American wild sheep. There is another group of hunters who weren't satisfied with that and wanted to hunt sheep worldwide. There are many obstacles to overcome in order to get you there, and get you back home with your sheep. Logistics, language barriers, bureaucracy, and corruption, or whatever else you want to call it, are just some of these obstacles. Sometimes all of these things affected the same hunt, resulting in costs much higher than expected. But, believe it or not, things are much better now.

Twenty-five years ago, somebody in the oil or mining business always had a connection somewhere that was going to lead to fabulous new hunting areas. Sometimes this did happen, mostly to a select few, but quite often enormous amounts of money were spent and not much happened at all. People would end up on lists, make payments, never see the money again, and never get to hunt.

Being a cautious soul, a hunter, and having some feeling for our clients, I limited our involvement to areas in Mongolia, Iran and Nepal — situations that we believed were realistic. For the most part, they worked. But, let me give you an interesting example of how some hunting developed partly on truth, and fact, and partly on fraud, corruption, and confusion. I will describe my initiation into the birth of hunting in Mongolia and Russia in about 1968.

As a successful booking agent you attract a lot of people with ideas, some well meaning, some not. There was a gentleman named Paul, who visited hunting clubs, travel agents, booking agents, and probably other road agents, and presented his very authentic looking credentials, written in English, Russian and Mongolian. With a little checking, it was concluded that Paul did have some connections with Russia and Mongolia, though I wasn't sure of all the details. But, I do know the sheep hunters were only too eager to put their money down to be one of the first people there to hunt these exotic species. However, any money I collected for Marco Polo sheep hunts in Russia I held in a separate account.

And, despite Paul's pleas, I would not give it to him. The Marco Polo carrot continued to dangle for a couple of years, and the deposits continued to flow. There was always a good reason and another letter stating why the Russian hunt did not take place that year. Sometimes it was politics, sometimes it was weather, all documented of course on more or less official looking stationary. So, we all waited. Paul let it be known that those who paid additional money would be elevated on the ladder to become part of the inner circle.

The Mongolian situation went a little smoother. You must keep in mind, in those days diplomatic relations with Russia, or any of its satellite countries, were extremely difficult — with none of the officials willing to commit themselves. But, I must say, the Mongolians did make some attempts to make things happen. And, some excellent rams were taken. However, being a taxidermy professional dealing with animal parts for many years, I discovered that many of the huge sheep coming out of Mongolia had been dead a long time. There was, however, no law against switching horns. And my job was to see that they were mounted and not question the hunter, as long as he had an import-export permit. Despite peer pressure to have the biggest and most ribbons, I'm pleased to say that most hunters did not switch horns.

After seeing those huge Argali horns I had to go hunt them and, in 1970, I would be among the first Americans to hunt in Mongolia. The cost

Mongolian hunting camp. Our yurt was quite comfortable. I don't know what the horses were eating.

in the Low Altai (Gobi Desert) was $3,750 for sheep and ibex, including licenses.

I decided to go with two of my friends, Bernard Meinerz and Henry Budney. In this case, we had to pay the deposits to Paul, and the balance before we would leave. As it happened, I was in San Francisco on a business trip and dropped into his office. There were numerous desks in a travel agency where he operated, but he was the only one there when I arrived. He took me to lunch. We primarily discussed the Russian situation and his plans for hunting in China.

Paul continually pressed me to turn over the Russian deposits to him. Paul also requested that we chip in and help finance some Chinese arrangement where the government would loan 200 soldiers to protect the hunter from bandits. Paul also discussed how busy his secretaries were, and that they had the day off, which is why he was there alone. In the back of my mind, something bothered me about this. But, it did not occur to me until we returned to his office. I already had decided that I was not going to go out on a limb asking people to finance his ventures until somebody actually hunted in Russia. He explained that all deposits for my hunt had been forwarded to the Mongolians in Moscow or London, and he gave me a receipt — including a copy written in Mongolian. I was going to take a taxi to the airport when he suggested his driver take me there — which

My good friend Henry Budney readies himself for tomorrow's sheep hunt.

sounded fine to me. I sat back, alone, in the back seat of this luxurious limousine and away we went.

Suddenly it occurred to me what had troubled me about Paul's office. His desk was the only one that was not covered with dust. He had been lying about the secretaries, and this really troubled me. Then, suddenly, I was startled by the driver who said, "How she goin' Jack?" Now, "How she goin'?" is Butte, Montana, lingo and I recognized it immediately. But, I didn't recognize this driver. He was the hairiest man I have ever seen. You could barely see his eyes or his nose. His whole head looked like a fur ball — and long hair hung from his fingers. He reminded me of the abominable snowman, or a gorilla. But, I don't remember meeting either kind of critter in Butte, Montana.

He went on to say, "You don't recognize me, do you?"

I laughed, and said to him, "I can't see you."

He laughed at this and told me who he was. I remembered immediately that he had graduated from grade school with my sister, but I don't remember him being quite so hairy. He inquired as to what I was doing there, and I expounded on what the big plans were. He said nothing. I asked him what he knew about Paul and the Russian adventures.

All he said was, "I like you Jack," and proceeded to discuss childhood events. This set off an alarm in my mind immediately. Something was wrong. I was being warned.

When I arrived at the airport, I called my office and told them to halt any more payments of any type to Paul on either Russian or Mongolian hunts. Make up any kind of excuse. Then I called all clients and related my fears to them. Oddly enough, most of them felt that I was being overly cautious, and were somewhat disturbed when I told them we were refunding their deposits and they would have to deal direct on the Russian situation.

I wanted no part of it. I felt okay about the Mongolian deal, as long as we had telex communication with the Mongolians in Ulan-Bator, Mongolia. And, we in fact had customers over and back, and it seemed to be working. I believed we would be able to work with the Mongolians ourselves without Paul. But it was a battle! The Atchesons, Klineburgers, and Roman Hapaloski were the primary agents to Mongolia.

After my Mongolian hunt, Paul, the gentlemen in question, dropped out of sight. I did not hear from him ever again. However, the postal inspectors came to visit me and asked if I had heard from him lately. I told them no. After some probing, the investigator said Paul had beat the Mongolians out of $80,000, and something like $250,000 of clients' deposits for nonexistent Russian sheep hunts. Fortunately, our clients lost nothing that I can recall.

My 1970 hunt turned out great, and went as follows:

Our flight from New York to Moscow was uneventful. Henry and

Here I sat on my padded saddle. These were the toughest horses I ever saw.

I had no problems and planned to spend several days in Moscow before going on to Mongolia. Unfortunately, Bernard had someone else handle his travel arrangements and they did not issue him a visa. Fortunately, Henry spoke Russian and we were able to secure a Mongolian visa for Bernard and he was able to accompany us to Mongolia. In the meanwhile, though, he was locked in a small room at the airport until the departure date. He had no Russian visa, and they would not issue him one.

At the airport we met four of Klineburgers' clients who had just returned from Mongolia. Each had two great sheep and two ibex. One ibex, although I did not measure it, may have been the world record at that time. The hunters complained bitterly that there was too much walking, and the prepared meals were not what they requested. Only vodka was available to drink. Glancing down at their trophies, I remarked, "I hope my luck is as bad as yours!"

We hired a guide in Moscow who called himself "Ted." He was a very knowledgeable individual, but Ted did not know that Henry spoke fluent Russian, which made it quite interesting to hear what Ted was really saying when he talked to other people. Although he was a good guide, he was also a drunk. He would drink a quart of water and a quart of vodka for lunch alone. By the time he showed us the town each evening, he would amble down the halls ricocheting off the walls. Once he staggered out into the street and a taxi cab came down upon him with the rear side door open. The door hit Ted square in the middle of the back and knocked him ass over tin cups! We rushed to Ted's aid, but he did not even know he had been hit. Nor did the cab stop.

We put Ted in another cab and sent him home. The next day Ted arrived late and complained to me that he had a terrible hangover. He said it was the worst hangover he had ever had. He said, "Oh my, is the worst hangover ever. Hurt is from back of head, back and legs. Must have been cheap vodka from Ukraine." We never did tell him that he had been hit by a taxi.

Ted had his humorous side, and told many Russian jokes about the Russian system. One day he pointed to a building in front of me and said, "That is the tallest building in the world." I looked at it and said, "Ted, it only looks like it is a few stories tall to me." He said, "That's not the point. That is the office of the KGB, and from the top of that building you can see all around the world!" Then, he doubled-up in laughter and insisted we have a drink.

Ted continued to expound on the greatness of Russia and the Russian system until on our final night the Russian police arrested him for having American currency in his wallet and beat the hell out of him. The next day we got him out of jail and I asked him what he thought of the system? All he could say was, "Poohy on the system. I don't like them anymore. Can you get me into America?" Henry refused to adopt him, despite my encouragement.

After Moscow, my notes show we arrived in Ulan-Bator, Mongolia, on September 30, 1970. The terrain appeared to be much like southwestern Montana — rolling hills and mountains. There was a river nearby, which I was told was good fishing. The city was larger than I thought — approximately 200,000 people. On the outskirts there were an endless number of round tents called Yurts or Gerrys. There were thousands of horses, sheep and camels in sight, scattered outside of the city.

The stewardess on the plane told us Ulan-Bator has 300 days of sunshine each year, and the trees that we were seeing were larch and poplar. And, that most of the beautifying of the city and labor work was done by women. She seemed very proud of this, and added that there were a number of Yugoslavians and Russians who did most of the building of apartment houses in the area. And that Americans were a novelty. She was right — we were stared at continually, but had no problems.

The first day we visited the Ulan-Bator museum, where I found some of the most horribly mounted animals I had ever seen. I was amazed, though, at the size of some of the sheep horns. The largest there was 66 inches long, with a 22-inch base. The guide added that, if anybody shot a bigger ram, it could not leave Mongolia.

The next day we went to visit Gandan Tekchinling Monastery, a religious site. We were told that the Grand Lama would be there that day. Perhaps he would bless our hunt.

All of the buildings had beautifully-shaped red tile roofs. The walls were plaster painted red and gold. Most of the Lamas were old people with shaven heads, some of them were very tall and heavy. We were given a tour guide who showed us around the outside area first. It was interesting to watch the people around the prayer wheels. There was considerable sing-song type chanting, which I taped on my recorder. The smell of incense was everywhere — inside and outside of the building. Besides the prayer wheels, there were a number of people praying on individual man-size platforms on the ground. The people would lay flat with their arms pointed forward. I assume they were praying, but there were a number of little kids who were lying on their back with their feet in the air. Some had crawled under the tables. Despite the chatter from their mothers, apparently the kids weren't buying the program.

One little boy peed on the prayer wheel, while his friend looked on and giggled. Alas — there is no respect left in the land! As the mothers moved on, I noticed, smiling, that here, just like home, there was a trail of kid's clothing, a couple of shoes, and pieces of broken cookies, upon which the hundreds of pigeons circling our heads would settle down in a great swirl.

It was interesting to note how the Lamas were careful to walk around us and not step on our shadows. In all of the buildings a number of Lamas were praying and chanting. Many of them were reading tablets, approximately eight inches wide, and two feet long. They would read one side, turn it over, and pass it to the Lama next to them. I inquired about what they were reading. They said they read about everything in the world that happens. They then took us to a library that was supposed to have information on everything in the world, kept up to date. They seemed to be particularly interested in medicines. I noticed that a number of people visiting the monastery were carrying little sacks of grain as offerings, I suppose both to the Lamas and the pigeons.

I have made it a habit to bring a Polaroid camera with me to all remote areas where I would travel. To open doors, I find giving people pictures is better than money. At first no one wanted their pictures taken, then when they discovered it took instant pictures, everybody wanted one. At one point a very tall gentlemen dressed in a great flowing red robe said that the Grand Lama had heard of our camera and wanted to know if we would like to have an audience with him at 2:00 p.m. We would also have tea and kumiss.

My friend, Henry, was particularly interested in the kumiss, as he was an historian and was familiar with the ways and means of the Mongolians for the past 1,000 years. The kumiss had been voted the top drink of the century. We had to have it!

We were escorted to a large round building. It was elaborately decorated inside and out. On the inside of the circular room, along the outside perimeter, were little benches to sit on and little tables in front of each bench, upon which loaves of bread were stacked upon each other. On top of this mound was a plate full of grain or incense. There were beautiful lanterns, vases and statues to be admired as we entered. A gong sounded — we were in the presence of a great man.

At the end of the aisle, down the middle of the room sat the Grand Lama, sitting cross-legged in a red robe. On each side of him sat two people — one, I assumed, was an interpreter and the other was a bodyguard and one of the largest men I have ever seen in my life and, undoubtedly, the meanest and ugliest. I noticed that the beautiful background behind the Lama was the same one I had seen in a picture in the *National Geographic* many years before in which U.S. Supreme Court Justice William O. Douglas had sat, possibly with this same Lama. I did feel humbled.

Henry was anxious to try the kumiss. Bernard decided to just watch and lit a cigar.

We each had our picture taken with the Grand Lama and I handed him my business card. I was amazed when he handed me his — written in Mongolian, Russian and English. This struck me as funny. I smiled, but sobered quickly when he didn't smile back. I never thought of holy people passing out business cards. I wondered if Pope John had a card.

Through the interpreter, the Grand Lama asked many polite questions, and we snapped away with pictures and left small donations. The Polaroid camera, though, is what truly amazed the Grand Lama. It sort of amazed me too, as I still hadn't figured out how it worked! Through the interpreter I told him this. I'll be darned if he didn't start telling the interpreter to inform me of what he knew about it and how it worked. Humbled again. It was obvious this guy had spent a lot time in the library.

I sat down by the interpreter. He elaborated on how pleased the Grand Lama was, and now we would have kumiss and tea. At long last, kumiss! A soup bowl filled with kumiss was set before me. The interpreter grasped my hand and warned, "Some like it, and some do not." He had a solemn face and voice that sounded like Rudy Valle singing through a megaphone. He advised me to drink it down and I could have another. My friend, Henry, had his back to me, taking pictures, as I took my first sip — and my last! Never have I tasted anything so awful! Kumiss is fermented horse milk with salt and urine in it! The ammonia was so strong I started to belch.

The Grand Lama sits on the right. Near his left hand is a bowl of the deadly kumiss.

I told the interpreter that I was allergic to milk - which I truly am. I grabbed the teacup to wash it down, only to find out the tea was similar, just a bit more salty. With this, I declined the second bowl and suggested that they bring two bowls for my unsuspecting friend, Henry. As Henry sat down next to me I told my friend that the interpreter had advised me that if you want to really impress the Lama, drink one of these bowls full of milk — nonstop! Henry was eager to please, until he was on about the third swallow! He glanced sideways at me, like I had deceived him! Rightfully so — I had! I guess the Devil made me do it!

I quickly said to Henry, "Don't spit it out or you'll offend the Grand Lama." Henry knew I was right and swallowed it down. But, that was the last thing I saw Henry drink on the entire trip. I don't even remember seeing him drink water.

Back at the hotel, we met a couple more hunters who had just returned from the field. It was very discouraging. They each had two fine sheep and ibex, but these people said they expected to take something far larger. One man had purchased several sets of long dead ram horns which he was taking along with him.

At this time Henry and I were hunting what was known as the low Altai. There was also a mid Altai and a high Altai. The high Altai being very expensive and the permits very limited, although this is where the largest sheep were. We each purchased permits in the Gobi for two rams and two ibex. Bernard went to the mid Altai. Only one permit was available.

At the airport we boarded a plane called Mongol 104, which kind of looked like a Russian version of our DC-3. Oil was leaking out of the engines, but we went anyway. We flew for some time, finally landing at Dalanzadgad, where Bernard would continue on the mid Altai. But, that's another story.

The area was as flat as a saucer. Except for some public land in America, I have never seen land more over-grazed. The town itself seemed to have considerable building going on, but also was surrounded with hundreds of yurts, horses, sheep and camels. Far in a distance I could see the low Altai mountains, the top half of which were covered with snow. I believe the mountains were about 7,000 to 8,000 feet in elevation.

We were met by seven safari cars — all Russian jeeps. They were immaculately clean. One of the guides, whose name was Provoja, spoke relatively good English. He told us there were so many poachers that he jokingly suggested they form their own poachers safari club. I began to worry that maybe game was going to be scarce, or nonexistent.

I was impressed with the size of the camels that hung around the airplane. All were the double hump — Bactrian camels. One of them was being loaded with crates of chickens. It was interesting that on the flight from Ulan-Bator a lady in front of me had carried a live sheep onto the plane and pushed it under the wooden seat in front of her. It kept glancing up at me now and again as if it were asking for help. Luckily, all of our baggage was there. We reloaded onto the jeeps and away we went, seven jeeps abreast. The Mongols enjoyed a good race.

We drove six hours to the camp on very poor roads. On every corner we nearly collided with a free-roaming camel. As we started to gain some elevation I saw a small patch of snow in the road and immediately got excited. There was a sheep track in it.

Much of the country reminded me of the terrain around Las Vegas. Quite barren. Barren as it was, we saw a number of gazelles. The drivers would take off and chase them in their vehicles for a few hundred yards — screaming and yelling at the top of their lungs. Once we chased a red fox, with jeeps converging on him from all sides. Fortunately for the fox, it made it to some rough ground and dove into a hole. And I thought that it was no wonder these people had overrun much of Europe. The thrill of the chase was with them.

It was still early afternoon when I saw my first ram. I cannot begin to relate how overwhelmed I was. There were about 10 females (ewes) and one ram with horns approximately 36 inches long. Then, our jeep nearly collided with a 40-inch ibex while it was crossing the road or trail, whatever you would like to call it. A truly magnificent animal, the ibex quickly scurried up what appeared to be a sheer rock wall, jumping from nothing to nothing, and still gaining elevation. No one had time to shoot. We did see 20 smaller rams, probably two or three years old, and for a Montana boy with very little money, I sure was seeing the world and loving every moment.

We were going on a slight detour to visit a village to obtain permission from the local chieftain to hunt. We waited for him for some time and he came roaring in on a motorcycle dressed in western style clothes with very shiny patent leather boots, and an Italian fedora with a bird feather on it. He looked so out of place among the rest of the Mongolians.

There was no doubt though, that he was a politician. We took more pictures and gave him several wristwatches. We were told that it had been very dry and the land had been grazed heavily by domestic sheep and that the wild sheep, at least the trophy ones, were going to be in rough country. Because of the poaching, he felt they were going to be very wild. He was sure right about that. I don't think I have hunted any wilder sheep than these Mongolian rams. Running fast and far was their defense.

Not far from the village, we came onto three huge rams all

together, but were told we could not hunt them as it was in another chieftain's area, whom I suspect must have been a relative of Genghis Khan, because our guides were sure unwilling to even step across the trail!

We arrived at the hunting camp in late afternoon. The camp consisted of one white, round yurt and one blue tent. The yurt was well made; obviously it could withstand a lot of wind, which there was plenty of. There were three steel-frame beds, blankets, carpets on the floors, and the building was beautifully painted white, green, yellow and red. It had an iron stove in the center, with a chimney going up through a hole in the center of the roof.

They fed us almost immediately, an excellent meal of rice and domestic sheep. Now I like rice and certain domestic meat. It's a good thing I did, because that's mostly what we ate. There were a lot of Mongolians staying in one tent — half a dozen, I guess. The cook wore a white suit and a white hat and had his own horse. While we were eating, he went for a short ride. When he returned he said he had spotted a magnificent ibex. Henry and I were immediately ready to go!

Just before dark we came upon fifty ibex, including two very good males. Henry made a beautiful offhand, 150-yard shot at a running ibex and we quickly photographed him before it was dark. To celebrate, a bowl of kumiss was set at the table — but we declined the honor.

I'll do anything to get my game, but the camel sure protested.

The next day Henry went one way and I went the other. Henry completely circled the camp area and had a shot at a nice ram, but the ram was partly concealed by a rock the same color as the sheep. I walked for a great distance through some very broken country and saw plenty of ram sign, but all of it was a day or two old. I was amazed at how badly over-grazed the country was.

My first night there, I was amazed at how clear the Milky Way was, and so close, as if you could almost touch individual stars. I could, of course, see the Big Dipper and the North Star.

The third day was much the same, driving out by jeep and hunting on foot, as the horses had not arrived but would be there in the afternoon. We hunted the morning and came back to camp. Provoja said sometimes they have a real rodeo.

We had no sooner arrived when half the village came yelling and screaming, chasing about 20 horses in our direction. I could see why the Mongols were so feared centuries ago. The horses were quickly herded up and hobbled. The Mongolians use a leather thong to tie three legs together so the horses could not move far. I honestly couldn't figure out what the horses were going to eat. Perhaps they had acquired a method of sucking dust out of the gravel and maybe found it very nourishing.

Apparently we had pleased the mayor, because he brought various

My ibex. Note the arid, rocky terrain.

bottles of "stuff" for us to drink that night. As I said, Henry was drinking nothing. Between Provoja, the mayor and I, we drank them all. I, of course, said they were all good, but in all honesty the first one tasted like turpentine, the second like some form of crankcase oil, the third was some kind of a yellow liquid with little white things floating through it. Somehow I had trouble drinking this one. My lips would part, but my teeth wouldn't. I barely touched the awful contents with the corner of my tongue, but could tell it was "White Lightning." Most of the Mongolians from the villages were hammered before bedtime.

In the morning, when I awoke, everyone was gone except our guide, who seemed to be in the best of condition. He said what a wonderful party we had and how pleased the mayor was with us. He said we must do it again before we left. Henry said in a hushed tone, "Don't hurry."

The next morning we had breakfast of fried eggs and mutton and some very tasty bread. There was a man and a couple of kids who were our wranglers. It was cold and I noticed that their coats had very long sleeves and you couldn't see their hands. A couple of the boys kept wiping their noses on their jacket, a trait I also have noticed among little Eskimo kids. I have often thought of bringing along Kleenex, as well as my Polaroid camera.

I am not much of a horseman compared to some others, but I have

Henry Budney and his great ibex.

been around horses quite a bit and was very interested in the gear being used. Mostly leather more or less tied onto the horses. I wondered how Genghis Khan had nearly captured the world using equipment that likely was identical to what we saw in use here. The wrangler picked out a nice gentle horse for me and got on to show me how gentle it was.

Now, I'm always suspect of a horse that humps its back, ears back and head held high and mean. The horse immediately pitched him clear over the other saddled horses. Everyone laughed. The wrangler was astounded. His kids giggled and ran in little circles. In Mongolia, everyone is a great horseman or an archer. I believe archery and wrestling are their national sports. The wrangler jumped on again, and the horse dumped him the second time. More laughter. The third time he stayed on, with obvious pride, and aimed a glance, sharp enough to kill, at his kids.

They roped another horse and brought him over to me, a red horse, with even redder eyes. These were small horses. I don't think they weighed over 600 to 700 pounds. They were very shaggy with thick manes and, obviously, very tough. I stepped into the saddle and immediately discovered why Mongolians like to ride high in the saddle. This is because the saddle's are so wedge-shaped that if you were to slouch down and let yourself relax, you would crush your testicles. These Mongols had a quick eye and could see that I was going to need some help and brought me a pillow, which I sat on. Maybe this wedge saddle was designed to keep the rider awake?

Although much of the area could readily be hunted by jeep and on foot, I could see that because of local poaching and encroachment by domestic sheep in the areas that we would have to get into some real rough country to find any of the older rams. Although the horses helped considerably, I found that I still preferred walking. The red-eyed horse preferred that too.

My walking ability impressed the Mongols because their belief was, never walk when you can ride, and added that their ancestors had learned to sleep while riding a horse. And, I believe that is true. There was nothing those tough little ponies couldn't do.

I must also say that the guides we had were some of the best I have ever seen. They had binoculars, and they knew how to use them. I also could see these folks were genuinely enthusiastic. We were going to country that even they had not ventured into. Our guide told me we might have to stay out overnight without any camp. I told them, if there were sheep there this was fine with me, for in my backpack I always carried enough food to last me an extra day.

One of the guides carried a .22 single-shot rifle that showed considerable wear. The entire rifle was covered with some sort of black tape, either to deflect light or perhaps to hold it together. I discovered later that this man made most of his living by shooting marmots and selling the skins. I saw quite a number of marmot and fox and occasionally borrowed the awesome little .22 and shot a couple of chukar partridges, or at least what looked like chukars. Later I impressed the Mongols when we shot at targets with the .22 and I shot as well as their best shot.

That day we saw a magnificent ibex lying under a cliff. All we could see was his head. Then, after the angle of the sun changed a bit, one of the guides pointed out the tail and shoulders of the ibex. About that time, the ibex saw us and, though he was still lying down, the guide urged me to shoot immediately, which was the right thing to do. I shot; the ibex took one jump and was gone. Unfortunately, what we saw was not the ibex's tail and shoulders at all — he was facing the other direction. That is the last I saw of this magnificent animal. The big one got away again!

We were seeing a few sheep every day — most of them young rams, but there were a number of very large tracks, always seeming to be a couple of days old. This had the guides all puzzled. We decided to make a wide circle off the mountain, and walk back to the horses. We had just reached a high plateau when we saw three large rams headed in our direction. They were still too far away to shoot.

The sheep stopped and laid down. Provoja suggested we pretend we were sheepherders and walk in one direction for a ways, then another direction and then back and forth, always working closer and closer to the rams. The sheep never took their eyes off of us, but the ploy did get me close to a small ditch-like depression in the ground. As the two guides continued to walk, I dropped down on my knees and started to crawl closer to the sheep. I do think they could see me, but at any rate, I got within 200 yards. The sheep stood up and I could see two of them were heavily broomed, with very heavy bases. The other one had much longer horns, which were relatively thin.

Since I had never seen this type of sheep before, I really had difficulty estimating the length of the horn. The guides had previously assured me that all three were exceptional — over 45 inches, which are good rams for the Gobi. These sheep walked more like a deer than a mountain sheep. The Gobi sheep were runners. Their legs and neck were longer and they had short ears and a longer face than a bighorn, and were kind of a mottled grey, white, brown and black in color, and weighed about 300 pounds.

Even though I felt the sheep horns were not as big as they said, I shot. The 180 grain Nosler from my .300 Winchester passed through both shoulders, killing the sheep instantly. The other two sheep disappeared as if they had been swallowed up into the ground. The ram had a very large base — approximately 17 inches and was 38 inches long and heavily broomed. I was very pleased with my trophy, but could see I had to rely on myself to estimate the size of any other rams we encountered.

We cleaned out the ram and they said they would get it out tomorrow while we were hunting in a different area.

The next day we were watching a beautiful red fox hunting rodents on a rocky ledge. He suddenly stopped and stared, then turned and ran like the devil himself was pursuing him. Hot on his tail was a female ibex. The pursuit was short, but the fox continued running as far as I could see him. We watched the female ibex pass between two gigantic boulders. She climbed the largest and stood there surveying all below her. In moments, there were a dozen ibex standing around her, seemingly taking it all in.

I was hoping to see a good male, and then I saw him — a really great ibex! He had very heavy horns, probably 38 inches in length. He was almost impossible to reach because of so many females high enough above him they could probably see everything in all directions. I suggested I would come around from behind if the Mongols could hold the ibex's attention by walking little circles, back and forth, up and down, and waving their arms.

This plan probably would have worked, except the male ibex apparently walked out of sight and when I reached the area I planned to shoot from, the females were still there watching, but no male.

In a situation like this, sometimes the best thing to do is just sit and wait for something to happen. The females had decided they had about enough of that entertainment and turned around and started trotting in my direction. There in the middle of the rocky bench, several male ibex stood up. They had been lying in some sort of depression I could not see. Had I walked toward them and not waited, I would have just run them off the hill without even knowing they were there. Patience is important.

Again, one shot through the shoulders stopped him.

I do believe an ibex is the strongest smelling and most perverted animal I have ever encountered. They seem to delight in peeing on themselves, rolling in it, rubbing their horns in it, and licking areas where the females have urinated. But, I suspect this is where the term "smelled like a goat" came from. I suppose I shouldn't knock something until I've tried it! Now that I think about it, I had a friend in the Army who fit the same mold and I bet he could also out-drink any Mongol.

We returned to camp early that day and found that Henry had shot an excellent ram down by a water hole several miles from camp. He had also been successful in taking a second ibex with an exceptionally beautiful hide. He decided on making life-size mounts of all of his trophies, which pleased his taxidermist to no end — that being me! Henry's ram was about 44 inches and his ibex 39 inches.

So far I had not seen a sheep that was 40 inches. The Mongols confided in me that there weren't many sheep over 40 inches in the area, and that many of the sheep that people claimed were low Altai rams were actually pickups or poached animals from the mid Altai area. The Mongols further advised that there was so much poaching in the mid Altai area that most of the surviving rams there were quite young and not as large as we were presently seeing. We would have to find an area too rough to herd domestic sheep, and we did.

The next day we decided to take the horses, leaving very early to reach a high ridge where we could see in all directions, even out into the plains. Time for some real spotting scope work. I rode that day. Both Provoja and I had agreed that perhaps the bigger rams were looking for ewes and it would be a good idea to hunt closer to some of the areas where female sheep might be found. This is where a good spotting scope and binoculars saved the day.

We had been spotting for several hours, and it was very cold. It was difficult to look down into the canyon because of the dark shadows. I had my spotting scope set up and was very slowly looking over all the surrounding area. Suddenly, right in the middle of the spotting scope, were three very big rams. I instantly knew one was far larger than anything I had

Provoja and I share a great moment, and yes, I suppose it was a lucky shot.

seen. And, they were headed more or less in our direction. We decided to wait.

Now, waiting has its merits, as I told you a few minutes ago. However, sometimes if you wait too long the opportunity is lost. I suggested to Provoja that the sheep had the option of going up three ridges in front of us. So, we moved and positioned ourselves so that, regardless of which ridge the rams started up, we would be able to make a good stalk. But, somehow, the sheep didn't get the message. I could see they had split up. But, in the glare of the rising sun and the dark shadows below us, I could not tell one sheep from the other. Instead of coming up the ridge, it appeared they were all walking up the bottoms.

One of the horse wranglers was waving frantically at us about 500 yards down the ridge. I was sure he saw a big sheep. But, judging from past experiences I'd had, all sheep were big sheep to the wrangler. I did not know whether to leave the high ground, or go where we were beckoned. I must admit I was about as close to buck fever as I could get. I was pleased to see Provoja was frustrated. He decided that I should stay where I was, and he would go a bit higher. I would stay where I was more mobile. At the rate the sheep were walking, I knew that if we did not see them shortly, they were going to pass by us on one side or the other.

Then, I saw Provoja jabbing his finger off to my right, and motioning with his hand to come quickly. In those days I could run a little faster, and I did just that. I ran approximately 100 yards up a very steep ridge. I was continually watching the hillside to my left, as it seemed the obvious direction the sheep would go. But again, the sheep did what it wanted to do. Sheep make a habit of changing the plan.

There I was, right out in the open ridge, when the sheep appeared in the draw below me, about 250 yards away. At first I could see nothing except the two smaller rams, who were both looking at me. I think it was a miracle they did not run. There wasn't any doubt in my mind that I had but seconds to shoot. Both were good rams.

I hesitated a second too long and they disappeared. I cursed myself for waiting, as this was our last day. At the same time, however, Provoja and I saw a giant sheep's head with wide horns raise above the rock. All I could see was the head and about four inches of neck through the 6X Weaver scope. I was breathing very hard. I never have been able to hold a rifle still for offhand shooting, so I have developed a method of aiming to the left of my target and swinging the rifle to the right. Just before the vertical cross-hairs pass the target, I squeeze the trigger. This may not sound too scientific, but when I shot, the sheep disappeared. I waited, perhaps fifteen minutes, to be sure he was not going to appear somewhere else. We slowly walked to the big boulder. Did I miss?

When we reached the great ram, I was absolutely astounded! I would guess he weighed between 350 to 400 pounds. Measured green, he was about 49 inches on one side, and a bit under a 16-inch base, still one of the very best rams ever taken in the low Altai. Provoja said it was the biggest ram he had ever seen in the low Altai. Provoja said, "You are one hell of a good shot!" Then, he hesitated and asked, "Or, are you just lucky?" He'll never really know.

THE THROW AWAY RIFLE

Recently, a magazine writer called and asked if I had ever screwed up or missed any game I'd gone after. I have been hunting about 55 years, including parts of Asia, Africa, Alaska, Canada and Mexico, etc. I've been out with many friends and clients. Hundreds of game animals were harvested and missed. But have I ever screwed up? I would have to say "Yes — many, many times."

I have probably screwed up on more big game animals than I ever shot. For example, I had just about given up finding a big buck that I had been specifically looking for. I knew he lived on a mountain face area where there was a series of rocky ledges. I had hunted all day and was on my way out and not too cautiously walked up over the last ledge and looked down over a cliff. At the base of the cliff, amid some juniper trees lay the big buck, casually looking out across the valley. But, the wind shifted and he looked up. In one bound he was up and moving.

It was late November and cold. I was wearing a pair of thick mittens and my new .270 Winchester was slung on my shoulder. I flipped the rifle off toward my waiting hand. Unfortunately, I flipped the rifle off the cliff. My rifle seemed to hang in space and then dropped rapidly about 200 feet below and landed with a loud crack.

The buck was gone. I recovered my rifle. The barrel was buried 10 inches into the semi-frozen ground and there struck solid rock. The stock had split clear up to the butt plate. The scope mounts must not have been real quality material, for the scope lay beside the rifle. The glass was broken out of both ends. Also, the barrel was bent, but aside from that, it was just another nice hunt.

The worst part, though, was that my hunting companion witnessed the event!

Jim Carmichel's best moose — 65 inches. We hope to improve on our moose, grizzly, and caribou collections this coming September in Alaska.

The Forkhorn Moose was too close to even aim my rifle — self defense.

AN ANGRY MOOSE WITHIN ARM'S REACH

Jim Carmichel, Shooting Editor of *Outdoor Life* magazine, was throwing rocks at a huge conglomerate boulder projecting out of the river. I had just focused in on him through my 45 power Bushnell scope. I could see water splash up occasionally, if it was a miss. Jim was probably bored and looking for something to do while waiting for Alaska outfitter Clark Engle's plane to arrive. I thought back a few days on how well our hunt had progressed. Jim collected a magnificent bull with a 65-inch spread, easily record class, and prior to shooting, passed up 20 other bulls most hunters would be elated to take. Now Jim had to leave early to make another hunt he had planned in British Columbia. I would miss his campfire wit and his supply of great, aged, vintage red wine.

Robert Gerlach, a guide and Clark's spike camp tender, and I were sitting on a brushy knob high above, and about one mile from camp. I still had my moose tag to fill, but was looking for a special bull or nothing. We had seen some dandies in the last few days. In fact, just below me, not 200 yards away, lay a jet black bull that might have been 60 inches with wide palms and exceptionally long dagger-like front points. He was watching over four or five cows, keeping a wary and suspect eye on three younger bulls, gathering courage, but smart enough to hang back. They knew that sniffing around any of the lady moose in this area could be hard on your body, resulting in loss of hair and blood. This awesome bull of the woods seemed to be a resident monarch of the area — no male visitors allowed. This bull was nicknamed the Dagger Bull.

It was a beautiful day — not a cloud in the sky and warm. I leaned back to savor the moment. Most of the leaves had fallen to the ground, which looked like golden carpet with splashes of red, grey, green and brown. There was a surprising number of robins, obviously migrating. Just to be here was great! Occasionally my eyelids would flutter and my mind would wander. I knew what I was looking for; I'd seen him yesterday — and I wasn't dreaming. This bull would be named the Forkhorn Bull.

We had scrutinized more big bull moose than I have ever seen in one area. A couple I would like to have examined up close for a better antler evaluation, but they disappeared into the spruce and alder-willow brush thickets higher than a moose's head. Occasionally, you could make out the flash of a whitish antler palm tipping to one side or another. Then they were gone. There was one moose in particular — probably very old — with a deep fork on the top of his left antler, which helped identify him at a glance. Thus his christened name — the Forkhorn Bull.

The palms were wide, the antler spread over 65 inches. He seemed very enamored with a surly cow that kept running away. She probably had a headache. Another cow and a peculiar mouse-colored calf browsed nearby on what appeared to be willow buds. I made an unsuccessful stalk. They winded me, and apparently left the area. Maybe I should have waited. But, on the other hand, maybe I waited too long. Lots of "maybes" in hunting.

Early that morning, after a goodbye to Jim, we started a long trek up the valley to a higher point of land where we could look down into several boggy benches dotted with black spruce, a place where a passionate moose might feel secure. I had forgotten my "long range" camera and was disappointed at the opportunity missed at the Dagger Bull and his flock. We emptied out our packboards and planned to bring back a load of Jim's moose upon our return that evening. And that day I was to witness a rarely seen event — and me with no camera.

Robert commented about the unending flocks of Canada geese flying overhead. Geese are so verbal I wondered what they were saying. Maybe talking about how they might spend their winter in Mexico, or who is flying out of formation. Reality returned. Something was happening, and very close by. I heard the clash of antlers. The 60-inch Dagger Bull was standing and facing another large bull of comparable size, their antlers almost touching. Another clash and the newcomer turned and walked a short distance, grunting with each step and moving his head in such a way as to show off his antlers. The cows were watching. The monarch was not putting up with this and charged after the intruder. Their antlers clashed briefly, but mostly they ran in circles hooking at each other's rear end. A considerable amount of hair was flying! Most sparring I've seen with antlered animals has been somewhat of a mismatch. One very large and powerful animal, and the other smaller and just hopeful. The sparring is usually over in a minute or two, the weaker animal taking off as fast as it can go, thankful to even survive, but promising to meet again next year. This was not to be the case in this instance — the match was equal.

The fighting intensified. There was a great deal of pushing and shoving whenever their antlers met. The Dagger Bull's antlers, which had considerably longer brow points, were inflicting some bloody body damage on the challenger, especially about the ear, eye and rump. But after a brief rest, he would return for more. This went on for well over an hour. Then the newcomer suddenly broke and walked away into a boggy area and laid down. I assumed the episode was over. The Dagger Bull casually walked up and laid down about 10 feet from the bleeding moose while continually watching his cows. The three young bulls kept edging in closer and closer — obviously eager to score and run, but afraid to try. I was watching through my 45 power telescope, when the newcomer moose, about 300 yards from me, stood up just gazing into space, his flank exposed, the fight gone out of his system. The Dagger Bull then got up, seeming most casual. Suddenly he turned and hit the other bull broadside and bowled him over! I could see that the long antlers' points had been driven deep into the newcomer's stomach. There was considerable grunting and bawling as the Dagger Bull laid siege on the other, actually lifting him off the ground, rolling him over with each powerful thrust.

The awesome power and fury of the Dagger Bull was amazing. The defeated bull lay still and the Dagger Bull casually returned to the cows, his antlers completely covered with blood. The loser struggled to his feet with a vast amount of blood draining from a multitude of stomach and chest wounds. He staggered away and then collapsed in the thick willows. I did not see him move again. Neither Robert nor I had ever witnessed such a battle.

Within 15 minutes a third big bull entered the arena, grunting and turning his head from side to side, shuffling along with that peculiar gait that moose use when trying to impress another moose. Upon reaching the spot where there was considerable blood, he altered his thinking and his course. He fled at high speed. I guess he decided against joining the rump-kicking party.

We mortals decided to swing around the combat zone, through some very thick willow, and pick up a load of Jim's moose meat and get back to camp before dark. We paused to watch a pine marten carrying some

Robert Gerlach looking for the Forkhorn Bull.

sort of mouse in his mouth. And lucky we did! From somewhere just ahead, I could hear a moose grunting and thrashing a spruce tree with great enthusiasm. We made a hasty retreat only to encounter still another young bull that decided that we were about the right size to fight. He gave us an impressive display of bad temper, tearing brush and tundra, then with antlers tipping to the left and right he came directly toward us, grunting with every step. I positioned my rifle and slipped off the safety. I hoped I was not going to have to use my license on a 40-inch bull. Fortunately for all concerned, a cow moose caught his attention and, with his tongue flicking in and out of his mouth, he too melted into the alders.

We picked up about eighty pounds of meat per pack and pushed hard to reach camp. Exhausted we just sat for a while realizing with all the sweat and grime on us that we needed a bath. I watched the darkening sky. Some of the geese had changed direction and were flying north. I wondered if they had run into a storm. The wind was picking up, and it occurred to me that I had not seen any sign of bears, even at Jim's moose kill site. It was good-looking bear country, too. Robert and I had a cup of Jim Carmichel's fine red wine and a peanut butter sandwich, then sacked out. Jim graciously left us a bottle of wine. How nice of him; it made me feel bad that I had pinched his other one.

The next morning the ridges were fogged in so we walked down the river and saw a black wolf and a number of ptarmigan. I pitched a couple of rocks at them, hoping to supplement our diet, but I missed. On the river bank we had previously found a vein of coal and filled my packsack. We needed fuel at camp, as most of the wood was green or wet. Robert continued on for a load of meat and I sat at a good moose trail, but saw nothing. A light snow started to fall. Then I saw a strange sight, a floating cow moose head — there was a narrow, dense strip of fog low over the river bed and I could not see the body, but the head was very distinct. The head just drifted upriver!

That night we had moose loin roast, which was a little tough. Robert had managed to make a thick gravy to pour over the mashed potatoes. We talked for a while. I slid into my two-man tent, and by candlelight read a few pages of "The Honey Badger." I could hear wolves howling downriver. It occurred to me that we had seen, and would only see, one calf moose and no calf tracks. In some areas, most moose calves are killed shortly after they are born. Bears and wolves prey heavily on moose. Eight-five percent of Alaska's wildlife that die each year are killed by other wild predators. Man takes about 2 to 7 percent.

If I wanted a giant moose we would have to find him soon. Clark would pick me up the next evening. We boiled some eggs for breakfast and watched the camp robbers eating away at the moose meat scraps. It was remarkable how tame these little jays had become in just a few days. There was a very light, cold rain, occasionally turning to snow. I felt we should try somewhere else — an area about half a mile from where Jim had taken his moose. The big forked-horn bull may have taken his girlfriend on a little vacation.

A bitter cold wind intensified as we worked our way up the ridge. I was glad I brought a heavy hat and mittens. There was a skim of ice on all standing water. We came upon an immense flock of white ptarmigan. They exploded like snowballs, flying in all directions, giving me a momentary scare. At that moment I wish I had brought my shotgun. I figured I could make a triple on this flock, but didn't have a shotgun, and this was a moose hunt. So, we continued to climb above timberline.

From our lofty perch we could see everything below us, but not a moose anywhere. We found a depression in the hillside where we could get out of the bitter wind. It was a very long day. I had made myself a half-a-dozen very thick moose meat sandwiches and ate them all. It is strange how you can see so many huge animals in one area and then a few days later, not a sign of anything. Trophy hunting means you come home empty-handed most of the time.

We had only six hours left — maybe I should have taken something smaller. But, if you shoot a smaller trophy, you aren't going to shoot a big one if the chance arises in the final hours on your last day of the hunt.

About four o'clock I could see an excellent bull following the timber line off to our right, coming from the same general area where the Dagger Horn moose lived. Through my spotting scope I could see a lot of ravens congregated in one area — perhaps they were there to feed on the moose that lost the battle. I brought my glass back to the moose 500 yards below me. I'll be darned! It was the Dagger Horn moose all alone — I recognized his antlers and wondered if he had been run off by a bigger bull? He started to display his antlers by turning his head and working into his familiar fighting stance before disappearing into some thick spruce. I assumed there was another bull in there somewhere about to catch hell. We concentrated our interest in that particular area, and all at once out walked that mouse-colored calf. Then I saw two cows. My blood pressure went up. I believed we were going to see the giant forkhorned bull! I had taken some of my best trophies during the last minutes of the last day. Maybe my luck would return.

We could hear the clash of antlers and a great deal of brush breaking, and then saw a bull moose apparently making a rapid escape — back humped and his hind legs almost passing the front. The wind was not in our favor, but we decided to head down for a quick look. It would soon be dark.

We moved rapidly downhill, with Robert off to my left about 50 feet. He seemed to be watching something on the other side of a clump of spruce. To my right I could hear a moose grunting and a great deal of thrashing and beating of brush. I glanced at Robert and he was pointing at something to my left which I could not see (three more bulls)! More grunting from both directions — then, 30 feet away — massive antlers, and then the shoulders of a great moose parted the dense willow looking first at Robert, then at me. It was our old friend, the Dagger Bull! I could see there was still blood on his antler.

My first thought was, "My God, moose are huge!" He stood over seven feet to his shoulder and was as blocky as a draft horse. He grunted continually. A few more steps and he stopped and turned his head toward me. The hair on his neck started to rise — a sure sign of an aggressive moose, yet he appeared to be looking past me. I glanced with a concerned eye over my right shoulder to see another moose! Twenty feet away I could see one massive antler, with a piece of willow brush hanging from the brow points. It seemed I was between two angry moose — a darned poor position. I started to back up only to find a short, thick, stand of spruce blocking my retreat. After that, a lot happened in a few seconds!

The forked-horn moose to my right stepped into a small clearing, antlers still covered with torn brush, which he shook from his head as he started to display his antlers, grunting as he was angling towards me, now only 15 feet away. I don't think he saw me at first, but in four steps we were going to meet head on! For whatever reason, I took my hat and threw it at him and hollered, "***HEY, STOP!***" The hat passed over the right antler, which he hooked at, but missed. His head whipped to my level with the left antler tipped down much lower than the right. His ears flattened, and his mane hair stood straight up, his eyes bulged and he lunged at me! I pointed my .338 Winchester and fired. The 250 grain Nosler passed through the left nostril, broke his jaw and passed into his neck. He spun around, his hind legs only six feet away, with his head and body quartering away. I took two quick steps forward and I fired somewhere behind his shoulder at near point blank range. He staggered forward about 10 yards and I shot him again. With only one cartridge in my rifle, I immediately turned toward the other bull. I expected him to charge the wounded bull or me. He was still grunting — mane up and ears back — but he appeared to be watching the wounded moose.

Robert had his rifle ready to shoot the Dagger Bull if he charged me. I made a rapid retreat to a tree I thought I might be able to climb. We did not want to shoot the other moose. The Forkhorn Bull collapsed to his knees. The Dagger Bull just walked away in the direction of two cow moose he had just inherited. It's a good thing, as I couldn't get up the tree. Robert's only words were, "I thought you were going to get hurt." I thought so too!

We dressed and quartered the bull, then attempted to carry the enormous antlers between us, but decided to leave them until daylight. We thought perhaps we might run into another moose who would mistake the dead moose's antlers rubbing against the brush as another challenge, something that we really didn't need in the dark. Truly there were too many moose.

Both Jim Carmichel's moose and mine would qualify for the record book, an unusual feat on one hunt. My bull was very old with several folds in the back of his antlers. And even though a portion of one antler and palm was freshly broken off, the antler spread measured 68 inches. My best moose ever, but yes, he was kind of ugly. What else can I say? I really had no choice.

Jerry Manley following an elk trail. To reach the best elk areas, we started at 4 a.m.

The rule for walking on snowshoes in soft snow or over underbrush is, "You fall down often."

HAKER 95 ©/

THE BUTTERKNIFE BULL

I like to hunt anything that is a challenge — rabbits, sage hens, cape buffalo, or anything else for that matter. But, I believe that hunting for big bull elk has to be my preference, especially on late season hunts, providing one doesn't mind deep snow, bitter cold weather and hunting on snowshoes.

Some years ago in the vicinity of Gardiner, Montana, just north of Yellowstone Park, elk hunting was open every weekend for three days until the end of February, and that is where I spent all of my spare time.

That particular year there seemed to be an unusual number of big bulls in the vicinity, but they were wild and hanging out on the high ridges above the Yellowstone River. Wild animals are tough. Some of the bigger bull elk and mule deer never do come down to lower elevations. They seem to survive on wind-blown ridges and even where the snow is very deep, they seem to do reasonably well by pawing at grass under pine trees. Then they will eat the pine boughs.

Seeing and getting close to these wary elk is a major problem. Sometimes as early as 3:00 in the morning we would start the long trek up the mountain. Depending on the weather and snow conditions, it would take from three to five hours to get to the top. Some parts of the mountain were just too steep to walk on while using snowshoes and we would head up the mountain, one man behind the other, placing our snowshoes in front of us. Then one of us would step on the snowshoe and the fellow behind you would hand you his snowshoes — and so on up the mountain, just like making steps as you go. We seldom saw any other hunters up there and we had chances that year at 104 large, six-point bulls over a two month period.

We would hunt until dark and by the time we got off the mountain, it was about 9:00 p.m. There was little time for sleep, period. Sometimes we would camp out, but that's not much fun when it's 30 degrees below zero. On one such hunt the temperature dropped to 55 degrees below zero. And, we were helped by the fact that most of the hunters did not leave town until 8:00 in the morning.

An outfitter friend of mine was staying at our motel. His name was Buck Sanford and his three sons, Ronny, Lonnie and Rick, were there too, along with two hunting clients and great friends of mine, Dr. Doug Kennemore and Dr. Kenneth Parham from Greenville, South Carolina. We were in adjoining cabins that had separate outside entrances, which was fortunate.

In this particular case, the doctors had taken two good bulls and were going home the next day. My hunting companion, Jerry Manley, and I went to bed at about 10:00. Two of Buck's sons decided to go to Livingston and enjoy the night life. About 3:00 a.m. the alarm went off and it was time to get moving. Just then we heard an awful commotion in the Sanford's room next door. Then hysterical laughing, swearing, and one loud, clear exclamation, "Oh, my God!"

I knew there was considerable mischief taking place somewhere and told Jerry to hurry and lock the door. Something hit the wall and I could hear furniture hitting the floor. Then I heard their front door opening and slamming shut. Immediately there was pounding on our door and the Sanford boys yelling, "Open up, we've got something for you." There was more laughter and pounding, then I heard someone say, "Damn it! He got away."

I wondered what got away, but was soon to find that the Sanford boys had gone to Livingston, and on their way back their truck skidded into a herd of deer and knocked one unconscious, but not too unconscious, as they tied it up and brought it back to the motel where they slipped it into bed with Doug Kennemore — and then turned on the light. The deer got loose immediately.

Doug later told me that he had been in a dead sleep when something woke him up and a deer was lying in bed next to him. But not for long! The doe leaped over the bed and landed on a dresser. Doug blinked his eyes as the deer jumped over him, then over to Buck's bed and back to Doug's. Furniture was flying in all directions. Buck was out of bed in a flash and, being an old rodeo man, it didn't take him long to bulldog the deer and shove the doe out the door. The Sanford boys, outside on the porch, grabbed it and were going to put her in our room for a repeat performance, but luckily, the doe got away.

We got a late start that day, but as it was bitter cold, many of the elk had come down off the big mountain near Trail Creek. There were tracks everywhere. I saw a couple of truly giant bulls. One I shall never forget. The royal point was about 25 inches long and instead of being round, it was quite flat like a butterknife. There was no mistaking that elk. His antlers towered over all other bulls. But then he was gone, apparently headed for the high country with Jerry and I in hot pursuit.

We followed a maze of elk tracks for hours. Eventually we looked over a ridge into Bassett Creek. A large herd of elk, about 200 cows, and about 40 bulls, were moving up out of the bottom onto the ridge across from us. Directly below us was a fantastic spectacle. The elk's antlers were frosted and sparkled like rare gems as the early morning sun touched them — a sight I will never forget.

Most of the bulls were five pointers. Two were exceptional with six points per side, but not as big as the two we had seen earlier. It looked as though they were coming right to us.

"This is crazy," Jerry said. "Those two bulls are the biggest we're going to get. We're running out of time." Both were easily record class. We decided to wait until the last elk was out of the timber and if the giant Butterknife Bull wasn't with them, we would shoot.

The rising sun seemed to turn everything a delicate pink and even the frost-covered trees were glittering like diamonds. The elk were coming single file and were breathing hard. A stream of frost hung two feet in front of their nostrils. Just as we were going to shoot, a high wind blew up a cloud of snow. When it cleared, the two big bulls were gone into a closed area. More frustration! I said to Jerry, "I don't think the Butterknife Bull came up this far anyway. We'll hunt up here for awhile and then you head down one ridge, and I'll head down the other, and we'll meet at dark. We just might jump him somewhere between us."

I spent the day working my way down to where I had originally seen the Butterknife Bull earlier that morning. The weather had warmed considerably. The snow had softened and now started to crust over as the shadows lengthened. With my binoculars I could see Jerry on the opposite ridge. I waved at him and then put on my snowshoes to keep from breaking through with every step. Walking on snowshoes on crusted and icy snow is somewhat precarious if you happen to be crossing a sidehill. Your snowshoes then suddenly become skis and you're off for a wild ride and that's exactly what happened. Just as I noticed a herd of elk moving toward me, no more than 50 feet away! They were coming out of the heavy timber. Apparently they had been there all day. There were about 50 head of cows and five bulls.

The second elk in the emerging herd was the giant Butterknife Bull and he was looking right at me. That's when I fell and went down the slope like a bobsled out of control. The elk turned and were running downhill parallel with me. I somersaulted a couple of times, then lost sight of the big bull. I knew he was headed toward Jerry. There was no use being quiet. The elk were already spooked. I yelled to Jerry, "He's coming!"

Just then I slammed into a tree and ended upside down in four feet of snow, fighting to get the snowshoes off. The elk saw Jerry and instead of going across and up, the bull went down the mountain on an old jeep road. Then I heard a single shot. Luck was about to change for someone else.

It seems an old hunter had driven his four-wheel drive vehicle as far as possible and built a fire to sit and watch — not a bad way to hunt. Jerry, who came through the area a few minutes later, found that the hunter had killed the Butterknife Bull.

"Not only did the old man get the bull," Jerry said, "but when the bull fell, its feet were actually in the fire."

I don't know if Jerry was just trying to make me feel bad, but I did hear later that the elk measured 390 points. So much for my bad luck. The good luck belonged to the guy who did the shooting, and that's how you get the big ones.

We stayed at the same motel every weekend. The manager, an elderly lady who obviously didn't understand trophy hunters, approached us one evening and said, "I feel so sorry for you boys coming so often and not getting an elk. Now I have good news for you. Tomorrow the Fish & Game Department is offering for free confiscated cow elk carcasses, and I'm sure they would give you one." We thanked her and said we'd look into it.

The next day was the last day of the season and we were back in the same area. There weren't many elk around. It had started to snow and the wind conditions were horrid. The thought of climbing that mountain again after so many weeks was just too much. We decided to hunt lower. We were following a couple of reasonably fresh tracks and decided that so far this season we had seen 103 very large, six-point bulls. Almost immediately Jerry pointed and said, "There's 104." Jerry and I saw him at about the same time, but the elk saw us and was gone. Tracks revealed he had a partner. We couldn't decide which way he had gone because there was a maze of tracks. We had to move quickly. Alarmed bull elk usually do only one thing — go uphill, fast! Jerry circled left and I to the right. I wasn't tired anymore.

I got down on my knees and looked under the tree boughs and could see legs moving. I was ready when the bull was visible between two trees. Through my telescope I could see giant antlers. I swung my .338

Winchester and fired. The bull dropped and rolled down the mountainside into some sage brush. I heard Jerry yell, "Yeah! I got him!"

Well, I knew my elk dropped and I assumed Jerry had shot one too. When I reached the elk, Jerry arrived there at about the same time. We had both shot the same bull. Later, while skinning, we were to find both bullets had entered the elk's heart area about an inch apart. As I recall, the green antler score was 372 points. The season was over for the year and I was glad. Jerry quickly tagged the elk and suggested that I put my name in for one of the confiscated cow elk.

After hunting for 40 days, we shot the 104th bull.

WORMS

As well as hunting, I like to fish — particularly with my children, or especially my grandchildren. Even though it is a frustrating experience, untangling lines or climbing trees to retrieve fishing hooks, there are moments that you remember with delight.

I recall I had two of my grandchildren with me on one occasion. The boy was perhaps three years old and the girl, probably two. I gave the boy a coffee can to hold while I dug the worms. He helped me pick up worms and would give them to the girl, who had another coffee can.

The digging was good, and in no time at all, I figured we had enough worms to catch a few brook trout that night. "Let me see that can, to see how many worms we have," I said. My grandson passed me the can that the granddaughter was holding. I said, "There are no worms here. What did you do with them?"

The grandson explained, "Well Papa, you said that the worms were really good looking worms. So we ate them."

SILENCE IS BLISS

I was hunting with a friend who brought a companion with him from Florida. This companion guy seemed to have some high ethical feelings about hunting, which is good. But as the hunt progressed I could see that he knew very little about the habits of wildlife.

One such example: at daylight we saw a nice bull feeding at the top of a clearing. I was familiar with the area and knew that elk feeding in this part would generally bed down in thick timber about half a mile away. We picked up his track in the snow and had gone only a few yards when I saw the bull lying under the tree just in front of us, facing in the opposite direction. I pointed him out and put my fingers in my ears expecting the hunter next to me to shoot, an easy shot — about 50 feet away.

Instead of a shot, a loud blast of a police whistle pierced the air. The elk was on his feet and gone in a second. The noise scared me too! I said, "What in God's name did you blow that whistle for?" He said, "Well I didn't think it was ethical to shoot an elk lying down and I wanted him to stand up."

I told the hunter that there was a thin line between ethics and foolishness, but that I did admire his high level of sportsmanship, and asked if he blew a predator call when calling geese? Unfortunately, we never saw another elk.

DEAD SURE RAM

Sure enough, there he was — the biggest ram on the mountain, hell-bent on catching a ewe, which obviously didn't want his affections. She had bounded up on a little pinnacle too narrow for an affair while the ram appeared to be standing on his hind legs, looking for a way to consummate the relationship. That was the top of the picture viewed through my 60 power Bausch & Lomb telescope.

At the bottom of that picture, I could see a house, and a vehicle with a man still sitting on the seat, but whose body was hanging out the door, his arms touching the ground. I was waiting for the sheriff to arrive. The man was dead.

There are two types of bighorn sheep hunting areas in Montana — the unlimited permit areas, which are very difficult, high and remote terrain requiring a lot of time to hunt. Sheep are not abundant. On the other hand, Montana has special areas, by drawn permit only, where sheep with huge horns are abundant. In fact, most of the recently-taken sheep listed in the Boone & Crockett record book came from Montana. I had one of those special permits in my pocket.

Unfortunately, part of this special permit area requires permission to cross narrow strips of private land to reach the public hunting land beyond. It is sometimes frustrating when 50 yards of private property keeps you away from hunting on thousands of acres of public land.

One landowner had said, "Okay, you can cross, but for $2,500.00." I said, "That's a lot of money for a 50-yard walk." The landowner beamed, "Sheep are valuable animals," as if the bighorn ram or the mountain belonged to him, a trend in trying to hunt Montana's wildlife.

But another landowner who worked at a sawmill told me to be at his place early the following morning and he would show me how to get to the area I wanted. Actually, I knew how to get there. All I needed was an okay. I said I would be there before daylight, and I was.

The next morning I drove into the lane. His car was parked and it appeared in my headlights that he was down on his knees, perhaps fixing a fuse under the steering wheel. I walked up to him and said, "How are you doing"? I had a flashlight in my hand, and I could immediately see he wasn't doing too well. He was dead. Instead of fixing a fuse, he was actually hanging out of the door with his arms touching the ground, with a giant pool of blood around his head. My flashlight revealed the car window was down, and the inside of the car was splattered everywhere with blood. I immediately assumed that someone had shot him in the head.

I retreated and went down the road to the first house, which incidently was where a lady had adamantly told me, "No access to hunt her sheep." I knocked at her door, and before she could exert her venom, I told her there was a dead man up the road and I wanted her to call the sheriff. "Okay," she said, "but you still can't cross my land to hunt my bighorn sheep, and you might shoot my cows on the public land."

The sheriff said he would be there shortly, and asked if I could keep my eye on the house, but at a distance in case anyone was still inside — which I did. I set my spotting scope up on the hood of my vehicle, where I could watch the dead man's house, which is where this story began. Through my spotting scope I could see the dead man and the big sheep!

I decided that since the dead man had already given me an okay to go across his land, nothing had changed except that he had died. After I gave my statement and the sheriff left, I went after the ram, which by now had followed a hot ewe far up the mountain. I pushed hard. To remain concealed, I had to stay in the bottom of a shallow draw that was full of thick brush, a few aspen trees and slippery rocks. Keeping quiet was impossible, but the wind was blowing downhill, in my favor for a change.

I had stalked this same great record class ram three days previously, but at another location where the wind unfortunately shifted and he was long gone. This old boy knew the plan and wanted no part of the program, and so it had gone just as on all the other stalks I made on other rams in the area. Sure, I could have shot just any ram but I wanted the best one.

Things were a little frustrating, this being my twentieth day of hunting. I had spotted rams every day, several of them quite respectable. On the first day I hunted, before the fog moved in, I saw this same big ram sparring with three or four other rams near a disinterested band of ewes.

Starting from the first day, the hunting had been particularly difficult because of wind. No matter which way I went, the wind was at my back. The long careful stalks yielded nothing. The big rams were always gone. Whenever the wind would quit blowing, a dense fog would form. I often used the fog to obscure my approach on that first day; when the fog moved out, I would stop. When the fog would drift back in, I would move hurriedly to the next cover. I was hoping to reach a higher ridge where I would have a good view of the entire canyon. I reached my goal, but this time the fog just hung there.

I knew rams were nearby because I could hear them butting heads. This butting sounds like two big rocks banging together and is part of the sex game. In fact, I have often aroused the curiosity of rams by banging rocks together, and they would come toward me.

It had started to sleet that morning and I was cold, wet, and was crouching in a very uncomfortable position. A squirrel came racing across a pine tree limb just over my head, spotted me, dropped its pine cone, ran up a couple limbs, and started to chatter wildly. The noisy bugger dodged all the pebbles I threw at him, but I couldn't quiet him; sometimes wary game animals take notice of squirrel talk.

In the case of heavy fog or snow, sometimes the best thing to do is just sit down and wait. You can't see anything anyway, and you'll probably scare away more game by stumbling around. But, most people are poor at sitting, especially if their feet are cold.

Then it started to snow big, wet flakes. A raven landed on a broken tree snag just below me, and was eating what appeared to be some sort of mushroom. After finishing his meal, he ran through a chorus of sounds, ranging from a bell, to a dog. I assumed he, too, was informing the sheep where I was. Between the raven and the squirrel, I think they told the sheep, "There he is! There he is! Beware! Beware!" A bored hunter thinks too much. I ate my last sandwich and thought about what I was doing up there.

It didn't seem like I had much to lose, so I picked up two rocks and thought I would try my hand again at attracting the attention of the rams. Who knows what would happen? My friend, Canadian guide Henry Fercho, believes that if you build a fire, sit around and watch carefully, sheep are often attracted, especially if you are hunting heavily timbered slopes.

At the clang of the rocks, the raven flew, another squirrel started to chatter, and I could hear the sheep running across the shale. The old rock trick hadn't worked this time and, to make things worse, I hurt my thumb. Also, I discovered that my new-fangled, breathable raincoat leaked in many places.

I stopped daydreaming. All that had occurred days ago and now, today, the sun came out. Things were looking up for me! I thought I had a long way to climb when, through a hole in the brush off to my left, I could see a ewe and a lamb standing on a shale slide about 10 yards away. They didn't seem to see me and were watching their backtrail. Several more sheep appeared. I figured a ram was somewhere not far away.

They disappeared and I could hear shale rocks sliding above me. I kept moving. The right hand side of the draw had some large boulders and ledges, to which I might crawl to get a better view of the area surrounding the sheep. I had to do something quickly, as the now-clouded sun was getting low. I had no choice but to make a quick approach. No sheep were in sight and it suddenly started to rain very hard.

As usual, I was carrying my .338 Winchester with 210 grain Nosler bullets, which should be plenty of rifle, especially when the target would probably only be 50 feet away.

I was just working my way over a huge, slick, wet boulder, gripping with my right hand so I would not slide off, when I caught the sweet smell of the sheep, so strong that I knew they could only be a few yards away. For a second I saw a huge horn between two aspen trees; then it was gone.

I had just attached a Harris bipod to my rifle the previous day to see how I liked it and, upon removing my rifle from my shoulder, I started to slide backwards. A branch caught in the bipod and one of the legs sprang open with a loud clang. The sheep did not know where the strange sound came from. Now I could see the head of a ewe no more than 15 yards away and looking the opposite direction. But, as her head turned toward me, her eyes looked wild and her nose was pointed upward. She was testing the air. She looked directly at me for a long minute, flipped her ears, and started to walk rapidly uphill, leaving a trail of sheep pellets on the shale rock. Another ewe, then another and another, emerged from between two boulders. I dared not move. My presence had been noted, but they apparently did not smell me.

Thirty feet away, I could see the head and shoulders of yet another big ram — "my big one," alert and watching the ewes above him. I could not let go with my right hand or I would slide out of sight of the sheep. I'm left-handed and I wished at that moment that I had my .44 magnum pistol, or a spear, instead of the .338 with the bipod with one extended leg.

Not a bad ram, especially when shooting with one hand. I think it was 38 x 16 1/2 bases.

The ram, no longer in love but still looking uphill, turned directly toward me. I knew I had to act in seconds or my chance would be gone and darkness would fall. I decided to shoot with one hand. I slipped the safety off and raised the rifle barrel to rest over a rock in front of me. Unfortunately, the right bipod leg was sticking out and I couldn't get the rifle to the rock unless I turned it sideways. This was a most insane predicament. There was only one thing to do — shoot! And I did, just as his eyes met mine. I don't know if I aimed or just pointed the rifle at the sheep. The ram dropped instantly. The rain stopped. The sun came out for a few minutes.

I took a couple of pictures, and then it was dark and I realized I was a long way from my truck with a bighorn sheep ram whose massive horn measured 38 inches, with a 16-inch base, and measured about 178 points. It took me 30 minutes to debone the ram and four hours to reach my truck.

Later it was determined the dead man at the bottom of the mountain had died naturally of a massive hemorrhage. I thank him for his courtesy of giving me (before he suffered his fate) permission to cross his land to my public land.

THE SITITUNGA AND A LEOPARD RETURNS

I had just completed a business trip to Zambia and was ready to go home, except there were no airplane seats available for two weeks. Now Africa is a great place to visit once you are outside of the big cities. Normally, that is where I spent most of my time. Unfortunately, all the hunting camps were occupied by our clients and there were no extra vehicles available, even to visit a game park. I was stuck at the bar at the Lusaka Hilton.

Then, in walked Rolf Rohwer. Rolf was one of the safari company managers who had filled out his client much earlier than expected so Rolf had nothing to do for the next two weeks either. His next client was Prince Abdorreza Pahlavi of Iran. The prince wanted a nice camp and expected to hunt in Kasonso-Busanga, an area where very few hunters had been before him. Rolf suggested we head into the bush where our time would be better spent investigating new hunting areas for the prince than drinking beer.

"I don't know how much time we will have to hunt," Rolf suggested, "but, maybe you should take out a hunting license." My license, for very little money, included, among other species, leopard and sititunga. Rolf, although an excellent guide for leopards, had never shot one himself, with the exception of leopards that clients wounded and he'd finished off. I suggested he use the leopard license and I the sititunga, and we would gear our hunting pretty much around these two species. I am more of a horn hunter; cats have never done much for me. I had taken one fine leopard and have had a strange experience of seeing leopards walking around in broad daylight — 14 at last count. That is unusual.

The sititunga is a swamp antelope about the size of a mule deer. The male carries spiral horns, wears a long brown coat of hair except for various small spots and white chevrons on his face and legs. The males can be very hostile, especially if wounded. The trackers refer to them as "The Old Man of The Water."

Like most hunting, it's generally safe enough, but sititunga hunting could be very dangerous for other reasons, as you are often hunting in areas where hippopotamus come out of the swamps and pools at night and graze inland from the water. Despite what you have heard about the ungainly hippopotamus, there have probably been far more people killed by hippopotamus than all of the rhino-elephant episodes in Africa put together. Some hippos weigh 5,000 pounds or more, and can move remarkably fast. Instead of peg-like teeth, the bottom teeth, about a foot long, clash with the upper tusk and form a very sharp chisel-type tooth. Biting people who invade their domain seems to appeal to the river horse.

Overturning and crunching canoes is another of their delights. Crocodile keep their eye on these episodes also, for crocodile enjoy eating nice soft Americans when the occasion arises. If you don't happen to like the canoe scenario, you can, of course, just wade around from your knees to your armpits, anticipating the thrill one gets when stepping into an unseen channel and disappearing completely for a few seconds.

On the other hand, the sititunga is well adapted to marshy living. Their toes, or hooves, are very long — six or eight inches. They have a peculiar gait, such that when walking their feet seem to reach ahead of them and push down the reeds and prevent their sinking into the swamp mud, which I was usually standing in up to my knees. If a tree is available, you can build a stand, but most likely there is no tree, at least not near the sititunga. In those days, few people knew much about their habits, mostly because few clients cared to spend that much time fiddling around when so many other species were available on dry ground. At that time we did not have the classy boats with an elevated shooting platform.

After a rough 18-hour drive, Rolf decided to make some lavish improvements on the camp, which required a rather large staff of laborers, thatching huts and smoothing down a field which would be used as an airstrip for the prince's plane. I was only too happy to shoot camp meat which included a pig, small antelope, a buffalo, a roan and a sable antelope. I shot a 45-inch bull out of a herd of 40 black bulls, and we saw what appeared to be a 50-inch plus bull. Two years later Jack Jonas of Denver shot a 50 1/2-inch bull in exactly the same clearing. Years later, one of our clients, Fernando Tover of Caracas, Venezuela, did kill the world record sable.

One day I shot an exceptional reedbuck, which in body greatly resemble whitetail deer, including a large white tail. Besides sporting a very impressive set of horns, reedbuck in general are the most tasty of all antelope in Africa to eat. Rolf was impressed, but also lamented that he knew of this reedbuck and was saving it for the prince. But, I guess that's the breaks of the game. For now the princely trophy hangs on my wall.

Also abundant was the tiny antelope called the Blue Duiker — about the size of a very large jackrabbit. The Blue Duiker, a food source for various predators, seldom comes out of the heavy brush. Bushbuck were everywhere and about as evasive as a heavily hunted whitetail. Bushbuck and Duiker were so abundant we felt that baiting a leopard would be impossible, and after placing a few bait, our suspicions were confirmed.

One morning I shot an excellent bushbuck, which we followed a short distance in the brush and discovered a small water hole, and many tracks of the Blue Duiker. We decided to build a blind out of grass and collect a Duiker. So there we sat at four o'clock that afternoon — I with a .22 rimfire, my Duiker rifle, and Rolf with a 7mm magnum. We were facing in two directions. I was looking across a small clearing. The grass was relatively high, though I could still see little open spaces. There was not a sound, not even a dove, which is unusual in Africa. Slightly above the

The sititunga hunted on foot is truly a tough hunt.

grass I could see the tip of a tail, which at first I assumed was a baboon. Then I realized that it was a leopard, very close; then it disappeared.

Before I could speak to Rolf I could see the tip of the tail again — now only a few yards away. It is often hard to explain to anyone how effective the beautiful and camouflaged pattern of the leopard can be. At first it was just his great yellow eyes, then I could see the complete image of the leopard coming into focus. A now complete leopard took two steps and I found myself staring eye-to-eye with a magnificent male. He was so close I could hear him breathing. There was nothing between the leopard and me but a few blades of thatched grass. I moved my hand ever so slightly to touch Rolf. The leopard disappeared as if he had been plucked completely out of the picture. We sat hardly breathing for about 30 minutes. Another large leopard appeared, slightly smaller than the first, about twenty feet away. Rolf slowly raised his rifle and fired, but the bullet struck a branch right at the muzzle of his rifle. The cat disappeared and Rolf quickly looked for blood — there was a lot of blood.

Climbing through the brush after a wounded leopard was not high on my agenda, especially with a .22 rimfire. We went to the truck for reinforcements. Rolf put on a heavy coat, wrapped a towel around his neck and picked up his shotgun loaded with double OO buckshot. I did not have a coat, but decided to keep Rolf in front of me. I have an aversion to deep puncture wounds. We followed the blood trail only a short way — crouched and facing us, the leopard was dead — a magnificent 7 foot, 6 inch male. Our luck was improving. Rolf was elated!

The next day we hunted an area where one of the Africans said they had seen a great sititunga the previous evening. We decided to have a drive, just like hunting whitetail in a lake full of snakes and crocodiles. I would follow a tracker a short ways into the swamp and our crew would fan out and drive in our direction. I had reached about the half-way point when what I believed to be a hippopotamus crashed through the reeds with a great splashing of water. Several female sititunga dashed out in front of us. I threw up my rifle — Rolf's 7mm magnum — and was aiming in their general direction. Then came a big sititunga ram! In spite of their peculiar gait, they can move rapidly. With just a second to shoot, I fired and was sure I hit him. But, he disappeared. I didn't like this place! There was too much hippo sign and it was too late in the evening. If we did not find him at once, the crocs would. The next day was to be my last on the hunt, but last days are lucky for me.

I don't know how some African trackers do it, but they seem to have the ability to track things when there are no tracks. I cannot express my elation when we found the elusive quarry partly submerged! The tracker and I each grabbed a horn and started to pull. We dragged and floated the

Suddenly the leopard's nose was so close to mine that I could hear him breathe. Rolf admires the other great cat.

I did not know this reedbuck was reserved for the prince — now, the princely trophy hangs on my wall.

sititunga toward dry ground at record speed. I kept imagining a crocodile picking up the blood trail in the hip deep water. Once we all went in over our heads and the tracker lost the rifle, and under those circumstances, diving to retrieve a lost item was one of the least desirable things I had done in a long time! We found it fast. Light was fading and we quickly set the sititunga into place for photographs. Rolf and I each had our trophy; a leopard and a sititunga.

The story should probably end there — but it doesn't! Upon return to my home in Butte, Montana, a hunting club requested that I show some pictures and I decided this latest African adventure would be ideal. I had not even seen the slides yet myself; I put on a grand show. The crowd was delighted! While showing the sititunga slide there was a great deal of cheering and laughter, which puzzled me somewhat until we returned home and my then young sons told Mom, "Tell dad not to use that picture again." It seems that in my struggle to retrieve the sititunga I had torn the crotch out of my pants, and in the slide I exposed myself to all of Butte, Montana!! And on a big screen! For some time I was referred to as the "White Mamba," unlike the large Black Mamba which is perhaps the deadliest and most aggressive snake in Africa. One night my sweet wife even went so far as to call in on a television talk show where I was answering calls, and asked, "How long is a white mamba supposed to be?" She and my children watched the silver screen with glee as I groped for a simple answer.

Many years later, while lying in a hospital bed recovering from heart surgery, and probably under a lot of medication, I saw a very large male leopard walking down the hallway to my room. His tail was upright and the tip of the tail twitching. His head was massive and swung from left to right as he walked toward me. At the side of my bed he stopped. I could hear him breathing. His huge yellow eyes and slightly pulsating black pupils looked directly into mine — then he was gone — just like it had happened 25 years earlier.

THE PRECISION RIFLEMAN

I had a Montana moose permit and tracked a bull into some thick jackpine timber. Just ahead of me I noticed four bull elk laying amid the deadfall. I slowly backed out and later informed my outfitter friend, Ray Rathie, about the elk, which were most likely going to be feeding in the morning on a certain open slope near Fourth of July Creek, a real elk hot spot.

Ray took in four California hunters before daylight. They were to follow him up the ridge and he would place them at certain vantage points and at the same time, they were all to ease up over the ridge and look down. Someone was bound to get a shot. Watches were synchronized. Three hunters took their places, but the fourth man was missing. We had no time to look for him; it was getting daylight and every second was important, so we started forward.

Suddenly, behind and below us a shot rang out. Then another. And then, three more shots. We hurriedly looked over the edge only to see the rumps of the bulls disappearing into the black timber. Ray and the three California hunters were unhappy, but not as unhappy as they were going to be when they caught up with their pal, the fourth hunter, who they assumed was lost and was firing signal shots into the air.

That did not turn out to be the case, however. It seems that the fourth hunter wasn't sure if his rifle was sighted in for such close range as we had described the shooting that morning most likely to be. So, he set up a paper bag and, using his flashlight, fired a couple of shots to check the accuracy. He could not understand why everyone was mad at him.

I kind of wondered why they brought him. It appears he was someone's brother-in-law, and judging from what the other hunters were saying, he was somehow related to a stupid female dog.

IRAN

     In January of 1979, Bob McDowell of Cardwell, Montana, and I decided we could not live without hunting sheep in Iran. Once called Persia, Iran is a bit larger than Texas and is known for its huge oil reserves and various species of wild sheep.

     At this time Iran and the United States were big buddies. The brother of the Shah (king), Prince Abdorreza Pahlavi, was a very avid hunter and had recently taken a muskox. He requested that when I arrived in Tehran we should have lunch together and talk about hunting. Hopefully, I would have time to officially measure his muskox horns. Of course, I was delighted to do so. Who would turn down a chance to visit Golestan Palace and perhaps sit in the Peacock Throne glittering with precious stones, and lunch with a prince!

     I had met the Prince previously, and found him to be a most interesting person. In fact, some years earlier, Jack O'Connor invited me to go to New York with him to attend a social function for hunters in a high class hotel. We all had to wear tuxedos. I, of course, was much younger than most of the participants, and probably looked out of place. The master of ceremonies actually suggested that I get the rest of the band together and start playing. He thought I was a musician! In fact, I was out of place, but the event was a great boost to my business — thanks to Jack O'Connor.

     But, there Bob and I were at the Hotel Tehran. We were late in clearing customs, and when we arrived at the hotel we discovered our paid and confirmed rooms had been given to someone else. The manager suggested we go sit in the lobby until 4:00 a.m. Apparently some airline personnel were leaving then. The manager also suggested that we get on a waiting list. To get on the waiting list, we would have to pay in full for another room for two hours — between 4:00 and 6:00 a.m. Then, if we wanted to use the room that night, we would have to pay again! I explained that I had already paid for one room, and they had given the room away. The smiling clod said it didn't matter, and if I wanted on the waiting list I would have to pay again up front. I did, but I didn't smile very much.

At 7:00 a.m. we were met by representatives of Persian Shikar and on the following day we would begin our hunt. First we would hunt red sheep just outside of Tehran in the rugged Alborz mountains where Mount Damavand towers at 19,000 feet. We were told the sheep live at a much lower elevation and because of heavy snow, we might see many big red sheep rams. We would hunt in the royal preserve — the same area Jack O'Connor hunted. Yes, it does pay to know the right people! It would be a long drive. After that hunt we would return to Tehran for a night, and the next day, on to the city of Shirvan in northeast Iran, near the Russian border. We would hunt the Kopet Daghs mountains for Urial sheep and ibex.

We were told the ibex live amid horrible cliffs upon which they could climb or descend, defying gravity. And, I would find that to be almost true! On the other hand, the Urial sheep prefer more rounded hills and, unlike American sheep, prefer to run rather than climb. Since we were on a late season hunt, the sheep would be found in large herds and would be wild and difficult to approach. That was an understatement! I was pleased that we would be driving, as I would get to see more of the countryside. There were many historical sights to see. I was overwhelmed with my good fortune.

But, before this hunt started, we would visit Prince Abdorreza. The Prince had given me a letter of introduction with his address upon it. When I handed it to the hotel manager, he suddenly became very helpful, even selecting the taxi that looked clean enough to enter the palace grounds. Upon arrival at the palace we were frisked from head to toe on two different occasions before we could enter the waiting room outside the Prince's office. After we had a cup of tea, the office door opened and the Prince invited us in. In the corner sat a machine gun and on his desk an automatic pistol. This man was ready! We measured the muskox and inspected his magnificent collection of wild game and rifles. We were not asked to try out the Peacock Throne, but spent about four hours discussing various hunting adventures. Then came a cold lunch and return to the hotel in the prince's royal limousine. I recall the prince's valet said as we left the palace, "You must be on a very important mission. Most visitors are limited to 20 minutes." Of course — we were hunters!

The next morning at 3:00 a.m. we drove through horrendous traffic — even at that hour, until we finally reached the city limits of Tehran. I truly have never seen such congestion or smog. It was 9:00 a.m. before we reached the hunting area. I was excited and eager, but I insisted that we stop and sight in our rifles. Both were shooting well. I was shooting a .270 Winchester, and Bob, a custom 25.06. Both sighted two inches high at 100 yards. I was using a 150 grain Winchester factory ammo, and Bob a handloaded 117 grain Nosler. Our guides were shouting and waving their arms about, a trend that would continue. Their jawbone and arm bone obviously were connected — if one moved, so did the other.

We drove up the road just a short ways and on the left side of the road we saw three beautiful red sheep rams, the first I ever saw, watching the vehicle. They then turned and disappeared over a ledge. This was a fairy tale come true — we were hunting the King's sheep! We continued until we came to a fork in the road — another argument erupted as to which direction we were going to go. The driver won out with a sneer at his companion, and just drove up the road. It was rough and covered with about four inches of fresh snow. We parked, got ready and started walking up the trail and had not gone far when we saw five more rams. Two of them looked very large and the guide, who could speak English very well, said that they were indeed good rams. Another argument erupted and our guide suddenly turned and walked back to the vehicle. We followed. Bob laughed and said, "I think we are missing a lot by not being able to understand the language!" But I think they said: "The prince granted permission for the two Yankees to shoot a sheep, but not his big sheep!"

Again, we stopped and hiked for about a mile through a small saddle. The terrain consisted of steep, broken foothills at the base of some very high cliffs, the tops of which were hidden in snow clouds. Considerable grass, low bushes, and numerous junipers grew in abundance; the king's sheep had no competition for forage. Up to our left a small band of rams was feeding. One animal was exceptional. Jaws and arms went into motion and away went the sheep; the rams had seen this act before! Fortunately, Bob is a seasoned hunter, and quick and accurate on the trigger. Bob shot and hit the ram, but before he could shoot again, the ram was out of sight, but going downhill. I was sure the great ram was hit hard.

Sheep generally aren't hard to kill, but sometimes they fool you. Eventually, Bob got another shot and down went the ram. Both guides were very impressed with the size of the ram — the best they had seen for some time, and perhaps a generous tip was in order, our man suggested. Bob was very pleased, and I was exceptionally happy that Bob took such a fine animal — a very old ram. And yes, we gave the guide a good tip.

It was a long hike back to the vehicle, walking into a driving snowstorm. On dead sheep the rule seems to be that you walk uphill to find sheep and then uphill again to pack them out — the rule is very consistent. After loading Bob's sheep, we had only driven a short distance when several rams trotted down the hillside, crossed the road and headed back into the general direction of where we had first seen rams — one looked very good to me. We followed on foot a short distance and I could have shot the ram within 200 yards — an easy broadside shot. But, for some reason the guides did not want me to shoot. We kept following for approximately one-half mile, with the sheep heading into some pretty rough country covered with snow. Then I noticed we were almost back at exactly the same place we were in the morning, where they would not allow me to shoot. Now they were encouraging me to shoot, which I did, taking a fine ram with one shot through both shoulders. An excellent ram, but Bob's ram horn was much larger than mine. Bob attributes this fact to the good he's done for humanity, but Bob also won the toss for first shot using his coin. Both sheep weighed about 130 pounds. I gave a lesser tip, of course.

The three of us took turns dragging the ram up the mountain (See rule on dead sheep) to the road. It took another six-hour drive to get back to the city and would be a short night, for we were to leave the next day and we would find that the rest of the hunt was not going to be so easy, nor game so plentiful. Actually, I prefer tough hunting and wild game. It's a challenge, and so it would be!

Again, at 3:00 a.m., after only a few hours sleep, we were on our way to the border of Turkmenistan, with two vehicles, arriving late that night at Shirvan to find our camp to be a military radio station. There were half a dozen soldiers and one officer, and a cook. The meals were excellent — eggs and bread for breakfast. The lunches throughout the hunt consisted of chicken, mutton, oranges, apples, eggs, cheese, candy, crackers and canned fish and unleavened bread. Although this is suppose to be dry country, there was considerable vodka consumed, mixed with pomegranate juice. I decided I was there to hunt, not to drink. I just sat back and watched. Bob doesn't drink at all. We went to bed early. The next morning, and most mornings, there were hangovers. I should add, dinner was mostly rice with stewed chicken or mutton of the Iranian Fat Tail sheep. It was excellent.

There was snow on the ground with more falling. It was to be one of the heaviest snowfalls in Iranian history. Although there was only about a foot of snow, footing on the steep mountainsides became very treacherous. Drifting snow would limit our access to many of the ridges. It would be a demanding hunt.

The first day or two we saw virtually nothing, but did a lot of

Bob McDowell with an exceptional Armenian sheep and Ali, a great person.

walking. I saw tracks along a ledge, while scouting with my binoculars, and insisted we go up and take a look. The guide declined because he was very cold. They did not have hats or gloves, and were not equipped for this kind of weather — but Bob and I were. After I started up the mountain, my guide followed me at a considerable distance. He thought I was going to turn around. But, I was used to mountains and used to mountain hunting. And, judging from the tracks, I was close to a ram, and I love to track game! Besides that, it was the only ram in the area!

The sun came out and soon it was an absolutely beautiful afternoon. As I came around the corner of the narrow ledge between two stunted junipers, there was an old ram laying in front of me about 30 feet away. He was immediately on his feet and running. But, I was ready. Although I seldom shoot at running game, I felt that at this distance I could make a good shot — and I did. The ram slid off the ledge down into one awesome ravine and out of sight below me. In the meantime, the guide hurriedly caught up and passed below me where he found the ram lying dead. Going down on slick snow-covered grass was quite a thrill. I sat down and used my rifle stock as a brake; my rifles have a used look. This Urial sheep was indeed a great ram. It weighed about 120 pounds and had a very long white mane. The horn base was triangular like Alaskan Dall. The guide was very impressed and kept telling me how lucky I was. I finally asked him why I was so lucky. He said because they didn't think I would see any sheep at all here because the sheep had moved, but we only had permission to hunt this particular valley. The military made the decision and the officer in charge obviously did not like Americans.

The next day Bob and I, and the whole crew of five or six trackers and packers were out again. Both Bob and I felt it was ridiculous to have such a crew behind us, as someone was always in sight and might scare game away, even though we had not seen any tracks at all. There was a good looking area just below us and I said I would go up to the left and do some spotting. Bob said he would walk down the bottom where there were numerous little benches covered with boulders and juniper — and a little spring, a great spot for a soft old ram. The guides did not want to do this, as they felt there would be nothing there. But Bob is a good sheep hunter, and sheep country in one part of the world looks like sheep country in another. Sure enough, there was a lone ram. Bob shot twice in rapid succession, and the guides shouted for joy. Again, the jaw and arms waved, but this time there was dancing — the leg bone was obviously connected to the arm bone. Another good tip, of course, was given. The dead sheep rule applied again, really uphill this time!

It is interesting to note that the ibex we were hunting did resemble, in some ways, domestic goats, and they smelled just as bad. And, understand that our domestic goat did indeed originate from the Iranian ibex, but that is where any resemblance ends. The ibex is a great trophy animal.

Now, we would look for ibex on the other side of the ridge. This proved to be some of the most rugged hunting terrain I had ever seen. It's a good thing we had our rams, because we never saw any more sign of sheep, just ibex. They were about as wild as any animal I have ever seen. We saw several, but they always seemed to see us first. I had heard about ibex, but I have never seen any animal that seemed to defy the laws of gravity — running straight up a cliff or running straight down. And, instead of running to the cliffs or up on a mountain when they would see you, most of them would run off the mountain out into a desert onto little pinnacles of rock where they would stand and look back — very unsporting of them. They were almost impossible to reach. If you went after them, they would go to the next pinnacle a couple of miles away. There was no way to get near them. On about the fourth day, we looked over a high cliff and there were four ibex laying on a sandy bench at the bottom — about 350-400 yards away. A long shot! I don't particularly like heights and shooting straight down, hanging over a cliff, was almost more than I could handle. But, if it's in the name of a good hunt, I guess I'll do it. I shot and the ibex jumped up and only went a short ways, obviously hit hard. I shot again and I had my ibex, but not before he reached a narrow shelf over the 1,000 foot drop off. I can never stress enough the importance of shooting cliff dwellers through both shoulders — stop them on the spot! Bob's ibex moved before he could shoot.

My ibex was bigger in horn and body than I expected. I thought we would cut the animal in pieces, but instead, one of the guides loaded the entire animal on his back and started up the mountain. I would guess the ibex weighed about 150 pounds. I could not believe they would carry out the entire animal up such a dangerous cliff, when we could have easily deboned it and only had a third of the weight. I was impressed. But, good impressions usually mean a better tip. These guides were sharp businessmen and great people, despite their fierce appearance, so I reached for my wallet (that's the American way).

The next day we started out again looking for Bob's ibex. The weather had turned cold and the wind was blowing. We made a very long climb to the top of a ridge not far from where I shot mine. On a ledge below us, Bob spotted an immense ibex. I do not believe I have ever seen a better one, and we have handled a lot of ibex in our taxidermy shop throughout the years. But this was the biggest! The horns were wide apart and deeply curled at the end. The animal was beautifully colored — dark and light browns, black legs and light colored shoulders. Bob leaned over a rock and fired twice, missing the ibex. Bob was very frustrated, as it was to be the last animal we would see in the ibex area. The guide clasped his hand over his head and chanted what I supposed was some sort of curse. No tip on this one!

Back at the truck the guide was discussing something with one of the meat packers who seemed very frustrated, waving his hands, and looking toward Bob. It seems that earlier that morning he had picked up Bob's rifle and had dropped it on a rock and had not told anyone until just then. We immediately set up a target and found Bob's rifle was shooting about two feet high and to the left. If we had only known, Bob would certainly have a world class ibex.

On our way back to Tehran, enroute to the Armenian sheep area, we found the trip most pleasant. There were a lot of pomegranate and pistachio trees and Lombardi poplar trees surrounding old villages and walled gardens. Our guide told us that most of the roads that we had been following were actually the same routes that had been used for thousands of years by the inhabitants of this area. Many of the old stone or mud buildings that we were looking at were the old camel caravan stations. One building was pointed out to us that was supposed to be over 2,000 years old and was still being used by the nomadic people in the area, mostly to smuggle in booze and cigarettes. Like it was 1,000 years ago, bootleggers moved merchandise on the back of a camel to avoid the police.

Water is precious in Iran and the wells were covered with a large beehive-shaped, mud and brick cone which is somehow supposed to keep the water cool. There was a great deal of tunneling in the area to build underground ducts. By continually digging a tunnel, sloping downhill, you could actually make the water run up closer to the mountains where it was pumped out by hand into irrigation canals. Digging was, of course, very hazardous, but there seemed to be people who specialized in that particular work. Their lives were short, but the pay was good!

We stayed one night in Tehran, then moved on to the Armenian sheep country. Fortunately, the snow was melting, but there were plenty of bad drifts. It was obvious this was indeed a catastrophe in an area not used to snow. It was possible that we would not be able to hunt! This time we drove southwest toward the ancient city of Qom and on to Arak and based at another military radio station, but I can't recall the name. Snow would be a major problem.

Wildlife in this area seemed considerably more abundant, although just as wild. In some cases, there was a bit more vegetation and some small shrub-like trees. But, at this time of the year, many of the mountain sheep were moving around in herds. One herd I would estimate to be approximately 400 animals. Approaching a herd of this size is nearly

I have never hunted wilder game and was lucky to take the great ibex.

impossible; there are 800 eyes watching from all directions. At the slightest noise, the leaders of the herd would stampede and run. The animals in the middle would see the ones in the front running and immediately follow. Then, when they stopped and looked back, the tail-end of the herd was running. This would alarm the animals in the front, as they thought the ones in the back were being pursued. And, again, the front of the herd would start to run. I always called this the "rubberband effect." When you see a large herd of animals it can be great, or a serious problem, for it also means there must be vast areas with no game.

Our new guide spoke perfect English and was very helpful. But, the local game guard seemed to be very much at odds with the whole situation, as you shall see. In this camp, we ate very well. Large breakfasts of eggs, sausages, potatoes, box lunches — more than enough for two. For dinner we usually had chicken prepared in various ways. I discovered I really enjoyed the mutton from Iran. This was usually prepared with rice and large pieces of mutton served with various types of gravies, canned fruit, jelly and bread. Again, the accommodations were military housing units, somewhat of a small outpost with four or five soldiers, a radio and a few vehicles. They never interfered with our hunting, and at one time told us where we could go to see a herd of wild asses that had been reintroduced into the area and apparently they were doing very well. They were being preyed on by leopards, which I did not expect to see. My luck was holding, and on two or three occasions I could hear leopards roaring, evidently calling for a mate, as this was that time of year. I was advised that permits were available to shoot two leopards in this area — males only. I wish now I would have done it, but at the time $2,000 seemed like far too much money.

For some reason I have a strange knack for running into leopards in broad daylight. On this particular hunt, I believe I saw three. All were large males, which looked similar to any other spotted leopard, except they were more grey in color and the hair was much longer. We were also fortunate enough to see a pair of cheetahs recently introduced to the area. Unfortunately, we saw the cheetahs in the same area as some very nice rams, and the game guards would not let us hunt there. This also cut off Bob's chance at ibex, which was his primary game.

I understand that the game department decided to return lions to northern Iran and about a dozen were placed in habitat used by lion years ago, but created so much havoc among the people and livestock that they all had to be hunted down and killed. I hoped the leopards and cheetah fared better.

The same game guards that were reluctant to let us shoot in one area, now virtually forced Bob to take a shot at a ram that was obviously too far away. I got the impression they were saying, "If you don't shoot at this one, we aren't going to look elsewhere." It was a good ram, and Bob

A fine Urial ram but the game guard would not allow me to shoot a larger one. Note the long white mane.

shot. And, at that distance, he missed. The game guard told him he hit it. I said, "I don't think so." I had been watching very closely with my binoculars. But, as my usual custom, I wanted to go look for blood. But, the game guard insisted he do it alone. He came back and confirmed that there was blood and was going to charge Bob $400 for a wounded sheep. Since there was plenty of snow, I said, "You are going to have to show me the blood first." He balked at going back, but with the encouragement of the guide, we did and found absolutely no blood, and later saw the sheep far out on a flat feeding comfortably, with no sign of injury. I suspect they just wanted to pocket the $400. Our guide was greatly disturbed by these antics, but said he could do nothing.

We did a lot of walking, trying to find individuals or small herds of sheep that we could stalk. These animals were unbelievably wild. Obviously they had been hunted from the beginning of time. As so often happens, while hiking up a long ridge, we unexpectedly came across a small herd of rams. The game guard pointed out the one he wished to be shot, even though it was not the best ram. I fired one time, and I had my Armenian ram shot through both shoulders. No more cliff hanging for me. I had filled my tags, unless I wanted to try for a leopard. I was really tempted, and wish now that I had.

We saw quite a few wolf tracks in the area, and the game guard said that they had been having a lot of problems with wolves. As we were driving out that night, there was a wolf pack standing in the road in front of us. The game guard took my rifle and fired twice, killing two of the wolves. They looked like an average grey wolf, except they weren't particularly large — probably around 75 pounds each. We saw very few Armenian sheep lambs in this area. The game guard claimed wolves had been introduced to the area to thin the herd, but had gone far beyond what was expected.

One afternoon we stopped at a sheepherder's corral, which was quite interesting. The area was enclosed by a six foot brick and mud wall. There were several burros eating barley out of a trough and I was surprised to learn that all of the sheep were being kept in a cave that had been dug out under the ground so that the sheep could survive in the winter and be protected from predators. We were given a tour, and with our flashlights ready, we opened the door and went inside. It reeked strongly of sheep. I was absolutely astounded at the size of this dugout. Bob McDowell is a rancher, and estimated there were at least 4,000 sheep bedded down. There were various vent holes up through the roof of the cave. It was obvious these people had put out a lot of effort for their herd. Outside there were 300 to 400 more sheep being fed on barley supplied by the government to prevent the sheep from dying because of the phenomenal snowfall. The sheepherder himself was living entirely on bread. He lived in a tiny cubical underground, about eight feet square. There was a heavy wooden door, and a huge heavy barred iron gate with a lock and chain on it to protect him from something. Most awesome were the sheep guard dogs — huge animals with their ears cut completely so as not to provide a tender spot for wolves or leopards to latch onto.

We saw a number of very good ibex, but were disappointed that licenses could not be obtained to hunt them in this area. Our hunt was nearing an end. It was frustrating working with these game guards. They seemed to feel we didn't know how to hunt, but they themselves continually kept walking on top of the ridges and scaring away the game as if on purpose — maybe they were. On one occasion Bob had an opportunity at four excellent rams that we noticed just as we were leaving the hunting vehicle. Even though they were in the same area that we had been hunting before, they declared that area closed and would not let Bob leave the vehicle. They continually wanted to carry his rifle, almost as if they wanted to be sure he didn't shoot. I could see our guide was disturbed, but Bob kept his cool.

The last day the guide and game guards seemed to come to an agreement; or "bribery" in layman's terms, and we did some real hunting. Bob made some good stalks, but the wind shifted and the animals took off like they had touched a lightning rod. As we were dropping down into one valley, Bob was walking up the trail just in front of me, when off to the left a ram appeared. He obviously did not see us, but was only 50 yards away on the same trail we were using. Bob leaned down over a mound of rock to shoot and one of the game guards walked in front of his rifle. I don't know if this was by design or accident, but I grabbed him by the arm and pulled him out of the way, and Bob immediately shot and took a fine ram. He was large bodied with a beautiful mane. The horns, for some reason, were good sized, but shaped somewhat different than most of the species. All agreed they had never seen a sheep in that area with such horns. Bob was very pleased, and said, "This is a great hunt, but I wish I knew what they were talking about!" I think it's better that we didn't know!

Iran at this time was a powder keg ready to blow. The same American Embassy that we visited in Tehran was soon to become the most famous building in the world when the Iranians took 63 American hostages in November, 1979, and demanded that the Shah Mohammed Reza Pahlavi be returned to Tehran for a trial. The Shah's brother, Abdorreza, and many other Iranians with whom I was familiar fled the country. Bob and I were among the last Americans to hunt in Iran, and probably will be the last for many years to come. Go hunting while you are physically able. Many people wait until they retire, then it's too late for all kinds of reasons.

ATCHESON CREEK STONE SHEEP

While fishing the Big Hole River in Montana, I met a famous sportsman named Jim Bond. Jim did a lot of hunting and made 16mm movies, then traveled around the country renting school auditoriums and packing them to the brim with his excellent wildlife photography. He had books which he would sell at the door. I asked him for details on sheep and he said Stone sheep (*Ovis Stoni*) had been named after a Montana hunter, Andrew J. Stone, who collected a couple of rams around 1897, which is about when they were first classified. He also mentioned one of the first outfitters in the area was a man named George Ball, who specialized in 40-day trips out of Telegraph Creek, British Columbia.

In those days, a sheep hunt cost about $45 a day, multiplied by 40 days, and that was more money than I could spend and more time than I could take. Then, one day, one of our clients brought in a Stone sheep that he had taken in the Cassiar Mountains, somewhere near the Stikine River. The outfitter was Bobby Ball, son of outfitter George Ball, now deceased. I attended a guide convention in Canada, and there I met Bobby, and we talked about sheep hunting.

Ever since I'd heard of Andrew J. Stone, I felt that if I was ever going to get a Stone sheep that the Stikine River was the area I would like to hunt. Bobby told me that his father had been operating in the area before 1919, and there were two other people with pack strings, Jack Highland and

Frank Callbreath.

In those days there were no outfitters or guide areas. Anyone that had extra horses could be commandeered into taking out hunters if the money was right. Probably the first booking agent in British Columbia was Brian Williams, who worked with the Game Department and was the man who generally lined up these non-resident hunts.

Bobby showed me a watch he carried that was given to his father by a Captain Bailey from Ireland, inscribed with facts about a moose he'd shot in 1919.

In 1930, George Ball bought a ranch in Glenora, just outside of Telegraph Creek. The clients would go by steamer into Wrangell, Alaska, where they would come up the turbulent Stikine River, a two and one-half to three-day boat trip up, and a fast nine hour trip down on the return trip. Depending on the species the client was after, it would take approximately a week on horseback through bog holes, downed timber and sidehills where there were virtually no trails, to reach the better hunting country. These were all 40-day hunts. Approximately 30 horses were used per hunt, and George Ball would sometimes have as many as three parties out at the same time.

In 1932, George took out two separate parties. One, with three brothers from Belgium who could not speak any English, and being guided by the Indians, took a 44 1/2 inch ram which, at the time, would be the world record ram — however the records were tallied in those days.

But, on the same day, George's other party had slightly better luck. In August of 1932, a Major Workman from Belfast, Ireland, shot a 45-inch ram, which was the world record. Later, in 1936, Mr. L. S. Chadwick, a rich man hunting with a .404 Jeffrey magnum, took the famous Chadwick ram, with one horn measuring 51 5/8 inches.

Bobby and I hit it off very well, and I believe in about 1958, made plans to hunt together. In the meanwhile I had sent him quite a few clients, all returning very satisfied.

Generally our clients were flown up to a mountain lake, which would save two or three weeks of rugged horseback riding. It would cut down the time involved to about 21 days. In those 21 days, most of the hunters would take good trophies. Bobby suggested that I come up and he and I would go and explore some new country. The idea was that we would take four or five horses, a tarp, enough food for 14 days, and hunt for a big ram and a goat.

Our floatplane landed at Telegraph Creek, then on to Glacier Lake where we would spend the night. While Bobby and several Indian guides were separating equipment, shoeing horses and completing all the other endless tasks that go with using horses for hunting, I went down to the lake and caught several trout, which we ate that evening. Eva Brown was the cook and probably the best tent camp cook I've ever met.

Crisp, light white rolls, a chocolate cake and a blueberry pie, all done in a dutch oven over a bed of coals. That night there was a wonderful display of Northern Lights. I was sure this was a sign of good luck and we would find a great ram! I felt lucky just to be here. I had damned little money in those days, but a great wife.

The next morning there was a several hour delay trying to round up some of the horses that had wandered off during the night. I think all that preparation of horse packing gear disturbed them considerably. They knew they were going to have to go to work. Actually I have always been amazed that such a beautiful animal as the horse would have anything to do with a man anyway. A horse is generally worked hard all his life, and then when he is old he is sold to a cannery and someone eats him, if not a man, then a wolf. Maybe that's why horses bite and kick so many people.

It was about noon before the pack string moved out. We would travel only a few miles when the other hunters, their two guides, horse wrangler and Eva, our great cook, would go their way and Bobby and I would go ours. The quality of the meals declined after that. My objective was to take a ram with heavy horns, and a mountain goat with 10 inch or better horns. I also had a moose tag and grizzly tag just in case something worthwhile crossed our path.

It started to rain, and continued to rain all night. There was considerable fog; we could see no more than 50 feet in any direction. So, we set up camp early, as we were passing through some excellent goat country. After setting up the lean-to, I took my small collapsible saw and cut up wood for our campfire. I am one of those people who does not sleep particularly well, and doesn't like to go to bed early. Just sitting and watching the campfire can help while away a long evening. Bobby and I were quite warm and snug from the heat that reflected back into our little nest under canvas. A campfire is great therapy.

I found Bobby to be one of the most interesting people that I have ever met in the North Country. We talked of many things and stared into the burning coals, which seemed to create an atmosphere for storytelling. I noticed at Glacier Lake that Bobby carried on all conservation with the Indian in their own language, Taltan. Bobby told me of their old beliefs and legends. Few white men have such insight, and I am a good listener.

Slightly before daylight I was awakened by a rustling sound very close to my head. I turned on my flashlight and was startled to see a great furry ball about a foot away. I thought it was the head of grizzly bear, but it was just a porcupine. I was instantly wide awake! Bobby and I later laughed about the incident; it was time to get up anyway.

While Bobby was tending to the horses I built up a nice bed of coals to cook breakfast, and glassed the area thoroughly with my 10 power Zeiss binoculars. I saw a couple of nanny goats and kids, but that was all and it was so quiet. One of the amazing things about the North Country is the vast amount of territory one covers compared to the small numbers of wildlife that one normally sees. Certainly, there are little hot spots, but overall it takes a lot of acres of land to support one animal in the northern part of this hemisphere. Besides limited winter range, predation by grizzlies and wolves was intense. About 85 percent of the wildlife that die each year are killed by these predators.

For breakfast we had fried eggs, bacon, sliced potatoes, bread, jam and, of course, peanut butter and a big pot of coffee. We were joined for breakfast by four Canadian jays. I have always been amazed how these birds appear out of nowhere and are always so tame. We broke camp and moved out along the ridge, but saw no game except a few marmots and parka squirrels, which announced our presence without whistles. There was still considerable fog and mist, which covered the tops of the mountains at exactly the same elevation all around us, giving the appearance that everything slightly above us was perfectly level.

We came to the area where Bobby wanted to camp. There was plenty of good horse feed, and we could stay for a day or two. There was a small stream running down from the steep slope to my right. Bobby said that hidden in the clouds was an awesome glacier. Since I couldn't do any spotting in the mountains, I looked down into the valleys and saw a black bear and a cow moose. Not far away, a raven flew over us and dived down at the moose. Bobby said the raven was "dropping his pack sack." The Indians firmly believe this dive means "I want my share — there is meat to be shot below!"

That night we had fresh goat ribs that we had brought from Glacier Lake. The goat was a nice billy that had been shot by an Austrian hunter a week previous. We leaned the ribs toward the hot coals and broke out a bottle of 10-year-old scotch and mixed it with water and ice chipped off a 10,000-year-old glacier.

The next morning we were up at daylight and were thrilled, seeing all of the fog was gone and in front of us a panoramic view of gigantic glaciers, deep valleys that had been carved out tens of thousands of years ago by other glaciers. In front of us was a long straight valley. In the shadows it appeared to be all purple and, along the valley floor, the stream shone like a silver thread. Higher in the mountains where the sun was shining, the fall colors of the willows blended with other shades of deep red, maroon, and various shades of green. The air was so clear that everything looked like it was only a few hundred yards away. The sawtooth mountains were indeed rugged, and actually looked more like goat country than sheep habitat.

I have noticed that Stone sheep and mountain goats seem to cohabit the same rugged areas, whereas mountain goats and Dall sheep are seldom seen in the same area. Through my spotting scope I could see dozens of ideal little pockets high up in the side of a mountain surrounded by cliffs on three sides — areas with lush feed where big old fat rams could lay around in the sun, yet easily escape if wolves happened upon them.

The abundance of predators in this country is what was keeping the wildlife at low levels. When there is a die-off of wolves, there is almost an immediate increase of all other species of wildlife. Although I do not remember seeing any wolves, I do remember hearing them howl occasionally, and saw considerable wolf droppings, all filled with goat and sheep hair. Occasionally there would be an indication that a squirrel, bird or rabbit had passed through the wolf. Once we found what looked to be grizzly bear hair. Must have been a tough wolf!

We did considerable glassing and walking that day, but now it was late afternoon and we decided to set up camp and do more spotting in the morning. There was a big build-up of ominous, dark clouds moving in our direction. It looked like rain for sure. Bobby hobbled the horses and turned them loose. After a good roll around in the brush and mud, the horses shook themselves and started filling their bellies, a six to eight hour process, plus they needed time to sleep. Using horses is not like using a Suburban and an ignition switch. It takes as long to pack a horse today as it did with the Pharaoh's horses 4,000 years ago. The horse has not been modified at all; only people change.

Using horses is a good way to cover ground, but nothing will take the place of setting on one ridge for many hours of spotting across the valleys. You must see the sheep before they see you.

I highly recommend that the client bring along a very warm sleeping bag, or at least an extra blanket. It is much cooler in the mountains than most people think, even in August. I also carry a six by eight piece of breathable, waterproof tarp to keep me dry if there is a leak in the tent, or the wind is blowing rain into a lean-to. It is almost impossible to dry out wet sleeping bags under the conditions we were hunting in. In those days waterproof leather boots did not exist. Wet feet were such a common phenomena that even if boots did dry out, I would have an urge to get down and walk into the creek so my feet would feel normal again. A good raincoat and rainpants are a must and synthetic fiber insulation is best in wet country because it's easier to dry than goose down.

I must say, that evening showed me some of the most spectacular sights I think I have ever seen, especially when a rainbow momentarily appeared. The sunlight shining on the huge cathedral-like peaks cast a purple hue over the black, shadowed valleys. The contrasting, shining white glaciers exhibited thousands of little silver ribbons of water trickling over the rocks down into the deep glacially-carved basins below. And the ominous grey and pink rain clouds rolling over the top of the mountains behind me was one of the most spectacular sights I think I have ever seen. But this was the end of good weather!

The next morning it was raining, and reality had returned. The scenic beauty of the night before was now just another dull grey, rainy day. After a hearty breakfast of scrambled eggs, bacon and bannock, we were on our way down into the valley to go to one of Bobby's secret places. The "Devil's Hole" he called it.

There was somewhat of a trail to follow and occasionally you would see the track of a moose. We decided to camp early and look over the area on foot. We had no sooner unpacked the horses when I could hear some grunting just behind our lean-to. It seems that a bull moose, on seeing our horses, must have thought he was in heaven with four cow moose moving into his bedroom. He was a very shootable bull, but we were on a sheep hunt and would perhaps shoot a moose the last day or two. It would be easier to pack out the meat.

Behind our camp I found an old and crumbling trapper's cabin. It probably had been used by Indian trappers many, many years ago. It was a three-sided affair built on the ground with no floor and, probably was about four feet high and six feet wide at its widest point — just enough room for two men to sleep. There was a flat hearth stone that was surrounded by rocks to form somewhat of a chimney so the smoke could escape. Actually, half of the fireplace was outside of the cabin. This is all the space two men would need. I could see why these trappers developed cabin fever. A rusty axe head was driven deeply into a corner post and mice and porcupines had eaten most of the handle. I wondered why the axe had been left in the cabin?

There seemed to be considerable grizzly sign near the creek. Apparently the bears were digging for squirrels or mice. One hole was deep enough to bury a horse. Early the next morning we just took the saddle horses and rode part way up a steep incline and headed towards a V-shaped notch between the mountain and a glacier. Bobby said we could walk through, and that it was a good place for old rams to hang out. We tied the horses up to a couple of stunted balsam spruce and took off on foot. It was about as rough a mixed-up country as I have ever seen. It kind of reminded me of walking into an ice volcano. The basin was surrounded with high jagged peaks and contrasting soil and rocks. There was a glacier up to our right which covered most of the top of the mountain. Ahead of us the soft rock had been eroded by dozens of little rivets and other forces of nature into deep crevices. There could be a hundred sheep here and you would never see them. Yet, nature always finds a way and anywhere the hillsides flattened out at all had little bunches of grass and arctic birch clumps. We worked our way up the mountain so we could look down into some of the crevices. The rams would be near the grass.

There were many sheep beds that had been dug out and used for centuries by sheep, as well as caves where sheep or goats could protect themselves from the elements and in some places, the sheep dung looked like it was at least two feet thick. Perhaps sheep had been sleeping in this very spot for a thousand years. There were a few ram tracks, but nothing appeared to be fresh. We decided to work our way around the mountain, but at this point we ran into trouble.

There was a great sheet of hard packed snow left over from the previous year that ran like a long carpet from the edge of a glacier above us, then down below us for another 1,000 feet. The snowfield was perhaps 300 to 400 yards wide. We had to get across it.

The snow was relatively soft on the surface, which was safe enough as long as you did not fall down. You could dig in your feet and move slowly. However, as we rounded the mountain, it obviously was becoming steeper and steeper. As I looked below I could see that if we started to slide, we were going to go for several hundred yards, perhaps ending up going over a cliff at the bottom. It was now so steep I was almost afraid to turn around and knew I could not go another step forward, but it was so precarious I did not think I could turn around. I usually have a walking stick, but this time I only had my rifle. The buttplate would not go deep into the snow and the only thing to do was turn the rifle over and jam the barrel down into the snowpack eight or ten inches to give me something to hold onto if I fell. Bobby agreed that we were in a bad place. Had it not been for my rifle, I am sure one or both of us would have taken a long fast ride to the bottom. Every time something like this happens, I say "never again," but the urge to see the other side always pushes me on.

Once back on safe ground we stopped and built a small fire and made some tea and used the fire to warm up my rifle barrel so that the snowpack would melt out of the barrel. I am sure Winchester never intended a rifle be used this way — but it's my rifle and I use it as I see fit.

We decided to go to the rocky bottom and look up to the top. By this time it was late afternoon and the snow was starting to crust over. Although we could hear water under the rocks, we could not reach it. For our late afternoon lunch we had brought along some freeze-dried hamburger, but we had no water to mix with it. But, we were hungry and mixed the bland mixture up with a little bit of snow. Still, it was so dry it was something like eating lumpy talcum powder. There was no wood for a fire.

A dense fog started to form around the glacier, and probably there was no use in staying. Then we saw a giant mountain goat about 400 yards above us — a candidate for the record book. He crossed the mountain just above where we had turned around earlier that morning. He stopped and smelled our tracks, then looked down at us. (Goats have eyes equal to my binoculars, but if you don't move they may not see you.) On his right hip there was a very large black circle, probably a mud stain. We named him something original, "Spot." Although we never got near enough for a shot, we were to see this same goat several times throughout the duration of our journey.

Although some goats live out most of their lives on the same mountain, it is obvious that some goats are also great travelers. As we were nearing the horses, I sat up my spotting scope to look on the opposite mountain, and almost immediately could see the rump of a sheep, which appeared to be a very white spot with a black spot near the top, which would be the sheep's tail. I could see several other sheep. They were so far away that at first I could not make out horns. All of the sheep were the same size. There were no lambs. Probably rams!

Momentously, a ray of the setting sun passed through a cloud onto the sheep almost as if you had turned a spotlight on center stage, I could see that they were the herd of four or five rams. These were the first Stone sheep rams I had ever seen. I must say, they inspired me greatly. But it was too late that evening to get to them. We would, however, be there the next morning. Sheep generally don't move much at night, but you have to be there early in the morning if you plan on seeing the same sheep near the same spot.

That night I did not sleep well. My air mattress leaked and was flat. From then on, each night I would make a bed on about six inches of moss, which is warm and soft. At daylight I was behind my spotting scope looking for rams, but saw nothing. There was a black bear feeding in almost exactly the same place — probably eating blueberries, so no doubt ran off the sheep. Above the bear I could see "Spot" the mountain goat. Maybe he traveled all night to warn the sheep!

We ran out of bread and made extra hot cakes, which I coated with peanut butter and jelly and rolled into a ball. I put four of them in my packsack for my lunch. We walked for three hours then stopped and looked back towards camp and could see the tiny specks which were our horses foraging around the lean-to, which appeared as a small, square white dot. Then I saw another white dot, far above and to the right. After setting up my spotting scope I found that it was the same goat with the black spot on his hip. He had moved several miles back to where we had seen him the night before!

Once across the valley, we found ourselves far above the timberline looking for the rams. There were clumps of heather, blueberries, grass and forbs, and an occasional patch of arctic birch. In the soft ground we could see where the sheep had run. Obviously the black bear had made a run on them and they left for parts unknown.

We looked for the sheep for several hours and then it started to rain and sleet. I put on my raingear, but it was such a long and vigorous hike back to camp that I was as wet inside from sweating as I would have been standing in the rain. Just at dark I could make out two billy goats on a cliff just above where we had seen the black bear in the morning. In all probability, we had walked around the cliff within 50 yards of them, and didn't know they were there. "Spot" was not with them.

That night Bobby made more bannock in his cast iron skillet. We had a large can of Dinty Moore's beef stew for dinner, Bobby played his harmonica, and we went to bed. Wolves were howling and Bobby said, "That's the end of another moose!"

The next morning it was raining again. In fact, it had rained all night. Everything was wet, the fog lifted off and on, and you could see that the tops of the mountains had been dusted with a coat of fresh snow. There was a skim of ice in the water bucket. Winter was introducing itself, but was not welcome as far as I was concerned. We waited until noon and the clouds raised. We decided to call in on our whereabouts. Bobby carried, in his saddlebags, a small radio — an SBX11, single side band that he used to successfully call Fort Nelson, British Columbia. This amazed me when you consider all the high rugged peaks around us.

We decided to investigate a couple of areas around us for sheep and, if we didn't do any good, we were going to come back and look for the rams that had been chased by the black bear.

About mid-day we reached a small lake and quickly set up camp and I started fishing. They were easy to catch, and as fast as I could flip my fly, I had one on, but they were only three to five inches long. I don't know what kind of fish they were, but they looked like both lake trout and eastern brook trout. We deep fried 30 or 40 of them and ate them, bones and all.

I decided I had better test-fire my rifle after the abuse it had taken on the snow slide. I was using a .270 Winchester, with 150 grain Winchester power point bullets. It was shooting perfect, two inches high at 100 yards.

That evening we saw a few sheep, apparently all young rams, quite far down the mountain in the timber. We saw one more bull moose, which would be the last bull we would see on that trip. It was not a big bull, and was too far away to even consider going after anyway. Packing the meat out through the bog holes would be a nightmare for the horses.

One of our pack horses already had slipped into what almost appeared to be a bottomless pit. We had to unload the horse and pull her out of the deep bog, which seemed to be sucking her down at an alarming rate. The horse was terrified.

Most of the time we went cross country, sometimes in places Bobby had never been himself. This type of hunt would not be particularly expensive nowadays, and is still available, but not many clients would really want to do it. They might think they would, but everything about the hunt was rough, spartan and demanding. Many of the sidehills were so steep, we led the horses up and down most of the time. On one particular day, in every direction, I could see a goat — all of them old billy goats. Most often, in long-hike, out-of-the-way places, it would require backpacking and spiking out overnight. This is tough to do when you have no one to care for the horses.

I decided I would shoot a goat after I got my ram, as I did not want any unnecessary shooting in the area. I did have a sling-shot, and once managed to get two grouse, which was a welcome change from our dried food dinners. Again, if it had not been for the rifle report, I could have shot a couple of marmots, which aren't bad eating at all. I've eaten porcupines, beavers, and once considered shooting a colt while out with another outfitter when we ran out of food.

Bobby decided the name of the creek we were camped by would be "Atcheson Creek." It is still called that to this day. And a lucky creek it is, for it was from this campsite far down the ridge we saw several rams feeding on the skyline. They were not going to be easy to reach. The whole area below the sheep was a series of pillar-like cliffs that had been eroded by the elements until below each cliff would be a huge alluvial fan ending up with a series of glacial moraine piles, all covered with buckbrush, heather, moss berry and various types of grasses.

We decided to scale two very sheer shale slides and try to reach the same plateau where the sheep were feeding. Although I am sure they did not see us or smell us, rams very often seem to detect danger where as ewes and lambs just go about their business feeding. That's what had happened — the rams were obviously alert and looking in all directions. Two of the rams had exceptionally nice horns. One ram had two dirty black spots on each side of his rump, and when you looked straight at it, the tail looked like a beak and the dark spots looked like eyes. It was as if you were looking at the head of an owl.

Bobby thought the sheep would move downhill, and it might be a lot easier to back off now and get back to Atcheson Creek, and move down the bottom to where another tributary on the right entered the creek. We hurriedly set up camp as fog started to raise from the valley and it started to snow. You couldn't see 10 feet; damn the luck! But, at daylight the fog lifted. It would only be a short one-hour walk to where we expected to see the rams. But, we were in for a surprise. The rams had moved downhill further than we thought they would, then swung to the left, and were more or less coming in our direction, but too far to shoot. Bobby felt that they were going to make somewhat of a giant circle and be back up in the cliffs by dark.

We dropped down into Atcheson Creek and started to skirt the shale slide above us; perhaps we would catch them on the same slide we climbed last evening. Actually, we couldn't move back, as the sheep would see us.

It started to rain and snow. Soon Bobby and I were both completely soaked to the skin and were huddled together behind a large boulder. There we sat for hours. I don't think I have ever been more miserable. We had missed lunch and I was very hungry. Our packs, containing food and rain gear, were only 25 yards away, but if we moved, the rams, now lying down, would see us.

It was getting towards late evening and we were about to bag it when we discovered that the sheep had progressed far enough that if we moved behind a bank we would not be seen. The sheep disappeared, but one small ram kept coming back and looking in our direction. We could not move. The light snow and rain continued. We had decided to wait until dark, then try to slip out without the sheep seeing us, and try in the morning if we didn't have pneumonia.

We were both looking straight up the ridge in front of us, when suddenly, out of nowhere, we could see four or five rams. The two largest rams were quite visible. Then, a fog bank moved across them. Although I could see the sheep, I could not tell one from the other through my rifle scope. The sheep were about 350 yards away, which is about as far as I normally shoot.

One ram's horns appeared to be very heavy — right out to the tips. The wind started to blow slightly and my 4 power Redfield telescope lens kept filling with water. I was shivering, both from cold and excitement. I decided to shoot.

"Which one is the big ram?" I asked Bobby.

Bobby said, looking through his binoculars, "The ram to the left that is starting to walk uphill."

The ram was quartering at such an angle that I would either hit his left hip, or just in front of it where I was aiming between the last two ribs towards his right shoulder. I would shoot as soon as a hole appeared in the

Bobby Ball and my great ram just above Atcheson Creek in the background.

fog.

I could see him! The ram was still standing where he was before. Had it not been for the fact that Bobby was watching through the powerful binoculars, I would have shot and would have killed a small 3/4 curl ram. Somehow they had changed places!

To the left I picked up the big ram standing at exactly the same angle. I quickly fired. The sheep dropped dead instantly and started rolling down the mountain. The other rams ran about 20 yards, turned around and watched for a few minutes, then they started up the mountain. Like a rising curtain, the fog lifted for a long minute. I noticed one of the rams going up the mountain had a very nice head. I wondered if I had shot the right one.

I asked Bobby, "Did I get the big ram?"

He said, "Actually no, Jack. You shot the next to the biggest ram. I saved the biggest one for your buddy, Sully, who's coming up on the next hunt."

He said this with such a straight face that for a moment I believed him. Then he started to laugh. Suddenly it occurred to me. I had my ram! Just the way I had it planned — with the same outfitter, the same area, and the same type of hunt! Everything had gone according to plan.

We hurried up to the ram, cut off his backstraps and opened him up so he wouldn't sour. We decided to leave the entire sheep there until the next day. The rocks were so slick and treacherous that we thought it unwise to attempt moving him in the dark. I hoped a grizzly would not find him.

That night we had a couple of scotch and waters, and more 10,000-year-old glacier ice. I was absolutely elated! Bobby broke out his harmonica and we started to sing some songs. Bobby is quite a musician and has a great singing voice. Scotch always improves mine.

The next morning we had bacon and eggs, and very fresh sheep loin deep fried in bacon fat. This, of course, was long before I ever heard of cholesterol.

This time we figured out a route where we could lead the horses up close to the ram. I believe this is the first time I ever ate the sheep meat before I had the cape and horns off the mountain. It continued to rain and we decided that we would head back to the ranch, which was about 40 miles away on horseback — and 16 miles as the raven flies. It would be a long hard ride and we would not get there until after midnight. We probably would have stopped, except the horses were so eager; it was obvious they knew they were going home.

I have never had a tape measure on this particular ram. What do you think he would measure?

THE DEATH OF SWEET WILLIAM

Jim's first words were, "Jack, we've got to get a couple of big bears."

"Yep," I replied, "that's a great idea. What kind of bears, and when do you want to go? I'm ready."

The caller was Jim Carmichel, gun editor of *Outdoor Life* magazine, a good friend and hunting companion with whom I had previously hunted in Africa and Alaska. "How about a big Canadian grizzly?"

"A great choice," I said, for oddly enough I had just been talking to outfitter Bobby Ball of Telegraph Creek, British Columbia, whose area is on the Stikine River, an area well known for big bears. I personally had hunted with Bobby before and, as a booking agent, had sent many clients to him, with great success on Stone sheep, enormous mountain goats, and, yes, big grizzlies. I laid it out to Jim.

I was thinking of going back to look for a big mountain goat, as I had passed up several beauties while in pursuit of a magnificent Stone ram, which I eventually took.

"I don't want to hear about your goat or your sheep," Carmichel said. "I'm hot after a bear."

I told him we could handle that. Bobby and I had just been talking about an immense bear track he had seen several times along the Stikine River, as big as an Alaskan brown bear he said, judging from the tracks in the sand. This was backed up by two of our clients who had taken big boars there the previous year. They agreed this Stikine monster had to be big, old and smart.

"Okay, Jim, it's a deal," I said. "I'll make the arrangements."

I was waiting at the airport for Jim Carmichel to show up, but was disappointed to learn that, at the last minute, Jim could not make the trip. But, on the bright side, I would concentrate on "the big bear."

I arrived in Telegraph Creek and found it a very small Taltan Indian village built on the banks of the Stikine River. I suspected that some day there would be a mudslide, and most of the town would disappear into 20 feet of water. I was lucky to be there that day, for a newsworthy event had just happened. Someone had blown the only safe in Telegraph Creek. Bobby Ball was part of the investigating team, and I went along to witness the crime scene. Sure enough, the bottom was blasted out of a small safe. I asked the owner what he had in the safe. He told me he had some medical items for the natives and a couple of bottles of old rye whiskey he was saving for a special occasion. The desperadoes took the rye and some of the drugs.

The idea of blowing a safe and escaping in a canoe fascinated me. "I think those hippies living along the river did it," someone commented.

After spending the night at Bobby's ranch, we took his jetboat down the river. We were well supplied for a 10 to 14 day hunt. We set up camp and did a little hiking and glassing on the steep mountain slopes descending into the opposite side of the river, as I also had tags for moose, goat and wolf. There were a lot of grizzly and wolf tracks. I eventually assumed the wolves were surviving on salmon that were migrating up the river. Throughout the trip, I saw one live moose. Every moose track we saw was from an adult, and not a single calf track. Bobby felt that between the grizzlies and the wolves, the survival rate on calf moose could not be more than 10 percent. Well, that is what I was there for, to help reduce the predator bear population.

Far up the mountain, I saw what I believed to be a black mountain goat. Then I saw one that was black and white. Sure enough, there were three goats rolling around in a mud hole. I had never seen goats do this before. Because of fog, we didn't see any more goats either.

That first night we roasted a salmon over hot coals, baked a few potatoes, drank a little scotch, and did a lot of reminiscing. Bobby is one of the most interesting and knowledgeable Canadian guides I have ever met and can pick a guitar better than Willy Nelson. Bobby lived all his life in the area and speaks fluent Taltan, the local language.

"What color is this big grizzly that has been making all these big tracks?" I asked.

Bobby said he didn't know; it seemed no one had ever seen him. Prospects didn't sound good for the hunt, but we were going to give it a try. Bobby strummed on his guitar. Two owls hooted back and forth until midnight. I hoped that it was a good sign.

About 1:00 a.m. we were besieged by an army of mice. In all the years I have slept in the forest, I have never encountered so many mice. We were sleeping on the ground and mice were running across my sleeping bag three or four at a time. I was yawning wide and once a mouse ran across my face and actually had his feet on my tongue. I covered my head with a shirt, went to sleep, and dreamed of a huge silvertip grizzly.

The next several days we walked along several secluded river channels. We sat for hours and glassed slide areas. Everywhere we looked there were grizzly tracks of all sizes, but after eight days of hard hunting, we had not seen a bear, a moose, or anything else for that matter. One day we stumbled onto an American hippie cabin, occupied by a man and three women. They planned to live off the land and had just shot a small moose that happened to wander into their camp — but they didn't know what to do with it. Bobby and I cleaned it up, cut the meat into small portions, then hung it up, though it was already starting to spoil. I could see that these people living off the land were in for a long and tough winter unless they were going to get CARE packages from home.

Bear tracks, in mud or snow, are awesome and never fail to catch your imagination, but I wanted to see a bear standing in the track. We hunted high, we hunted low. Nothing! There were, however, fresh grizzly tracks on top of ours each day that we went out, but apparently all the bears were moving at night.

During the day, it was interesting to watch the salmon migrating right up to the end of a small stream. In their attempt to go a bit further, some of them actually would lay on their sides and flop upstream to follow a tiny trickle of water. Eagles, ravens and other small predators were eating on the fish while the fish made a valiant attempt to gain just a few more inches. The final days for a salmon are not a pleasant picture.

Bobby pointed out a beaver pond where he had watched two moose standing in water up to their bellies for five days while a pack of wolves waited around hoping they would wander out. Eventually the wolves gave up. The moose survived, only to be eaten by wolves a few days later. We thought about trying to hunt goats, but big bear fever had me. However, we were yet to see his track!

"I know one place we haven't tried yet," said Bobby. "It's kind of different."

Hidden back from the river was a large cabin built and abandoned by some other back-to-nature people. The log cabin was two stories, and was very well built. We climbed up onto a split wood shingle roof to watch a long meadow behind the cabin. This was another of the areas where the big bear's track was frequently seen. It started to rain and I crawled into the upper story where I could look out the window. I was actually sitting in a rocking chair and eating apples. There were books and papers scattered everywhere. At my feet I noticed a manila folder with a label on it that read, *"The Death of Sweet William."* I picked it up and started to read.

I thought, "My God, I have discovered the outline of a murder." Written in beautiful longhand, I found that the clan had met that day and agreed that Sweet William was getting out of hand. Since previous reprimands had failed, the consensus of opinion was that Sweet William be put to death. Straws were drawn and Sister Elaine had drawn the short straw. As the hit person, she would knock off Sweet William the following morning while he was eating his breakfast.

Unfortunately, the first shot had not killed poor William. He died very hard. Five shots were required before the end. Between bullets, his body was massaged and he was consoled by the other sisters to ease the pain. Songs were sung and the women cried. The members were so shocked by Sweet William's will to live that it was determined there would be no further executions. William was buried behind the house. There were prayers and flowers and a pledge to God that, from that point on, these pilgrims would be total vegetarians. So much blood and suffering was just too much for them.

I sat there in shock and was planning to turn the article over to the Mounties. But the next page revealed a picture of Sweet William and a copy of registration papers. It seems that Sweet William was actually one of the domestic goats the Colony had been raising. Sweet William's crimes consisted of destroying the garden, and attempting to copulate with anyone when the mood struck him.

The next day we hunted up the same river channel. I wanted to pick up the copy of the Sweet William caper, but I had forgotten to take it with me. We heard moose grunting somewhere off to our left. Bobby immediately called. The bull came crashing through the brush. I fired, and although it was hit high in the lungs, the moose turned around and ran 400 or 500 yards before collapsing. Oddly enough, there were only a few drops of blood on the ground. We cleaned him out, and went for packboards. We had time for one trip before dark. The bull had a 52-inch spread and Bobby had his winter's meat supply.

Upon our return to the moose, up jumped a pack of seven wolves truly pigging out on the carcass. It is unbelievable how much of the animal these wolves had already eaten. We filled the pack and covered the remains with brush, even left a coat on either end, hoping this would deter the wolves from coming back and eating everything. We even peed on the brush — plenty of man smell!!

Early the following morning we were back. Through my binoculars

His 5-inch shining white claws reminded me of knives. My best grizzly.

I could see that some of the brush had been moved. Bobby said, "Well, let's go and see what we can salvage." As we boldly approached the moose, right in front of me was the largest grizzly bear track I have ever seen. Muddy water was still oozing into eight-inch-wide tracks. I knew the bear had to be just a hundred yards or so in front of us.

"Damn," said Bobby. "We're out in the open."

Two ravens abruptly left the moose and landed in a tree. I said, "Let's just stand still for a minute and see what happens." Bobby said he thought the bear was headed for the moose. Sure enough, 150 yards ahead of us a gigantic silvertip bear lumbered onto a sandbar. Sometimes it is hard to tell an average bear from a big one. But when you see a monster, there is no doubt. They look different and your heart takes on a new beat!

I dropped down behind a log. Bobby said, "Can you hit him solid?"

"I sure hope so," I said. I fired, and the bear collapsed, but raised up. I shot again. He rolled down a bank into a pool of water.

"My God, what a bear. The biggest I've ever seen," Bobby said.

My .338 Winchester with 250 grain Nosler bullets proved itself again. It was all we could do to roll the bear out of the water pool to take pictures and skin him. I have never seen such claws. The longest were well over five inches and pure white. The bear was very old, badly scarred, with teeth badly worn and decayed. The skin squared almost nine feet.

I was later to learn that the bear was probably between 25 and 30 years old. He qualified for the Boone & Crockett record book. It was a good thing Jim Carmichel didn't show up. I would have had to arm wrestle him for the shot at the only bear we saw on the trip.

THE GREAT ZEMLJAK DEER HUNTERS

As a hunting consultant I received volumes of calls and letters from people desperately trying to find a good mule deer. Most wanted a buck of phenomenal dimensions in just a few days hunting, and at a low cost. Unfortunately, those days, if they really once existed, are now over. For a while at least.

There certainly are select areas where nice mule deer bucks can be had, but those big mountain, mossy horned old bucks just don't seem to be around much anymore. I am told by biologists it is a combination of habitat and bad winters that has brought this about. I think they have omitted a few other major factors — predators, coyotes and mountain lions that prey heavily on old bucks during the late season, and of course, bullets. If you shoot all the forkhorns, they are never going to live long enough to ever reach full maturity, let alone become the monster buck you want to hang on the wall.

If you are not content until you get your share of big bucks, then you had best plan on putting in a lot of time hunting. Plan on several trips a year, and eventually you will get lucky. There are still a few survivors. Actually, there never really were a lot of giant mule deer bucks. When I started hunting deer 50 years ago, there were far more deer in Montana than there were elk for sure. It was common to see 300 to 400 mule deer a day. Seeing 20 average four-point per side bucks was not uncommon at all. Mostly in November, but even in September, I have seen 30 big bucks in one herd.

Guy George, a guide I know, saw 57 bucks together near Yellow Bear Lake in the upper Ruby Valley.

I recall one day at daylight on a post-season hunt at Bear Creek near Ennis, Montana, through our spotting scopes we could count 1,400 deer scattered in small herds. There were many bucks, but as I recall, there were only 25 that we could see that were big bucks. And only a couple of those were exceptional. There were about 50 elk.

Quite recently I hunted the same area with a friend who had a post-season cow elk permit, and spotting from the same site we could see 137 deer, but only three small bucks. But, there were 3,000 elk occupying the same area. Whatever the reason, adult mule deer bucks are scarce in western Montana.

Some of my favorite places to hunt were the upper Ruby Valley and surrounding Gravelly Range and upper Blacktail Creek. Someone would take a deer or two with phenomenal antlers out of the area every year. They were also some very large-bodied deer. I remember one buck I helped pack out weighed 267 pounds. A fellow by the name of Aldrich shot another enormous-bodied buck in the Fossil Creek drainage. We pulled the animal over a log to cool and the next morning, before we picked him up, a badger had eaten the entire hind leg, but still the balance of the animal weighed 290 pounds.

But the vast majority of the mature bucks that we weighed, with just their insides removed, averaged out to 159 pounds. Finding a buck that weighed 190 pounds was rare. Anything weighing over that left people gasping or doubtful, with some unusual exceptions.

I recall in 1949 that, while making a stalk on a six-point bull elk, I jumped a herd of five better-than-average mule deer bucks on a sagebrush ridge just to my left. The sixth buck's antlers were similar to the other five, but body size-wise it was like comparing Wilt Chamberlain to a midget. I had the option of shooting perhaps the heaviest bodied mule deer that ever lived in Montana, or taking two more steps ahead and shooting a very large-antlered bull elk. I cleverly decided to wait until both animals were in the open and shoot them both! But greed was my downfall. The wind shifted and they were both gone, never to be seen again.

My greatest screw-up on giant-antlered mule deer happened in 1959. I was hunting at the head of Warm Springs Creek in the upper Ruby drainage. These higher elevations seem to attract old bucks before the sex lure came upon them. Most of the hunting took place above timber line in what most people would call sheep country; rocky, broken areas with deep ravines and shale slides where a misstep could give you the ride of the century. Timber was scattered, mostly limber pine twisted and distorted by the wind. The wind never seemed to cease blowing — from one direction, then the other, and then in circles. Seeing a big buck was one thing; getting near him was something else. But one great day all things were in my favor — or so it seemed.

There was a light snow on the ground, the sky was blue, and best of all, favorable wind. But I had only one day; at daylight I would do some spotting, and then walk along a ridge watching both sides and, hopefully running a big buck up onto the finger ridges where I could blast him. I also carried a slingshot and would lob pebbles into suspected clumps of trees. I chased out seven bucks that any hunter would have been proud to shoot.

One running deer accidently dislodged an enormous boulder that went crashing down the mountain, bouncing and disintegrating dead trees and headed toward a big buck bedded amid some mountain mahogany. Right in line with the granite missile! The buck glanced uphill to see trees, brush and shale rock flying in all directions above him. At the very last second he leaped as the boulder crashed onto his bed. Then he calmly laid down again, as if it were just one of those things that happened every day. That is, until my scent drifted down between his massive antlers. That was something that did scare him.

The last time I saw the buck he was bouncing down the mountain towards thick timber, with downhill leaps that covered 20 feet at a time. I would have taken that buck if he would have held one more second. Such is fate!

I worked on up the mountain, where the wind still seemed to be somewhat in my favor, and sat down on a rocky knob that allowed me to look down into a timbered basin. To my right were scattered patches of limber pine and juniper. To my left was an enormous shale slide with a series of broken draws and benches — ideal habitat for big bucks that wanted to see almost everything around them, and yet be virtually unapproachable across the open sidehills or through noisy shale rock that would trickle down the mountain with every step an intruder would take.

It was late afternoon and I decided just to sit and have a sandwich. I set up my spotting scope and leaned back and watched a couple of noisy Clark's nutcrackers working over some pine cones. A family of ravens rode the air currents up and down the mountain in front of me, their croaking sounding like anything from a bell to a dog. One raven did a peculiar roll that ended just over a large juniper patch directly below me. I was startled to see a white animal stepping out into the final yellowish-red rays of the setting sun. An albino mule deer buck!

Except for a couple of brown spots on his shoulders and neck, the albino was completely white. He walked out about 100 yards below me and looked down into the valley. I could see he had four points on one side and five on the other. The antlers were heavy, the forks deep, with a spread of about 26 or 28 inches. The antlers appeared to be almost black. Two smaller bucks walked between me and the albino, making a shot impossible.

I had no time to lose, as darkness was near, and decided to move a couple of feet to my left and hopefully get a shot. The basin below me was rapidly disappearing into an enormous dark shadow. I slipped off the safety of my 308 Norma magnum. But then I saw another buck. He just seemed to have stepped right out of the ground and was standing under a dead tree. I was about to return my attention to the albino, when suddenly the tree seemed to move. I thought, "My God, those are antlers." I had never in my life seen antlers so large. The buck laid down and all I could see were his antlers, which were as wide as his body from his brisket to his tail. His antler spread had to approach 50 inches! What I had thought to be a brush pile was a maze of antlers.

What a horrible choice — a chance to shoot the only albino mule deer I had ever seen, or to make a stalk on the biggest buck I had ever seen. The wide spread won the toss. I counted nine small ridges which would put me about 100 feet above the buck. I was so excited that I forgot my pack and spotting scope and began my assault on the giant deer. I had only a few minutes of daylight left to cover 300 yards. I probably should have waited until the next day, but I didn't. As I reached the ninth finger ridge, I suddenly could feel on the back of my neck the cold evening wind starting to drift down into the canyon. I was sure the buck was only 100 feet below me. I had him for sure!

Looking straight ahead I crept out and looked down. I instantly realized that I had made a terrible mistake. Instead of being above the buck, I had come out at exactly the same level as the buck, and only 50 feet from where he had been laying. Perhaps he saw me, as I do not recall even looking right or left, I was so sure I was above him. I heard an all too familiar thump, thump of a large animal bouncing down the slope. I ran to the edge knowing that I had just made one of the greatest blunders of my life. And then, it was totally dark.

I hunted the same area the rest of the season until the heavy snow made access impossible. Oddly enough, I never saw any of the bucks that I could remember seeing that day. The deer could have gone 20 miles in either direction, but I was to see the monster deer one more time, under a very different circumstance. The longevity of the big buck was very much dependent on the filling of a cow elk permit a year later.

Two of my friends, Pete Zemljak, Jr., who was about my age at the time, and Pete Zemljak, Sr., both very avid hunters and fishermen, had taken their share of nice bucks and bulls, but really weren't trophy hunters. When a nice buck came by, they would thump him. As far as Pete Sr. was concerned, a cow elk was a lot better eating than a big bull elk. The antlers were just too tough to eat.

Both Zemljaks had cow elk permits and were hunting the lower drainages of Warm Springs Creek and Poison Creek, just a couple of miles from where I had seen the big buck the year before. Pete Sr. gave instructions that nobody was to shoot any deer until the cow elk tags were filled, which is pretty much a normal procedure of Montana people. The party split up, and Pete Jr. proceeded up the ridge.

Not long after daylight Pete Jr. stopped near a stand of quaking aspens and watched a couple of does walking slowly up the ridge in front of him. Behind the last doe, standing broadside and looking directly at him, no more than a hundred yards away, stood the largest buck Pete Jr. had ever seen. An easy shot, but the sound of the shot may have sent the small herd of cow elk into the timber and away from his hunting companions. Pete did not shoot. The cow elk won out over the giant buck. The buck disappeared over the ridge.

Pete thought to himself, "I think I made a mistake," but the opportunity had passed. The worst part of the situation was that the elk had departed too. Nobody had seen a cow. Later that afternoon Pete Jr. laid back in the sagebrush where he could see 200 yards towards a low saddle and hoped somebody would run something to him. Then came the surprise of surprises! The biggest buck on the mountain walked across an open sagebrush hillside — his mind only on female deer. Pete's second chance at the big buck was handed to him on a platter.

"This is too much," he said to his companion. "I don't think there are any elk here anyway. That's the biggest buck that I'm ever going to see." One shot from Pete's .270 Winchester downed one of the finest bucks ever killed in Montana, ranking high in the Boone & Crockett record book — a 49 inch spread. Score 275 1/8 nontypical.

As soon as I saw the buck's head in my taxidermy shop, I knew that "my big buck" had been accounted for. But, the story doesn't end there. In fact, it gets a little awesome.

Like I said, Pete Sr. had taken his share of big bucks and bull elk in his time. Although not above shooting another big buck if it happened to come by his way, the meat was more important. While hunting in an area about 25 miles south of Butte amid an old mining claim, pock-marked with holes, abandoned ore dumps and old cabins, and only a couple of miles from the main highway, Zemljak saw what could have passed for the twin of his son's big buck. But the buck was wary. From his perch upon the old ore dump he could see in all directions. When the hunters would emerge from the timber, the buck was always gone. But, Pete Sr. noticed the buck always left in the same direction. A plan was formed.

Pete Sr. would make a circle around the dump before daylight and wait in ambush at a small clearing. Pete Jr. and party began a drive that ended with one shot — the big buck was a creature of habit one time too many. The deer's luck was bad, for Pete Sr. told me that he would have shot any buck or any size elk that happened to break cover. Since it happened to be the big buck with a 48 inch spread — all the better. And that is how most big trophies are taken. The antlers are listed in the Boone & Crockett Record book. Score 270 6/8 nontypical.

Pete Jr.'s buck was the largest ever taken in Montana; Pete Sr.'s the second largest! I was so close, yet not close enough!

The greatest mule deer ever taken in Montana — 49" spread and I missed him! But Pete Zemljak didn't. Bottom buck taken by Pete Zemljak Sr. Photo by DeWayne A. Williams

SHEEP FEVER

By Jack Atcheson Jr.

North America's highest mountain, Mt. McKinley, towering over 20,000 feet high, is located about midway in the Alaskan Range in central Alaska — the heart of Alaska's big game country! South and west of this towering, ice-capped peak is Farewell Lake. To this very day, Farewell Lake is a jumping-off spot for hunters seeking adventure in Alaska's back country. As our chartered bush plane circled Farewell Lake Lodge in August of 1970, I was filled with the anticipation of hunting Dall sheep, grizzly, moose, caribou and black bear.

Our aircraft buzzed the gravel landing strip twice to make certain that the bison that had been frequenting the area were not using the airstrip for their daily dust bath.

Bob and Gayle Curtis were operating Farewell Lake Lodge at that time and had organized a two week hunt for my dad and I. Earlier that day we had stopped at the McGrath, Alaska, Post Office where I had purchased just over $100 worth of hunting licenses, with which I could shoot all species.

Bob Curtis was known as the "Bald Eagle of the North" for both his bald head and his uncanny flying abilities. His trademark was a cartoon bald eagle painted on the side of his aircraft.

Dad had arrived at Farewell Lake the day before from his British Columbia Stone sheep hunt which began in early August, where he had taken an extremely heavy horned Stone sheep ram with a beautiful black pelt. Before our 206 came to a halt I could see Bob Curtis and Dad waiting at the end of the airstrip. I was thrilled to see Dad. He had planned three sheep hunts this year and was planning on hunting from August 1 through mid-September. I couldn't believe that anyone would want to do that much hard hunting, but he had sheep fever!

My mother was along as well, as she and Gayle Curtis were the best of friends. While Dad and I hunted with Bob, Gayle and Mom could keep each other entertained back at base camp.

Hunting season was already in full swing and a new group of hunters, all as anxious as I to begin their hunt, were gathered at the main lodge. I met famous guides that I had heard of for years, like Phillip Esai and Junior Gregory. They had been assigned their hunters and all were headed for hunting camps that I'd also heard of for years. The Hartman camp, the Dillinger camp and the Rhone River camp. Bob would begin flying these anxious nimrods out that afternoon. He explained to Dad and I that we would be opening up the Rhone River camp.

Heavy snows the season before had forced them to abandon the Rhone River camp. The first step of our hunt was to rebuild the camp for our own hunt and those that followed. We were joined by Edna Craver, a camp cook from McGrath, Alaska. We circled the camp twice from the air, seeing that all the tents had been flattened by last winter's snow.

We landed and immediately set to work re-erecting the tents. After a couple of hours we had the camp liveable and Bob flew back to Farewell Lake to take care of some last minute business. As Edna made supper I finally had time to examine our hunting area. The Rhone River camp was surrounded by towering mountains. The camp itself was situated on the river bank near a large gravel bar. Common in Alaska, these gravel bars can stretch a mile or more across and run for miles along a small glacially-fed river. Bob assured me that all sorts of game could be found within a short distance of camp: Dall sheep in the highest peaks, bull caribou summering in the higher alpine basins. Lower on the mountains in heavy spruce forests, moose, grizzly and black bear could be found. Wolf, lynx and wolverines could be taken as well. A hunter's dreamland!

The mountains were steeper and far rougher than I imagined. Naturally, my first thought as nightfall approached that first day in camp, was the thought of bears. Black bears, grizzly bears — large and small. I knew there were lots of them out there. Talk of bear dominated the evening at Farewell Lake Lodge, and now again here at Rhone River camp. The very thought of bears made this 14-year-old boy very nervous. I asked our cook Edna about bears. She assured me that I had nothing to worry about, as she always heard them first when they came in the camp. She brought along her iron sighted ".06" to handle any problems that might occur. Dad was more concerned about Edna and her rifle than he was about the bears.

The first five days of our hunt we were to hunt unguided for moose and caribou in the foothills surrounding camp. As opening day began to break, the first sounds I heard were of Edna snoring in the nearby tent. But, there was another noise too — a sniffing and snorting and the sound of padded feet shuffling.

I called to Dad and asked him what it was. He whispered back that he thought there was a bear in camp. Day was just breaking and light was dim. Our tent was an army pyramid tent with dark green walls so the interior was blacker than black. He crawled to the tent door and raised the zipper. I rolled in alongside him to peer out onto an astonishing sight of a sow grizzly with her nearly full-grown two-year-old cubs.

One of the bears stood peering at us from its hind legs while the other two watched on all four feet. An instant later, the bears wheeled to run. The sow ran past the meat pole where she leapt off the ground to grab a hind quarter of moose meat Bob had flown in to feed us. The parachute cord it hung by snapped and cracked like a rifle shot. The sow ran away with the 150-pound quarter in its mouth, like a dog would run with a stick. Then, there was no sound at all other than the sound of Edna's snores. What a start for my hunt!

We called out to Edna and told her that there had been a bear in camp. The snores stopped. No question about it — Edna was quick. She was out of the tent faster than Dad and I, ready and loaded for bear. What they had left was not pretty. Edna's pot of camp beans that I had enjoyed the night before had been placed in a wooden box about six feet off the ground, alongside a 10-pound slab of bacon. Two quarters of moose meat had been hung alongside this kitchen box as well. We had not heard the bears carefully lift this three-gallon pot of beans from its perch. Undetected, they had eaten the beans and bacon and had pulled down one of the quarters of meat and devoured it.

Berry season was in full swing at that time. The combination of gallons of blueberries, rich bacon and Edna's beans, along with about 150 pounds of raw moose meat had combined to create a gastric disaster for these three bears. There were piles of bear dung everywhere!

I was shocked that there were bears in camp and we hadn't heard them. Dad handed me a square-point shovel and told me to get shoveling. My awe for grizzly bears increased more and more with each load that I carted from camp.

The greatest indignity of all was suffered when I examined the bean pot and there was the biggest pile of bear dung of all! Right in the bottom of the pot. And, so started my first day of hunting in Alaska.

We walked for miles that day, and for the next four days, seeing very little game. No caribou was spotted. A few Dall sheep — all ewes and lambs. Tracks of our camp grizzlies were found daily. Had they not eaten all of our moose meat already, I am sure they would have been back for more. We had no fresh meat. We ate Spam! And my desire to shoot bears increased with each meal of Spam!

One day we spotted one fine bull moose just across the river from camp. The river looked small — maybe 10 to 15 yards across. But, it was deep and swift — impossible to cross on foot. So, we could only watch him stripping his antlers free of velvet.

Each day we had been walking 10 to 12 miles out and 10 to 12 miles back. We decided it was time to try and see if we could fire up the tundra buggy. Curtis' tundra buggy was an early attempt at developing an all-terrain vehicle. Bits and pieces of various machines had been cleverly crafted into a four-wheel-drive machine that had been driven into the Rhone River camp several years before — the box of a pickup truck, along with the axles of a Willy's Jeep.

The machine was hinged in the middle to bend and twist with the terrain. It hadn't been started in years, so we cleaned the gas lines, changed the spark plugs, and drained the fuel tank. It was equipped with a crank starter and it took two people to make this beast run; one to drive and the other to run the throttle lever and tranny. But, it would cross water five feet deep. This meant access to a lot more hunting country for us.

What impresses me most about Alaska is the lack of game, rather than the abundance. We had hunted for five days and had seen only a few animals at this point. The game wasn't in the areas in which we were looking. The only fresh meat we had a chance at was collected by my slingshot. Flocks of ptarmigan were found everywhere and both Dad and I amused ourselves by attempting to subsidize our Spam diet. After days of trying, an unfortunate bird finally got in the way of one of our missiles.

Dad stuck the lifeless bird in this pocket, but 15 minutes later the bird revived in his pocket. We didn't have the heart to kill it, so we let it go. Again, we had no fresh meat. Spam for dinner again.

Bob was flying in that night and we knew we would be going out to a spike camp. Bob suggested moving downriver to a drainage that ran to the east. He had seen some rams earlier in the season and felt it would be a good area. He suggested that we load our tundra buggy with our equipment, drive five miles down the river and he would meet us there the next day after we packed in and established a camp.

Backpacking equipment was in its infancy then. There were no internal frame packs. Our equipment was all army surplus from heavy army surplus down bags, to iron framed backpacks. We hadn't heard of freeze-dried food at that point, and were expecting to carry heavy canned food like we had back home in Montana. Bob surprised us by whipping out the first freeze-dried food I'd seen at that point. We had packages of freeze-dried porkchops — worse than Spam. Our tent was a sheet of plastic that we used in the style of a lean-to.

We started our hike into that promising drainage. We had walked less than an hour when we encountered a huge bull moose. This lone monster spotted us and grunted a few times, then went back to feeding. Undoubtedly, he had never seen a hunter before. The moose looked like a taker to everyone. Bob grunted twice when the moose started to move away, stopping the bull in his tracks. I chose a neck shot at a range of about 80 yards. I was using a .308 Norma magnum, a rifle I had commandeered from Dad a couple of years before. One shot into the bull's neck dropped him onto the tundra.

Oh, the size of that beast! Nothing could be moved on the animal other than lifting its foot from the ground. The moose had to weigh at least 1,500 pounds. He carried an antler spread of over 63 inches. I had never seen such a big animal in all my days, and he was my moose. I had taken my first Alaskan game.

Each quarter was removed and hung in a different pine tree around camp to try and salvage the meat from bears. I looked at all this meat in wonder. My mouth watered! I asked Dad if we could try moose tenderloin that night. He said fresh meat would do the same thing to me that it did to those bears the first night in camp! No fresh meat again.

We had no saw to remove the antlers, so Bob suggested a couple of well-placed shots into the skull, which allowed us to remove the antlers, which we lashed into a tall tree as well.

Four hours later, we were headed deeper into this wondrous canyon. We saw seven black bears at one time feeding on blueberries so thick they would stain your pants purple to your knees. We watched one huge black bear so lazy and content that he never bothered to walk. He laid on his belly and crawled along feeding on clumps of berries that appeared in front of his berry-stained muzzle.

We finally found a level spot to pitch our lean-to. As we erected camp, Dad looked to the north on a steep slope where he spotted a lone ram.

Not many quality spotting scopes were available at that point. A 20X scope was as powerful as you could find. The images often were fuzzy. We could still see that this was a big old ram. We planned tomorrow's hunt for him while we sampled our first dehydrated food. These freeze-dried porkchops did resemble meat — but tasted like cardboard.

At daylight we saw that the ram had moved slightly down the mountain. A long detour was required to allow us to make our stalk while keeping out of sight. We came in above the sheep and were able to get within 75 yards of the ram. But, the sheep had laid down and all we could see were the tops of his horns as he gazed into the valley below. We were forced to drop lower onto the mountain. And, unbeknownst to us, the sheep got up and moved uphill towards us.

As we eased up a small drainage, the ram suddenly came into sight, less than 25 yards away. Bob's only word was "shoot." I raised my rifle and fired a shot into the largest part of the ram, hitting him hard and immobilizing him, the advantage of a powerful rifle caliber.

Dad hollered, "Shoot him again!"

And I tried. In fact, I emptied my rifle without ever touching this ram. I was so smitten by "sheep fever" that my shaking knees forced me to sit down.

Reloading an empty rifle with a case of sheep fever is a nightmare! Fumbling around I finally got one shell to stay in the magazine and pumped it into the chamber. Meanwhile, Bob and Dad were hollering at me to shoot again.

I fired and the ram immediately collapsed and began tumbling down the mountain, bouncing 10 feet off the ground. The ram passed by us, crashing down the rocky chasm, around the corner and out of sight. What excitement! I had taken my first ram.

I had been hunting sheep with Dad since I was nine years old, but this is the first time that I had been able to take one myself. The big moose was like nothing I had ever seen before, but the hunt for this ram, oh, it was even more. I also knew fresh sheep meat was excellent. No more Spam!

We worked our way down the rotten talus slope to the fallen ram where I admired his incredible horns, which were over a curl and a half, both wide spread and perfectly tipped. Each side measured 40 inches. After posing for pictures, we boned out the meat. I demanded that I pack the head and horns myself. It was my prize. Bob and Dad could carry the meat.

One of the most important rituals of sheep hunting was to follow that night. That is the eating of the ram. We ate half the sheep that night ourselves, sitting around a small alder wood fire roasting tidbits of succulent sheep tenderloin and ribs until well into the night. I knew at that point that I wanted to hunt a lot more sheep.

The next morning, Bob made the decision to leave as he had more clients that needed his attention. Dad and I would pack out the moose and ram meat, which promised to take several days to do, as we had hundreds of pounds of meat, horns and capes to deal with.

We left some sheep meat on the mountain and decided our first step of the monumental packing task would be to retrieve it. I was doing my best to eat sheep meat to make the load more manageable. We hiked to the location of my fallen ram and decided to go the remaining few hundred yards to the top of the peak.

It was a gorgeous day — not a cloud in the sky and about 50 degrees with no wind. As we approached the top, we tried to cross a long snowfield that ran at least 2,000 feet down the mountain below us. Dad chipped footholds into the rock-hard snow. We got about halfway through the snow patch and couldn't go any further. Dad kicked a rock and it skidded downhill at an incredible speed, bursting into 1,000 pieces at the bottom. Mortified at the possibility of us taking the same trip down the mountain, we retreated to better footing.

We headed to a lower peak just to the north where we sat down to rest and take in some of the breathtaking scenery that surrounded us. Let me tell you, sheep country is like no other hunting country. I was hooked.

At that point we hadn't seen a caribou. But, upon glassing far into the valley below, I made out the two grey-black forms of two animals.

"Caribou, Dad!" I said.

I pointed out the animals in the valley below just as they walked onto a small patch of snow and bedded down. One was very large and the other small. My heart sank as I thought it might be a cow and calf. Dad pulled his spotting scope out of the pack and looked down and said, "They're caribou, and one of them is a good bull."

These caribou were in the opposite direction of camp and 2,500 feet below us.

Dad pointed out that "we" had a ram and a moose to pack out. "We" sure didn't need another animal to pack, he said. I began pleading with Dad to make a stalk on this big bull, which he finally agreed to. We stalked within 100 yards of the two bulls, which were still were laying on the snowfield unaware of our presence. Caribou often bed on a snowfield to stay cool on hot days or escape flies.

One shot from my magnum and the big bull rolled over. Three days, three trophies! I was ecstatic! The caribou lay in an area of unbelievable beauty. He was at the head of the same drainage where I had taken the moose. More pictures, more boning, and another giant load. A caribou bull boned out weighs about 150 pounds. Add a cape and horns and you've got a 200 pound load.

With this strapped on our backs, we headed down the drainage where we started to run into waist-deep willow, which tripped and fought us at every step. Suddenly a group of moose appeared out of nowhere. Five giant bulls! An unbelievable sight. The smallest bull had antlers greater than the one I had shot earlier. The largest was the best moose I'd ever seen, or have seen since.

Dad felt the bull would go close to 80 inches in spread. It had more than 40 points on its horns and great wide paddles. I pleaded with Dad to take the moose. He could have shot it — no problem! But, he declined as we had three animals to pack out at that point. So, we let the herd of giant bulls go unscathed.

Curtis later flew in to look at that giant bull. His hunters had taken two bulls that are still in the top 10 ever taken. He felt this bull was in that class.

We finally found a couple of tall trees suitable to cache our meat. We then stumbled up the canyon to our base camp where we feasted on more sheep meat and then collapsed into a deep slumber. The next morning we started on a marathon of packing. It was five miles one way to our tundra buggy. I knew we were going to have to make many trips in order to get the hundreds of pounds of meat, hides and antlers out to the river.

We'd eaten better than half of the sheep meat at that point. We loaded what was left of the ram, along with our camp, sheep horns and cape — a heavy load in itself — and hiked down the canyon to the heap of game we'd left the night before. We decided to try and pack out as much as possible on the first trip. Unable to even stand up straight, we staggered out of the canyon towards our tundra buggy. It would take us two days of packing.

Our walk out took us past the site where we had taken the moose. We decided to check on the meat and perhaps bone some of it out to make it a bit lighter for the remaining trips. Dad was very concerned about the abundance of bears in the area, and we approached the kill site with our rifles ready. As we approached, we could see the same sow grizzly and two cubs that had visited our camp some days before. The bears were heading away from us, leaving the valley and climbing a steep mountain.

Behind the grizzlies was a very large black bear, which was bound and determined to drive the grizzlies out of the area, which it succeeded in doing. Some black bear, I thought!

The grizzlies had found our moose kill and claimed it for their own. Black bears climbed the trees in which we'd hung the moose meat and ripped two rear quarters from the trees, dragging all of the meat into a giant pile of guts and dirt.

On top of this pile, the large black bear climbed and laid down to survey his prize. We tried to drive the black bear from the area, but he'd have none of it. The bear approached us stiff legged, making a whiffing noise and popping his teeth. The hair on the back of his neck stood straight up! He was prepared to fight for his moose.

We could see that all the moose meat and cape pulled from the trees was destroyed. The untouched items included the moose antlers, which were tied high in a tree.

While Dad climbed the tree the black bear approached closer. Dad hollered to me to shoot the black bear if it moved another 10 yards. I stood with the crosshairs on his chest. He made a few more steps, more deep growls and then turned around and walked back to the moose kill, climbed the giant pile of gore and laid down content that we were no threat to his prize. But the bear kept his eye on us as we deboned the moose shoulders.

The last two miles of each trip was an ordeal I'll never forget. We were so tired we could only walk a few hundred yards before having to sit down, and the spongy tundra didn't make it easy to get up after collapsing. My shoulders hurt so bad I felt like they were on fire. When it was almost dark, we finally reached the tundra buggy where we unloaded all our gear, threw our sleeping bags on the gravel and went to sleep.

We woke up early in the morning and threw on the torture devices known as backpacks, and headed back into the valley. There was still meat left, which filled Dad's pack. I took meat, caribou cape, sheep cape, and the caribou horns. Together with my rifle, the load felt even heavier than the one I'd carried the day before.

We passed the moose kill at a safe distance and could see the big black bear still lording it over the other bears; what remained of the moose

Sixty-three inch moose, 40-inch ram and a good caribou. Not bad for your first Alaska hunt.

was his.

Packing a set of moose horns almost six feet wide on your back, and then carrying it through waist deep brush is an experience in itself. Rarely does one want to do it more than once. But Dad now regrets passing up his chance at that huge moose!

We finally got the last load to our tundra buggy with about two hours of daylight left. I could barely turn the hand crank to fire up the engine. Finally, we were off and running. But, unknown to us, the warm weather of the last few days had raised the level of the river. We started into the Rhone River in low gear, only to see the front end of our tundra buggy almost completely submerge. Dad slammed on the brakes and I let off the throttle. Since the tundra buggy had no muffler, it sounded like a big Mercury outboard engine. Dad carefully eased the machine into reverse and backed out of the river.

The river was so full of silt and mud that it looked like you could plow it. We couldn't tell if the water was three inches deep or three feet deep. Slowly, but surely, we found a safe crossing and finally made it back to the base camp just as it was getting dark. As we entered the deserted camp, we had our guns loaded and ready, wondering if the camp grizzly bears had moved in. But, the camp was empty.

Curtis was flying in the next day and my hunt was over. I now clearly understood why Dad had planned three sheep hunts in a row — I had sheep fever like him! I couldn't wait to get back to Montana. Bighorn sheep season had been open there for five days and I was already thinking about sheep country. And I knew that the only cure for sheep fever is sheep hunting!

ALASKAN RAIN GOATS

By Keith Atcheson

In August, 1977, our ambitious group of six hunters boarded a flight in Butte, Montana that would eventually take us into wild and remote southeast Alaska. We were on a "do it yourself" backpack mountain goat hunt. The members of our party consisted of my father, Jack Sr., my brothers, Jack Jr. (older), and Brian (younger), family friends Terry Scott and Bob Bushmaker, and myself.

Upon "dropping" into Yakutat on a commercial jet, we were greeted by plenty of wet, rainy weather and the dreaded fact that three quarters of our luggage was somewhere on a trip of its own. This is one reason why travelers should always allow extra time for such circumstances. Our rifles had arrived, but no gear bags.

We checked in with our charter flight company that would fly us. Anxiously, we made our baggage claims and then the driver taking us to Yakutat Lodge said it rains over 300 days a year there. He had no trouble convincing our group of that! The salt-eroded Chevy Suburban was a skeleton of its former self. Water and mud actually splashed into the vehicle at every pothole. It was rather amusing.

Soon we were settled into our rooms. My dad was immediately on the phone with some of our local contacts and friends, forming Plan B, just in case our luggage didn't arrive. My father is extremely resourceful, and I had no doubt whatsoever that he would have all the equipment we would need. When you can't buy it or borrow it, you make it!

We met with a local guide friend of ours that night for advice and went over the maps and game plan. It should have been called "Plan of Attack." I'll elaborate more on this later.

Until recently, and undeservingly so, mountain goats have been an underrated species by hunters. They have always taken a back seat to their neighbors, the mountain sheep. It is partly for this reason that at the time of this hunt, very few locals knew anything about goats, and exactly where they could be found in good numbers. After discussing our goals with our resident friend, we decided we should pool some money and pay for one of us to do some aerial surveillance of several potential areas. Jack Jr. was chosen to be our spotter.

The next day we all went down to the airport and saw Jack fly out in a Supercub. Visibility didn't look good, as rain and fog persisted. After he left, we headed over to the terminal to wait for the morning flight inbound from Seattle. We were disappointed again. Some of our gear arrived, but not all of it.

Several hours passed, and our chances of getting out to goat country that day were rapidly diminishing. We were all starting to worry about Jack's whereabouts when they finally showed up. They had flown for well over six hours and he had good news. They saw lots of game animals, including brown bears, moose and lots of mountain goats in one remote area in particular. Things were looking better, especially when the rest of our gear arrived on the afternoon flight.

We would be heading into an isolated area known as Icy Bay. To reach it, we would fly north across the gigantic icefield of the Malaspina Glacier and into Federal lands now closed except to local subsistence hunters. The plan called for splitting the group in half. Jack Jr., Terry, and Bob would fly by floatplane to the north side of the bay, land in the ocean, and ascend from sea level. My dad, Brian, and I opted for the south side and would land by fixed wheel aircraft on a strip that was about 400 feet or so above sea level. I thought it was great, because on the map our climb into the goat area looked fairly easy. But sometimes the way terrain appears on a map can be a far cry from reality.·

Early the next morning we were on our way. Jack Jr.'s group left in a 206 on floats while our group had to make two separate flights, as all our gear, myself and the pilot was all the Cessna 172 could handle. After a spectacular hour of flying, we landed, unloaded and the pilot was off back to Yakutat to pick up Brian and my dad. The definition of lonely is redefined when the whine of an airplane engine disappears in this country. The first thing I did was load my .300 Winchester magnum, as I was now in true brown bear country, and my imagination was becoming active.

The rain was coming down steady so I pulled out my raingear and put it on. The weather wasn't cooperating unless you were a goat or a duck. I chewed on a granola bar as I studied the topo map and the huge ridge that lay in front of me. The escarpment was seemingly featureless and unbroken. It was about two miles to the base of the ridge where we could start a climb. The terrain rose sharply into the clouds and fog some 3,000 feet before we would reach the areas where the goats had been seen. There didn't appear to be any easy route such as natural openings or dry creek beds. Just one continuous thick lush forest. It would soon prove to be nearly impenetrable as well.

It wasn't long before I noticed a huge swarm of noseums gathering around me. These are very small flying insects that carry a nasty bite. We had been warned and were equipped with lots of repellant and military style headnets.

About two hours later I could hear an airplane approaching. Soon Brian and my dad were unloading themselves and the rest of their gear and the plane was on its way back to Yakutat.

My dad, being the leader that he is, had us go through our gear to lighten the loads. People tend to overpack, and Brian and I were no exception. There is a definitive difference between what you think you will need and what you actually do need on this type of trip.

Our food was the freeze-dried type for the next seven days. This trip, among many others, has contributed to my extreme dislike of freeze-dried anything.

We fired a few shots from our rifles to make sure we were zeroed in, one inch high at 100 yards. Perfect!

We then stowed away extra gear in an old dilapidated shed. Then we threw on our 45-pound packs and started out on a walk that soon turned into an absolute nightmare.

The lower area was a complete and total rain forest. It was so thick and dense that sometimes you couldn't see the man five feet in front of you. All types of vegetation flourished in this area, including the treacherous "devil's club." This vine-like growth is up to eight feet tall and is completely covered with cactus-like spikes. Even heavy leather gloves can't resist it. At times it was so thick we had to chop a path through it with our ice axes. As we pushed on, the mountain became steeper and steeper. The rain continued, hard at times. Sweat poured from our bodies, attracting more and more insects. These things were literally driving us nuts. The bugs were in our eyes, ears, nostrils and mouths. We had to put on our headnets, which were a godsend, but provided poor ventilation and even more sweating. I had heard of such stories, but never experienced it. They could easily drive a human temporarily insane and they were doing a good job of it with us.

It had been our plan to hike up out of the thick brush and into sub-alpine terrain in three or four hours. But we were not even half way up and we had been climbing for over six hours. Brian and I were becoming exhausted and displaying fits of rage as an occasional devils club vine would smack us across the face, or bugs would penetrate our headnets.. Adding another interesting element to our predicament was the fact that we were in prime brown bear habitat. There was sign everywhere. Once in a while we got some relief in the climb, as over time, these bears had carved rounded tunnel paths through the thick brush. Huge prints of bear tracks have been pressed into the ground. We were genuinely concerned about having a face to face encounter and one can only imagine how difficult it would be to defend yourself with your gun strapped on your backpack, an ice axe in one hand and grasping for a handhold with the other, while a headnet obscured most of your view. This was, and still is, the toughest situation I have ever been in. It was a physical and mental hell. My partners are quick to agree.

My dad and I literally cut a path up the mountain with our ice axes. A machete would have been more useful. We were three quarters up the mountain as darkness approached. I suggested we make camp, and all were in favor.

Finding a flat spot to erect our tent was impossible. We put it up in an unlevel hole that was created by an enormous spruce tree that had been toppled by time and high winds. Little sunlight ever penetrated and all of the trees and brush were covered in a green mold. There was a small stream nearby so we boiled some water to make a cup of soup. All I could think about was getting into that sleeping bag away from the bugs, and sleep. My dad said the water was ready so I held out my cup and let him pour. It was nearly dark and we should have been using a flashlight. I must have moved, or he missed the cup, as the boiling water poured all over my hand. My reaction was predictable, and so was the damage that occurs when 212 degree water hits human skin. My thumb took the worst of it, second and third degree burns from the thumbnail back to the knuckle, and first degree burns on the rest of my hand. I literally slept that night with my hand in a coffeepot of cold water. The last thing I can remember about that night was the exploding sounds of huge pieces of ice pounding the ocean waters of Icy Bay. The glacier at the head of the bay was spawning icebergs into the sea. This is the same site that several years later would be blocked by icebergs, thus trapping three or four whales, which resulted in a massive human effort to rescue the trapped whales. It was a semi-successful effort.

None of us slept well that night. The presence of bears, pounding rain and lack of a comfortable bed made it tough.

Before dawn we got up and bandaged my thumb, which was throbbing with pain. We ate some gourmet freeze-dried food and we were all sorer than hell. But a little rest, food and my dad's unswerving motivation had us back on the warpath, up, up, up. Around noon we finally broke out of the thick brush and into more open alpine country and very steep terrain. A steady breeze took care of the pesky noseums. No words could express our joy to be up and out of the hellish jungle we had come through in the last day and a half, but it was a great adventure where few, if any, humans had ever been before.

Although rain and fog continued, at times we could see several hundred yards. It was absolutely spectacular country. We stopped to take it all in. The great forces of nature were at work far below us in Icy Bay. What we had heard happening the night before we were now viewing in panorama. House-sized chucks of ice and rock were separating from the main glacier and falling hundreds of feet before crashing into the ocean. It was an awesome sight to witness. We decided to keep working up the ridge and find a stream so we could heat some water and have some lunch, gourmet of course!

Occasionally we would stop and glass for animals, and we did see one brown bear about a mile away, wandering aimlessly in search of food. At one point we found the remains of a couple of goat carcasses lying on the tundra. My father felt they had been caught by brown bears or wolves.

The terrain now was more of a brilliant green, rolling and gradual ascending steppes. Huge snowdrifts, or as we called them "mini glaciers," riddled the landscape. These icy formations seemed to have developed in draws or depressions where more snow and ice would gather in the winter. No doubt they were also remnants of the much larger glacier that had existed eons ago. The land we now walked on was undoubtedly covered by ice just a few years prior.

We found a good place to have lunch at the head of a mini glacier. Brian went to retrieve water while I was trying to light a temperamental stove. My dad was rummaging through the food sacks selecting a freeze-dried entree. Visibility was very poor, perhaps 50 yards or so, due to the continuous misting fog.

Suddenly my irritated concentration was broken as my father loudly whispered, "Keith, get your rifle." There was a genuine urgency in his voice. I bounced to my feet subconsciously knowing that it had to be a bear. I was armed in seconds. I glanced in the direction that my dad was pointing his .338 Winchester magnum. There, on the opposite side of the creek, perhaps 40 yards away, he appeared from nowhere out of the hazy fog. Heading directly toward us, a huge brown bear was ambling along on top of the mini glacier. My father's concern doubled when he noticed

Brian's .270 lying on his pack, and he was nowhere in sight. Brian had headed in the same general direction where the bear now stood. The bear was unaware of our presence until my dad started yelling frantically for Brian. This startled the nine-foot-plus bruin and instead of turning 180 degrees and taking flight, he stiffened, laid back his ears, and immediately charged.

Bears possess stunning explosive speed so in a few short seconds he leaped off the snowdrift, bounded across the creek, and scaled the sharp embankment directly in front of us. Hoping it was a mock charge, my dad was saying, "Don't shoot, don't shoot, until he passes that rock." I was having a hard time with this, as I was just squeezing the trigger, when sure enough the bear stopped some 13 paces away, just beside the large rock. Brian suddenly appeared behind us. The beast raised to full height on its hind legs. His head was huge. My crosshairs were trained firmly on the middle of his chest and my dad was lined up on his head. His great nose caught our scent and he let out a loud "woof" as he swayed back and forth. He spun around as he fell back to all fours and galloped out on the same path as he came in on, defecating for 100 feet or so as he disappeared into the mist. I guess we scared the hell out of him but I can assure you, the feeling was the same.

Thirty seconds, and the whole event was over. Brian caught a few choice phrases for breaking the No. 1 rule in bear country — never leave your rifle. It was quite an experience for all of us. Bears are unpredictable and horribly maul and kill people every year.

We ate, packed up, and headed up the mountain. The fog and rain had set back in and we couldn't see more than 20 to 30 yards. We decided to find a place to set up camp and wait it out. Little did we know, as it didn't clear up until six days later!

Try spending that amount of time with someone in a small mountain tent sometime. You really learn a lot about yourself and others in these conditions. Everything was wet. Our tent developed a real distinct odor of biblical proportions. All we could do was read a few books, eat freeze-dried foods, relieve ourselves once in a while, and wander around in the fog. The continuous salty mist wreaked havoc on our rifles. They were literally rusting before our eyes, but we did manage to keep the barrels clean.

Very little brush could be found to burn, and what we did find was soaked. There was no sign of any human ever having been there before, which was nice. During this time, my dad broke one of his teeth in half on a prune seed, but he had his first aid kit and was able to get by.

Our time was almost out. We had to meet our plane in two days and the same obstacles had to be dealt with going back down. However, the next day there was a glimmer of hope. Clouds were lifting and we could see better now than we could any of the previous days. Within an hour we had a group of 35 plus goats spotted, all nannies and kids, and one average billy. This was it. There was no time to look for large old billys. We were going to be lucky to get anything.

Using the available terrain to stalk the goats, we were on our prey within 45 minutes. We were extremely pleased to find them down low and out of the steep cliff areas above them. More often than not, after shooting a goat in this type of terrain, they can take terrible plunging falls that can destroy the cape, horns and meat, and we didn't have much time as the fog was moving in again.

Brian decided to shoot the billy while I concentrated on a large nanny that had no kid with it. My dad said he would wait and see what happened with our goats. I don't think he really ever intended to shoot one. He knew better. After all, we had to carry them out on our backs, and two goats and all our gear, well, that's a no-brainer.

The herd was spread out on a steep lush hillside above us, and off to an angle. Right below them was a huge mini glacier that was 300 yards across the top, but narrowed dramatically as it pitched off steeply down the mountain ravine some 500 yards.

Brian shot first. His goat was about 200 yards away feeding in a small depression. Two shots about a hand's width apart were placed perfectly behind the shoulders. Surprisingly, it anchored right then and there. The .270 bullets, 150 grain Winchester power points had performed well.

Mountain goats are by far the toughest North American game animal that I have ever hunted. They can be extremely hard to kill. I later told Brian that his goat was weak and feeble. Why else would it be with a bunch of nannies and kids? After Brian shot, the goats were quite spooked and off to the races, running in all directions.

I picked out the goat I was after and fired as it was trotting upward. The 180 grain Nosler bullet from my .300 Winchester broke its back and killed it instantly and it was down and tumbling head over heels fast and furiously toward the glacier below. It angled off toward the edge of the glacier, hit the tundra bank and simply disappeared. Gone! We all looked at each other in dismay. Obviously it had dropped off the edge of the ice and would be lying there when we arrived. However, that was definitely not the case.

Over time, these mini glaciers are slowly melting, and in some places the ice has receded back from the earthen bank by several feet. What is left is a frozen dangerous tunnel that leads deep underneath the depths of the ice. That is where my goat had gone. At first, we couldn't see it. We figured it was long gone, but as I stared down into the hole, my eyes

Brian and Keith show off the Rain Goats.

adjusted to the darker light, and I could barely pick out the horns and head. We pulled out a flashlight and could see that luckily its sharp points had acted as icepicks, and it was hanging precariously. My dad's instinct was to leave it, and for good reason. Once you fall into this hole, it is very unlikely that you will be coming out.

I finally convinced my dad and Brian to tie a tough nylon climbing rope around me and I would crawl down into the hole and tie another rope around the goat's neck. Using my ice axe, I was able to reach the goat without much difficulty, although it was extremely slick. It was reassuring to have a rope on me, as it was an eerie feeling. As far as I could see, the icy cavern continued into oblivion.

I got the rope tied on the goat's neck and they pulled me out. Then all three of us latched on and pulled the nanny out, and well away from the glacier. Brian and I decided to throw a rock down the hole and it confirmed our fears that it was almost endless. My father said, in a stern voice, not to talk him into any more precarious acts such as this, as my mother would kill him if she knew.

We went back over to the goat and field-dressed it, and then eventually dragged the two goats together and took dual pictures. We then caped out the goats, boned out the meat, and loaded them on our backpacks. An hour later we were back at camp breaking down, repacking and loading up for the big descent off the mountain where we had spent a long, wet week.

The packs were very heavy, but it was all downhill. As expected, it was easier going until we dropped into the devil's club jungle. We tried a different route, but it was almost as bad going down as it was coming up. There was bear sign everywhere and to a bear, we reeked with the smell of a goat dinner. The bugs returned with the same fury. All we could do was keep moving toward the bottom. At one point, we did attract one bear when we were in heavy brush, but he reconsidered. We heard him grunting and crashing through the brush. At that point, we decided to make plenty of noise so we blew on police whistles and attached a pan and a couple of spoons to our packs with a rope, which banged along behind, warning any other bears of our presence.

We reached the airstrip, such as it was, late that evening, right at dark. Brian and I could barely function, but we finally erected the tent and the lights were out for that night, after we cooked up some chewy goat steaks.

My dad figured the fog would keep us there for days, but our charter flight arrived early the next morning, and once again we took turns flying back to Yakutat, where the sun was shining brightly. When we arrived, we learned that Jack Jr., Bob and Terry had all been successful in taking very large billy goats. For some reason, the weather for them wasn't nearly as severe as in our location, rain but no fog. They dropped off the mountain and walked down the beach about 10 or 15 miles to a logging camp and called in a plane. My dad certainly could have been successful in taking a goat, but as he has done in many cases, he went without, making sure that everyone else was successful. This has always been his nature.

I have always wondered how we ended up on the side of the valley where all the fog, nannies and kids were, while Jr.'s group went to where all the billys lived. We have asked Jack Jr. about that and he just shakes his head and smiles. Somehow I think he knew more, but then next time we reversed the scenario. But that's another story!

THE MAGNIFICENT SEVEN

By Kerry Constan and Jack Atcheson

The sight below me was one that a sheep hunter dreams of — seven large old Dall rams. Two were bedded down and the others were peacefully feeding. However, one of the bedded rams was alert and staring directly at us.

To get to Alaska and hunt Dall sheep was the answer to my fondest dreams. Thanks to Jack Atcheson, my very close friend, hunting partner, internationally known hunting consultant and fanatic big game hunter, I was able to book a sheep and caribou hunt with Clark Engle in the Alaska range. But, Jack, with his rifle scope fogged, was at that moment a very frustrated and wet sheep hunter.

Jack had also booked me a Stone sheep hunt in British Columbia's Northern Cascades. That hunt had ended and I was still excited about killing a beautiful Stone with 40 3/4 inch horns that were unusually flared, 35 inches tip to tip spread.

After my Stone sheep hunt I flew directly to Anchorage, Alaska, for the Dall sheep hunt. I was still in a slight state of shock over having taken a 40-inch ram. My Alaska adventure was starting out in high gear.

After a dinner celebration with Jack and his hunting guide friend, Bob Curtis, Bob said he'd be happy to fly us to Clark's camp on the Tonzona River with a grand tour of Alaska. I was overwhelmed with the awesome splendor. The trip was highlighted by my first sight of the "white" sheep. I was impressed with how easy it was to see them against the green hillsides. It was a relief after my many years of hunting bighorn sheep in Montana where they blended into their background as if they were invisible. On the flight I also saw my first wolf, a large black one.

Bob eased his Helio-courier onto Engle's landing strip, a gravel bar in the Tonzona River, and we were greeted with the good news that three of the four hunters present had killed their rams during the first two days of the season. Bad luck plagued the fourth hunter; however, he did get his ram later.

Clark suggested that we hunt out of the main camp for the first day. Our guide, Ray, was new to the area and sheep hunting, and suggested we all participate in the hunt plan. Our first day hunt revealed the beauty of this part of Alaska. Steep hillsides covered with lush green vegetation extending up to perpetually snow-covered peaks with glaciers hanging in the high valleys and winding down several larger valleys. The heads of the glaciers headed out in basins which were nearly 15,000 feet high. The glaciers fed streams, causing an added difficulty since you need hipboots to wade them. However, I found hipboots to be uncomfortable to wear while climbing. Jack and I therefore carried hiking shoes in our backpacks. The first day we ran directly into five young rams, 1/2 to 3/4 curl. This was my first close-up view of these beautiful animals. A few minutes later a band of ewes and lambs filed past us less than 100 yards and then disappeared like ghosts into an extremely rough piece of real estate.

On the way back to camp we came upon a dozen cow caribou. They stared and trotted in a small circle, then reared on their hind legs and dashed off when our scent drifted to them.

Early the next day we were moved to the spike camp down the Tonzona River. After a hurried lunch we took off uphill. This drainage had a deep, swift glacial fed stream roaring down a narrow rock strewn valley. It was named Hell Bender Creek and it was correctly named. Within minutes of camp we spotted three full curl rams across the creek and about a mile and a half away. The rams were lying on a rocky point that gave them an unobstructed view of the surrounding country. A stalk looked impossible but we decided to get closer to evaluate their horns. If they were large enough we could leave them and hope to relocate and stalk them the next day. Dropping down into the creek bottom we waded the milling stream and moved into a willow and alder thicket.

As we followed a small channel I saw my first fresh grizzly bear sign. On a sandbar was a huge perfect foot print of a grizzly. Jack verified that it was very large and probably less than a day old. As we worked through the thick brush I couldn't forget that track when suddenly a huge black body leaped up in front of me not 30 yards away. Jack was off to my left about 30 yards. My heart stopped in the split second before I saw that it was a cow moose very anxious to get away from me. An hour later we were nearly in position to get a good look at the three rams.

"I believe that I see more sheep a long way up the valley and back on the side of the stream which we just came from," stated Jack.

We set up our B&L-15-60-X spotting scope to check these sheep and Jack located another herd of sheep nearly three miles away. There was a band of nineteen ewes and lambs. However, a half-mile from them were seven rams and they really looked good, even at that extreme distance. There seemed to be sheep everywhere. Jack said, "We can reach those rams if we hurry and if they don't move. It will take us at least three hours to get in position."

Those were the words that Jack used to bring me down from my excitement of finding more and possibly larger rams. Three hours of crossing Hell Bender again and climbing through rough country going at top speed to beat the fading daylight didn't appeal to me as my tired body was beginning to complain. We reached camp about 9:00 p.m., heated up some canned stew and crawled into our cozy little tent. I counted Dall sheep jumping over Hell Bender Creek until about 2:00 a.m. Tomorrow seemed so far away. My lifetime ambition was only hours away.

At daylight we were on our way and had to cross a very steep side canyon that was perpendicular to the main stream. As we approached the deep canyon, two bull caribou came into view on the far side. One of the bulls looked huge to me, but I was not familiar with judging caribou. Jack confirmed my initial guess when he said that one of the bulls would go high in the record book.

"Well, Kerry, we're going to go right by that bull on our way to the rams. You can decide then if you want to take him," suggested Jack.

What a decision to make — pass up a record book bull, or take him and maybe blow the rams. It was soon decided as we dropped into the steep canyon; it happened before we could do anything. Six large rams stood on the opposite side of the steep canyon near the canyon floor about 600 yards away. They appeared to be aware of our presence, but they weren't spooked as they slowly climbed out of the canyon. The lead ram was monstrous, probably 42 inches and heavily broomed. As the rams topped out of the canyon they passed within 50 yards of the caribou, which were also drifting away. A record book ram and a record book caribou only yards apart, and we were pinned down 600 yards away.

Rain started to fall and the canyon filled with fog — all we could do was sit and wait and think of rams.

I figured I had finally made it to "Ram Heaven." Rams seemed to be everywhere. Wow! The fog sort of lifted and we hightailed it toward the "Magnificent Seven" rams. When we were within a mile of them we could see that they had shifted to a slope that made the stalk more difficult and tedious. Also, time was running out on us. We now had a good look at the rams and they all looked very large. But, daylight was fading. We reluctantly started back to camp.

We had high hopes that we would find them the following day, where they were now grazing. We arrived at camp at 10:00 p.m., which meant we had been going for nearly 18 hours. I didn't even dream of the next days hunt as I was too tired.

Fog greeted us in the morning and it looked like the rams had won the day. Though visibility was less than 200 yards we started our long walk to where we had last seen the rams. The hike became a drag as the fog continued, and our spirits were sinking rapidly. Nearing the vicinity of where we last saw the rams, I suddenly heard an animal let out a bawl.

My first impression was that it was a domestic cow but I knew that there weren't any cattle anywhere within a hundred miles. Jack heard it too, but shrugged his shoulders when I asked what it was. Less than a minute later Jack softly called me and said, "It's a grizzly." I was excited and I tripped over an alder branch and fell flat on my face as I tried to cover the 15 feet between Jack and I. Jack quickly pointed out a sow and two cubs standing about 125 yards above us.

The wind was blowing directly from us to them. Within seconds she reared up on her hind legs and began slowly swinging her head from side to side. One cub imitated its mother and did the same thing. The sow's head suddenly stopped in the middle of a sweep and she locked in directly on us. Her wonderful nose had located us as accurately as a good set of eyes.

In another instant she whirled around and took off running with her cubs trailing behind. Jack commented that she was only an average size bear, but since it was my first grizzly up close, she looked like a Volkswagen.

We picked a high vantage point to rest and to wait out the fog. Weather had beaten us many times when hunting sheep in Montana and other places, so we tried to maintain a positive outlook. Two hours later and after 1,000 weather forecasts, such as, "I think the fog is lifting" or "Damn, the fog is getting thicker," the fog began to rapidly lift. We anxiously glassed the mountain where we last saw the rams, but only spotted a herd of ewes and lambs. We decided to eat lunch, after which Jack suggested that we head further up the Hell Bender.

In 15 minutes we came to another vantage point where we could continue glassing. Excitement gripped me as I smugly yelled, "I have found the seven rams." The reason I was so smug is that when Jack and I hunt together the rule is that whoever spots the game first gets his choice and first shot. This friendly competition causes both of us to work very hard at trying to find game each day.

The seven rams were less than a mile away and on the other side of Hell Bender Creek. They were feeding peacefully and had not seen us. Jack set up our spotting scope and began to evaluate the rams. When I got my chance to look, all I could say was, "They are a magnificent seven."

All seven rams had heavy horns. Six of them had tight curls and three of these six had some brooming on their tips. The seventh ram had perfect unbroomed tips and wide, flaring horns very similar to the Stone ram I had taken two weeks before. I told Jack that I wanted the ram with the wide flaring horns.

It looked like it would be a relatively easy stalk. Since the sheep were across the creek we had to wade old Hell Bender again, work up a side gulch until we were higher than the rams, then out and across the ridge until we were directly above them. The stream crossing was again terrifying. As the day warms up the glacier melts faster and the creek raises and roars. The wind kept swirling and it rained during the entire stalk, which seemed to take forever as the excitement mounted. We picked the wrong side of the gulch and had to retreat and go up another gulch which was the right one. But now it started to rain and the wind shifted. With each step we were sure that the sheep would smell us. But the wind didn't betray us and we finally arrived at the place where I started this story — cold and soaking wet after a long crawl.

We were lying prone on a ledge only 100 yards above the rams, yet we could do nothing as both our rifle scopes were fogged up. We had agreed that I would shoot first with Jack firing just a second later. My ram was bedded down and Jack's pick was feeding. Jack said in an irritated voice, "Go on and shoot." Since I could now see clearly through my rifle scope, I said, "Okay," and squeezed off a shot. The bedded ram rolled over and didn't move.

Being excited, I shouted loudly, "I got him Jack!" At that instant, instead of hearing Jack shoot, I heard him cuss softly and I looked over and there he was still trying to clean the fogged lens. My heart sank. I looked down at the rams and they were bolting. None of the rams ran for more than 15 to 20 yards before they stopped. Obviously confused as to which direction my shot had come from, they didn't know which way led to safety. It seemed like an eternity before Jack finally shot.

Lady Luck was with us, as the rams waited and Jack's well-placed shot behind the shoulder sent his ram tumbling down the steep slope. Then, as if on cue, my dead ram kicked and also began rolling down the mountain. The rams came to rest within 25 feet of each other. I could barely see them.

It had been a lucky shot! Our rams were truly magnificent. Jack's broomed ram measured 40 inches even. My ram was over 39 inches. Both rams had good bases and were 11 and 10 years old respectively. The other

I guess the smiles tell it all.

five rams were just as large and old as the two we took.

According to our topo map, we were miles from camp. The trip back, even though complicated by the weight of the horns, cape and boned out meat was not excessively difficult as we were both in good condition and in high spirits. The crossings of old Hell Bender were even more terrifying with our heavy backpacks, and at the last crossing we waited until 2 a.m. for the creek to subside to a mere torrent. We went one person at a time while the other held the rope. To fall down would mean possible disaster.

During the next two days Jack and I took two large caribou bulls. However, it was anti-climatic after the sheep hunt. Jack now went back to Bob Curtis' camp to be with Jack Jr., who took a 40-inch ram, a 63-inch moose and a caribou — meaning we had taken four rams right at 40 inches in 10 days. That must be some kind of record itself.

PS: Jack described our hunt as a hunt that will be remembered as "It doesn't get any better." After 25 years I still agree. The picture of us hangs on my wall and always brings me the fondest of memories. Thanks Jack!!

DAD, YOU'RE AN ELK HUNTER

I couldn't believe it. I had a heart attack. There must be a mistake. Dr. Hubbard said, "No. And, if you had not been so active, you would have had this heart attack 20 years ago."

Dr. Hubbard and Dr. Corbett liked to hunt and we discussed hunting possibilities as much as we did the pending surgery. Dr. Corbett wanted to know which area I would suggest to apply for sheep. I responded, "I'll tell you after I come through the surgery."

Well, the fellows did a good job. Dr. Corbett drew a sheep permit and shot a magnificent ram and by September of that fall I was hunting elk in Idaho. That was in 1989.

Then in May of 1994, another heart attack. The grim word was I would probably have to cut back on my mountain hunting. My response was, "You mean I will be a rabbit hunter and not an elk hunter?"

And, that was the general consensus of opinion. I didn't like that response, and a guy can only eat so many rabbits. I had a couple of good things going for me — my heart was very strong and I had no heart damage. The anesthetist, and my friend, Dr. Lance Parks of Billings, Montana, carried on a conversation concerning a hunting trip that he was taking to Australia when I drifted off into a very dark world. When I woke up, I realized the operation was over. But, was it a success? I thought of myself as a rabbit hunter, perhaps with a shawl over my shoulders and a hot water bottle for my cold feet. I very well remembered my predicament.

Dr. Dernbach had to operate and by-pass an artery that was almost inoperable. If the operation was a success, I would probably be an elk hunter. If it was not a success, I would be a rabbit hunter. I was very alert, and this crippled mental image troubled me greatly. I managed to open my left eye and almost immediately another eye appeared almost next to mine.

A familiar voice, that of my son, Jack Jr., whispered into my ear, "Dad, you're an elk hunter." They were the magic words I wanted to hear.

That was the first of June, 1994. On the 10th of August in Alaska I watched our pilot, Kelly Vrem, fly into the shadows. I stood on a high windswept ridge with two of my friends, Vince Fischer and Tony Schoonen of Butte, Montana. We had been dropped off to hunt caribou. I felt great and thought to myself, this would not be a good place to have a relapse. On the other hand, what greater place to die?

I wasn't figuring on dying. I figured on hunting caribou. I just wasn't going to push it too hard. Tony did the cooking, Vince did the dishes and pumped up the stove, and both promised to carry out my caribou meat. That was the up side of surgery — you can get more work out of your friends if you practice looking peaked.

My partners got their caribou and left, but I stayed on and hunted out of Kelly's spike camp with another hunter and his wife, Dick and Becky Goodwill of Yerington, Nevada, very pleasant people. Their guide was Ken Robertson. These folks were looking for a record book caribou bull or nothing — and Becky took a magnificent bull caribou and a giant record book moose.

I made a great stalk on a moose over 65 inches, but I was not hunting moose and played tag with a grizzly that hung out near camp. We came close to butting heads twice; I must admit that a little huffing and snapping of bear teeth can alter your thinking real fast. I wanted to avoid any wear and tear on my body.

There was considerable wolf sign at the lower end of the main ridge and I suppose that is why the caribou departed. The wolf tracks told me that they were spending a lot of time around some beaver dams. I slowly glassed the valley. I could see a partly chewed tree, and at its base, a bloody spot in the snow — the end of the beaver.

Patience paid off, though, for with the same sweep of my binoculars, here came one lone bull caribou. I thumped him with one shot behind the shoulder with my .338 Winchester. I loaded up about 30 pounds and put on the pack. It didn't seem to bother me, and since I was wired together, my heart probably wouldn't fall out! I headed back to camp. I took my time and felt great, and would return tomorrow.

Later that year, on October 15, at 5:00 a.m., flashlight in hand, I was walking up a trail at one of my secret spots in Idaho. The country was rough, steep and mostly thick timber and deadfall. I decided I'd only shoot a bull with six points per side, or a deer with four points per side.

On the first morning Chad Magness of Kalispell busted an excellent six point per side bull. A week later his father, Jim, shot a heavy, hog fat five-point bull.

Jim was the elected cook and camp manager who rules with an iron hand, but he's first up and gets the fire and coffee going. You have to like a guy that does that! We had three horses, which we were using exclusively for packing meat, although a lot of human backpacking was required to get the elk quarters to the horses. Since Pat Maloney, of Butte, owned the horses, he graciously accompanied everyone who got an elk to and from the kill site. By graciously, I mean we worked the hell out of him. But, he's a big guy and can take it — at least that's how we have it figured, and isn't that what friends are for?

That morning I was hunting with Jack Jr. and we bypassed (a nasty word) a couple of small five-point bulls. There was also a lot of mountain lion sign. We found kills of two deer and one elk. Lions kill about one elk or deer, or more, per week, and old bucks are very vulnerable.

The next day I decided to work the thick timber below camp alone, so Jack Jr. and Pat were hunting together. Just at daylight two bulls were spotted standing right on the trail. Pat made a perfect heart shot with his 300 Winchester.

I was tracking a very large bull, but blundered onto him in the fog and couldn't get a shot. I also saw a couple of huge Pileated woodpeckers and noted in the snow that a small mountain lion was following me.

Just at dark, far in the distance, I could hear Jack Jr. shooting. And, about 10:00 at night the tent flap drew back and I said, "Are you a yep or a nope?" His response was, "You heard me shoot, of course I'm a yep." He produced from his pocket a couple of the most beautiful elk ivories I had ever seen.

The next day after packing out Pat's bull, Jack and Pat took the horses to Jack's Hell Hole to bring back part of his elk, or at least get it to the trail. While backpacking an elk quarter through the trees, Pat, who is an exceptionally good hunter and a good judge of trophies, said he came upon a 30-inch mule deer with massive horns and deep forks — something none of us had seen for years. But, before he had an opportunity to get to his rifle, the deer was gone. He thought I might want to go after the buck, but I knew the buck would still be there the next year and maybe I'll dust him then! I will, however, let Pat carry him out. It's the least I could do for the hot tip.

The last day of the hunt came and, while I was looking at one ridge, Jack spotted a big five-point bull just over the hill from our camp, bedded at the edge of a clearing. I could have gone after him, but everyone was packed up and ready to leave. I already had passed up a couple of bulls, and I'd had a really great time so I decided not to go after him. Besides that, I had to get to Montana because I was packing into a remote area with horses the day after I got home for another elk hunt. And this time just Jack Jr. and I would be on the hunt.

The first two days we saw no tracks at all. An earlier, and now crusted, snowfall combined with drought conditions had caused the elk to move. Elk hunting is like that. Enough time makes all the difference.

Although the mating season was over, elk do occasionally bugle, and sometimes answer bugles or cow calls, which at least gives you an idea where they are and how many there are. And, upon occasion curiosity gets the best of them, and bulls actually come to you. On the third day, within 500 feet of our tent, Jack Jr. heard a bull bugle and eventually the bull came out in response to his calls. Jack carries a variety of cow, calf and young bull calls and created a phantom herd with calls that, like each human voice, sound slightly different. I heard the familiar crack of his vented .338 and he had taken another excellent bull — six points per side.

The next morning was very cold with a light snow, which eventually turned into a bad, windy day. We sat on a ridge piling wood on the fire, boiling tea and toasting sandwiches until about 4:00 p.m., the magic elk hour, when we simultaneously spotted two bulls far across the valley on another ridge. Snow was about 10 inches deep and crusted, but I decided to give it a try.

As the big bull moved up the slope, a cow was blocking my shooting lane. Then, a very large five-point bull with exceptionally heavy black antlers emerged between the trees 200 yards away. I could have busted him easy and might have, if I hadn't known of the big six-point just above him. Unfortunately, the cows stayed where they were, preventing me from going any further or moving. The bulls proceeded to ease up the hill.

The five-point walked broadside most of the time, but always between me and the six-point. I could easily have shot the bigger bull in the rear end, but that may have just wounded him, leaving him to die a long death. I hesitated — and then both bulls were gone.

Some of the tremendous elk country I hunted on the trip.

The next day it snowed. The temperature was dropping rapidly and the wind was awesome. We located two more six-points, not quite so large, and three or four smaller bulls that were located in a slide area.

I made various stalks over the next two days, and could have easily shot a couple of five-point bulls. I only saw tracks of the bigger six-point. That night, in the tent, we cooked up some tough elk loin and decided to move because Jack had to go back to work. I would continue to play.

Although I was doing very well, a lot of people were concerned that I would wander off into the mountains somewhere, drop dead and nobody would find me until my body washed out in the spring. I was not exactly pushing myself that much anyway. In fact, if you are a slow hunter, you look around yourself more and you may actually see even more game behind you than in front of you.

I was hunting alone, but stayed at the hunting lodge run by Keith and Leah Rush, mostly because they are good, friendly people, and Leah is a phenomenal cook. Plus, they had horses I could use to pack out my elk — if and when! I was still looking, on public land, for a big bull with six points per side. Public land hunting is the best hunting. It's all your land, though some of it is badly overgrazed. In all I spent 33 days hunting elk and passed up 35 legal bulls.

It had been a week since I had seen a six point. I wanted to get the elk hunting over with and go on to hunt deer and pheasants in other areas. But, since I was an elk hunter, this can be a curse and a crazy obsession, I decided that I was going to hunt until the end — elk or no elk. And it had to be a bull with six points per side.

The weather couldn't get much worse than it had been. It was very cold, with the wind blowing in all directions. On the higher ridges it appeared as if the tops of the mountains were moving.

Long before daylight I was working up the ridge on what was to be my final morning in this area when I came across a very large bull track and decided to give him a run for his money. Although the wind was bad, the fresh snow made quiet tracking. My long hunt began just a few minutes after daylight.

I carefully circled around two four-point bulls that were digging grass from under a pine tree. I don't know why they didn't smell me. Elk were all around me, calling back and forth to one another, while moving to higher elevations to bed. The bull track seemed to be going in the same direction, which compounded matters. And for the next six hours I slowly followed the big bull. He seemed to be going nowhere in particular.

When tracking elk, if you plan to shoot them in the timber, you constantly look for pieces of elk hide or antlers.

Luckily, the wind seemed to be staying in my face. I moved very slowly. Three times the bull had bedded and had gotten up on his own, rubbed his antlers against trees, and nibbled on isolated clumps of sagebrush, and the tips of spruce boughs.

I built a fire, leaned up against a tree and went to sleep for about 20 minutes. I melted snow, made tea, and toasted my foil-wrapped turkey sandwich over the fire. In fact, I had two turkey sandwiches and had two more in my pack. I believe in bringing more than enough.

I moved across the mountain to one of my favorite elk hideaways. Then I found a dead cow elk being eaten by a mountain lion. The lion was following the same bull I'd been tracking all day. We had made a great circle; the elk was headed back toward my truck. The lion saw me and departed.

The bull was moving slowly, and I even more slowly. In front of me I could see two spike bulls feeding heavily on spruce boughs. I could see no way around them. If I scared the spikes, I would perhaps scare the big bull.

While I was pondering this dilemma, a raven swooped down right over the elk and I believe he told them where I was standing. I am sure the elk could not smell me. Nevertheless, the bulls looked in my direction and slowly started to walk away.

There was only about 45 minutes of daylight left, so something would have to happen soon — or not at all. Off to my right I saw an out-of-place color behind some brush, between a couple of large spruce trees. I stopped instantly and did not move.

I guess I can still count myself as an elk hunter.

I was convinced from the color that it was a bull. By moving and leaning a few inches in either direction, I was able to make out which direction he was facing. I could see the tip of his brow-points. He was at least a legal bull — and only 100 yards away.

I decided to get down on my stomach and slide to my left, for I now determined the bull was lying down. I had to reach a point where I could see him, and shoot him where he was, or shoot him when he jumped up. His nose tipped into the air — I believe he sensed the presence of danger. As his antlers went back I could plainly see six points on one side and seven on the other, but I couldn't see his body and I don't like head shots.

I slowly stood up, as tight to a tree as I could get, so as not to silhouette myself. I could make out a spot through the brush about the size of a saucer. There was one limb right in the middle, about as thick as your thumb. Right in line with the stick was a hairline — the type of hair that grows on an elk back at the top of the shoulder blade. To hit the elk, I was going to have to shoot through an area about the size of a business card. I would either hit the elk's backbone, or shoot over him. I was offered a clean kill, or a clean miss!

I raised my .338 and fired. The bull never moved.

Before I walked up to the elk, I reflected on the experience, and said to myself, "Just a few months ago I thought I would never be able to hunt elk again. Now, I have shot a lot of elk in my life, but this elk was as important to me as was the first one I shot over 50 years ago."

I was elated to know that Jack Jr. had been right. I was, once again, an elk hunter.